"Steven Félix-Jäger has cr
church. His book presents
on in the wider culture and responds to the salient issues of the day
from its fidelity to covenantal freedom, proclaiming God's vision
of shalom, and embodying a new form of public witness. The responsible church lives out a public theology that is rooted in God's
covenant of abundance. Félix-Jäger's brilliant book is both a thesis
and a manual for churches willing to be 'responsible' in today's controversial Western societies."

—**Nimi Wariboko**, Boston University

"The concept of 'freedom'—particularly for those in the Western
world—is fraught with misunderstanding, misapplication, and mis-
appropriation. Especially for the Christian. Too often, we see our
freedom in Christ as a kind of libertine Americanism where we can
do whatever we want under the banner of empire. Thankfully, Félix-
Jäger has offered us a substantive alternative. To be free, it seems,
is to be submitted to Christ. And this book paves a way forward to
understand how that is more about freedom than anything a nation
could ever construct on its own."

—**A. J. Swoboda**, Bushnell University; author of
The Gift of Thorns

"This book rejects conservative Christianity's culture-war stance
against secular liberalism and instead advances a vibrant Pentecostal public theology of renewal and abundance. Rooted in the biblical
themes of covenant, jubilee, and Pentecost (interpreted as a cosmic
jubilee), this book presents a constructive theological alternative to
secular liberal ideologies of freedom and the free-market economy.
Written with conceptual clarity, academic rigor, and fresh insights,
this work makes a significant contribution to public theology."

—**Hak Joon Lee**, Fuller Theological Seminary

The
PROBLEM
and PROMISE
of FREEDOM

The
PROBLEM
and PROMISE
of FREEDOM

A Public Theology
for the Church

STEVEN FÉLIX-JÄGER

Baker Academic
a division of Baker Publishing Group
Grand Rapids, Michigan

Published by Baker Academic
a division of Baker Publishing Group
Grand Rapids, Michigan
BakerAcademic.com

Printed in the United States of America

Library of Congress Cataloging-in-Publication Data
Names: Félix-Jäger, Steven, author.
Title: The problem and promise of freedom : a public theology for the church / Steven Félix-Jäger.
Description: Grand Rapids, Michigan : Baker Academic, a division of Baker Publishing Group, [2025] | Includes index.
Identifiers: LCCN 2024029184 | ISBN 9781540968142 (paperback) | ISBN 9781540969156 (casebound) | ISBN 9781493449972 (ebook) | ISBN 9781493449989 (pdf)
Subjects: LCSH: Public theology. | Freedom—Religious aspects—Christianity. | Generosity—Religious aspects—Christianity.
Classification: LCC BT83.63 .F65 2025 | DDC 230—dc23/eng/20240807
LC record available at https://lccn.loc.gov/2024029184

Cover design by Paula Gibson

Baker Publishing Group publications use paper produced from sustainable forestry practices and postconsumer waste whenever possible.

25 26 27 28 29 30 31   7 6 5 4 3 2 1

CONTENTS

PROLOGUE

A Public Theology for the Church

Whenever I hear a preacher ask, "You know what's wrong with our culture today?"[1] I typically turn to whoever's sitting next to me and say something like, "Oh boy, here we go." Time and time again, this opening line precedes a political rant about how our nation has lost its way. Sighting a few examples from pop culture, the preacher diagnoses our moral decay before painting a rather narrow view of what our culture would look like if we lived in a Christian nation. This vision usually harks back to a time in our collective history when things were better. One glaring issue is that the preacher's vision of a moral society is often limited and perspectival. The preacher might, for instance, call us to return to 1950s America, when the family unit was respected and celebrated. But this moral vision only reflects that of the privileged majority that enjoyed middle-class stability at this time. It was, after all, the 1950s, when black people and white people couldn't even drink from the same water fountain. Diagnosing a culture tends to be one-sided—the good ol' days weren't good for everyone.

1. As will be discussed next chapter, this book engages a Western public discourse. In particular, it focuses on the Western church's relationship to classical liberalism.

The preacher's pessimistic take on culture usually serves as a call to arms to be a force for Christ in a morally bankrupt society. While the preacher's intent may be to embolden congregants to be an intentional Christian influence in the world, a "culture war" approach to Christian public witness misses the mark on a few accounts. First, *it confuses the role of the church by waging war on the wrong thing.* Culture consists of the shared beliefs, customs, traditions, values, and even language of a society. The church's war should be not against culture per se but against the "cosmic powers of this present darkness" that affect the world (Eph. 6:12).[2] Culture is the product of its influences, and Christians in a society already *help shape* culture. Rather than condemning the outcome (culture), the church should offer a compelling vision of what the world could be. When a society truly sees the goodness of a Christian witness, culture condemns its own practices.

This leads us to a second point: *A culture war approach confuses what it means to be a public witness.* Being a public witness for Christ means being Christ's ambassador—a citizen of the kingdom of God who demonstrates what it means to live a Spirit-filled life in the world (2 Cor. 5:20). Instead of focusing on winning cultural battles, we should emphasize living out the values of the kingdom of God, such as love, grace, generosity, and reconciliation. People need spiritual and emotional help; they need Jesus. Should we spend our energy arguing over superfluous matters like whether we call it a "holiday tree" or a "Christmas tree"? Such arguments are futile, especially since, last I checked, evergreen trees don't grow in Bethlehem!

Furthermore, the church was never commissioned to go and make a "Christian nation" but was commissioned to go and make "disciples of all nations" (Matt. 28:19). This means Christ's followers must spread the good news to all cultures, backgrounds, and nations, in hopes of leading people to Christ. Making disciples involves evangelism, teaching, mentoring, encouragement, and providing support (emotional and material), as people cultivate relationships with

---

2. All Scripture references are from the NRSVue unless otherwise stated.

Christ. Discipleship also involves building and sustaining communities of believers who support and help each other along their faith journeys. These communities also band together to do good works in the world—feed the hungry, help the poor and disenfranchised, and care for the hurting. In fact, Jesus describes his own public ministry as doing just that:

> The Spirit of the Lord is upon me,
>   because he has anointed me
>   to bring good news to the poor.
> He has sent me to proclaim release to the captives
>   and recovery of sight to the blind,
>   to set free those who are oppressed,
> to proclaim the year of the Lord's favor. (Luke 4:18–19)

The church should minister like Jesus in word *and* deed. Jesus's kingdom is concerned for the *whole* person.

Third, *a culture war approach confuses what it means to enter a public discourse.* In a pluralist society, public discourse is the exchange of ideas between members of the society on topics of public interest. This sort of interaction is crucial for a democratic society that strives to govern according to the needs and desires of its citizens. The goal of members of a society is to use *persuasion*—the act of influencing someone's beliefs and actions through debate—to convince others that their particular vision for the world is the most compelling and beneficial path for making the world better. The Christian perspective is welcome in a pluralist, democratic society, but it is one vision among many other competing visions. Our goal as the church should be to demonstrate the truth, goodness, and beauty of the gospel in such a compelling way that we win the public debate. This happens not through force but by faithful witness to the gospel, which *is* true, good, and beautiful. By living out the gospel, the church will demonstrate to the world what living in peace with God and others looks like. The church will create a compelling alternative vision for the world that truly emulates the good news of the gospel.

Fourth and finally, *a culture war approach to public witness doesn't recognize that society has shaped the culture of the church*. Culture war preachers believe that they are living out the gospel in purity—in a way untouched by the influences and demands of contemporary secular society. They fail to see that *they too* are products of Western liberalism and that much of what they think is plain text and biblical actually bears the marks of their modern interpretive lens.

This last point inspired my approach to public theology in this book. Rather than calling for the world to be different, I want a public theology to call *the church to be different in the world*. This seems simple enough, but as we'll see throughout the pages of this book, in many instances the church condemns secular society even while it adopts and perpetuates many of its tenets. This sort of hypocrisy works against the witness of the church as it, ironically, attempts to be an emboldened witness. Thus the church must first work to make its own polity reflect that of God's kingdom before it hopes to be an effective witness to any other polities.

While the task of *any* theology is first and foremost to study the nature of God in relation to humanity, *public theologies* attempt to understand God's relation to humanity across the pressing social, cultural, and political issues of the times. Public theologies seek to foster dialogue across religious and secular boundaries. They bridge the gap between Christianity and public life in two ways: (1) by offering a critical perspective that challenges the church's role in society, particularly its relationship to power structures and its response to social and political issues, and (2) by offering a constructive voice in shaping socioreligious discourse. When theologians promote a particular type of government (i.e., a liberal democracy or a populist autocracy), I believe they are doing too much. Public theologies should focus not on what sorts of political environments are conducive for Christian flourishing but on how to be a faithful witness in *any* political environment. Since every nation needs ambassadors for the kingdom of God, our job is to faithfully represent the kingdom.

This is not to say that Christians should not have a political voice. As democratic voters in a pluralist society, Christians can and should be informed by the values of their own faith tradition. Likewise, elected officials who are transparent about their moral and religious commitments have full right to take positioned stances in public discourse, so long as they adequately represent the wills and desires of those who elected them. While we should never coerce others, we all have the right to persuade each other through genuine public discourse. As we craft a public theology of renewal in this book, we will be less concerned with the particular government or ideals of a secular society than with the church's Christian witness in society. As such, this book spends a lot of time critiquing the Western church's embrace of liberal ideology[3] before offering constructive recommendations for the church's public engagement in the world. In particular, this book challenges the church to live up to its mission of advancing love, generosity, and reconciliation in the world by promoting a theology of abundance.

---

3. See my definition of "liberalism" and discussion of liberal theology in the introduction.

ACKNOWLEDGMENTS

While *The Problem and Promise of Freedom* is my first book-length foray into public theology, I have, for decades, been thinking through and teaching on many of the issues discussed throughout these pages. When I was a youth and college group pastor at various churches, students would invariably ask me about the church's role in politics and the public realm. Similar questions have come up throughout my years of teaching theology, philosophy, and ethics courses at various universities. Thus the first group I'd like to acknowledge consists of the hundreds of students, colleagues, and parishioners I've had the privilege of engaging with.

The second group I'd like to acknowledge consists of the wonderful people who helped make this book a reality. First, I'd like to say thank you to Brandy Scritchfield, Melisa Blok, and all the other rock star editors at Baker Academic. I am so blessed to have worked with you again. I'd also like to thank my friends A. J. Swoboda, Bill Oliverio, and Chris E. W. Green for writing wonderful recommendations for me to help get this book published. I'd like to thank several friends who were kind enough to read parts of the book and offer me feedback. In particular, two colleagues at Life Pacific University, Jim W. Adams and Luci Sanders, were such a huge help for me! They helped make this book significantly better. My friends

Josh Edwards, Chandler Sargent, and Yoon Shin gave me valuable insight as well. I'm also thankful for Meagan Lord, Tim Lee, and Jen Thigpenn (colleagues and podcaster friends), who have talked through several of these issues with me! I'd like to thank all of my friends at the Society for Pentecostal Studies (my favorite academic society!) for giving me the space to work out many of these ideas. A few of my all-time favorite dialogue partners on matters of the church and the public are my dad Wilfredo, my uncle Luis, and my sister and brother-in-law Jessica and Kevin.

Finally, I'd like to acknowledge a third group that consists of my personal support system. My wife, Connie, and daughter, Mila, always support me and even offer feedback to my random, off-the-cuff soliloquies that nobody asked for! Finally, I thank God, the subject of all my work, for the clarity and strength needed to write this book.

INTRODUCTION

The Problem of Freedom

After the Enlightenment, one could argue that "freedom" emerged as *the* hallmark of modern Western civilization. The American and French Revolutions gave rise to democratic societies that sought to protect the individual rights and freedoms of their citizens. Many of these nations erected monuments to commemorate their unwavering pursuits of liberation. For instance, parallel Statues of Liberty stand in the US and in France as iconic symbols of freedom and democracy. Many replicas of the Statue of Liberty can be found around Europe and Canada, including Spanish artist Salvador Dalí's famous renditions of the statue in Vascœuil, France, and Cadaqués, Spain, where lady liberty holds up both arms as if she's cheering on a team at a sporting event. Other examples of freedom monuments include the historical Brandenburg Gate in Berlin, Germany, which has come to symbolize unity and freedom in post–Cold War Europe, and the Freedom Monument in Riga, Latvia, which has come to symbolize the state's independence, sovereignty, and freedom in Eastern Europe. As symbols of social and political victory, these monuments attest to and honor what has perhaps become Westerners' greatest modern ideal: liberty.

Indeed, classical liberalism animates the Western psyche so completely that notions of freedom have been favored not only in political discourse but in religious sympathies as well. For instance, American flags commonly adorn the altars of church sanctuaries. For many Americans, the flag is closely associated with their God-given freedoms—both political and spiritual. Facing the flag and with their hands over their hearts, American schoolchildren are asked to daily commit their allegiance to "one nation under God" before affirming the cherished American values of liberty and justice. But at what point does the reverence of a national symbol of freedom turn from a gesture of patriotic unity to the veneration of a false idol? When we let nationalizing symbols physically enter our churches and conceptually enter our confessions of faith, are we erecting temples to foreign gods throughout the kingdom of God? Throughout this chapter, and as a main premise of this book, I suggest that the Western church's movement toward liberalism (see my definition below) is a form of syncretic idolization.[1]

Before diving into these deeply important issues, a few definitions are in order. Throughout this book I use the term "liberalism" in the historical, political sense, which is sometimes called "classical liberalism." By liberalism I do not mean leftist politics but instead refer to the liberalism of the Enlightenment—a political ideology that emphasizes individual liberty, equality, and the protection of individual rights and freedoms. In the context of government, liberalism promotes democracy and a limited role for government, with the primary goal of protecting individual rights and promoting a free-market economy. The term "freedom" refers to actions without restraints, but throughout this book, and especially in chapter 1, I am careful to distinguish various concepts of freedom (i.e., voluntarist freedom and covenantal freedom). In fact, one of the main premises of this book is that the church confuses varying concepts of freedom. "Voluntarism" refers to the idea that political authority comes from the human will, so "voluntarist freedom" refers to a person's willful political action. This book proposes a public theology of renewal. The Pew Research Center has defined "renewal" and "renewalist" to refer collectively to

---

1. Syncretic worship involves the blending of rituals and symbols from different traditions, creating a new form of worship that reflects elements from both participating communities.

classical Pentecostal, charismatic, and neo-Pentecostal expressions of the Christian faith. In like manner, I will use "renewal" as an umbrella term that encompasses Christians around the world who identify as any sort of Pentecostal or charismatic.[2] Finally, I use the term "theology of abundance" to frame a theological social ethics based on personal and communal flourishing in covenant with God.

Throughout this book I extend a two-part argument—one part critical and the other part constructive. Critically, I contend that the Western church's "golden calf" is the liberal notion of freedom and that this idol has two faces: *voluntarist freedom* and *free-market reasoning*. Neither of these "faces" are bad in themselves, but they are treacherous when idolized. Put succinctly, the church is at fault when it embraces the *social* constructs of voluntarist freedom and the *economic* "neutrality" of market reasoning. If the church seeks to reflect the polity of the kingdom of God, it must resist the idols of the liberal tradition. Constructively, I contend that a theology of abundance can help us generate a renewal public theology that resists these idols. Theologies of abundance are not exclusive to renewal theology; in fact, major public theologians from other traditions have written robustly on the subject.[3] While I certainly draw from many non-Pentecostal sources, I rely heavily on the Acts 2 account of Pentecost to present a distinctively Pentecostal theology of abundance for a public theology of renewal.

For the remainder of this introduction, I lay out the biblical foundations for part 1's critical arguments against the church's embrace of liberal concepts of freedom, and I then provide a summary of part 1's structure. Next, I repeat this process for part 2: I first provide the biblical foundations for part 2's constructive arguments for a generative theology of abundance, and then I summarize the structure

2. "Spirit and Power—A 10-Country Survey of Pentecostals," Pew Research Center, October 5, 2006, http://www.pewforum.org/2006/10/05/spirit-and-power.

3. See Sallie McFague, *Life Abundant: Rethinking Theology and Economy for a Planet in Peril* (Minneapolis: Fortress, 2001); Walter Brueggemann, "The Liturgy of Abundance, the Myth of Scarcity," *Christian Century* 116, no. 10 (1999): 342–47; and Miroslav Volf, *Free of Charge: Giving and Forgiving in a Culture Stripped of Grace* (Grand Rapids: Zondervan, 2005).

of part 2. Together, these critical and constructive arguments form what I call a "public theology of renewal."

The Biblical Foundations for Part 1: Critiquing the Idol of Freedom

As we will discuss further in chapter 1, it is not hyperbole to call liberal freedom the Western church's golden calf, nor is it a false analogy. The idolization of liberty is a serious issue that has far-reaching ramifications for the Western church. When ideals extrinsic to the Christian faith are venerated by a society and adopted by the church, what inevitably follows is a spurious, syncretic form of the faith that's biblically unrecognizable. A diplomatic Jesus who preaches a gospel of individual liberty, free markets, the protection of property rights, and limited government intervention stands in place of the miracle-working, Jewish rabbi who preached redemption, reconciliation, loving kindness, and covenantal fidelity in the kingdom of God. Church pulpits become platforms for political persuasion, and a straw-man image of a "Christian" stands in place of a cruciforming disciple.[4] The church's witness is compromised through a subtle yet pervasive idolatry. While the veneration of freedom is *our* problem as a late modern, Western church, it is not a new problem. In fact, we can see striking parallels between us and the newly liberated Israelites throughout the book of Exodus.

The Israelites' Golden Calf

The account of the golden calf in Exodus 32 serves as a cautionary tale about the dangers of idolatry, faithlessness, and the consequences of turning away from true worship of God:

> When the people saw that Moses delayed to come down from the mountain, the people gathered around Aaron and said to him, "Come, make

---

4. "Cruciform" literally means "cross-shaped," so "cruciforming discipleship" refers to a type of discipleship that is humble, loving, and sacrificial. In other words, it is discipleship that is shaped by and centered on the cross.

gods for us, who shall go before us; as for this Moses, the man who brought us up out of the land of Egypt, we do not know what has become of him." Aaron said to them, "Take off the gold rings that are on the ears of your wives, your sons, and your daughters, and bring them to me." So all the people took off the gold rings from their ears and brought them to Aaron. He took these from them, formed them in a mold, and cast an image of a calf, and they said, "These are your gods, O Israel, who brought you up out of the land of Egypt!" When Aaron saw this, he built an altar before it, and Aaron made a proclamation and said, "Tomorrow shall be a festival to the Lord." They rose early the next day and offered burnt-offerings and brought sacrifices of well-being, and the people sat down to eat and drink and rose up to revel. (Exod. 32:1–6)

Growing impatient in Moses's absence, the Israelites approached Aaron and requested a tangible representation of God's presence to worship. Thus the golden calf became an object of worship for the Israelites, and they engaged in revelry and idolatry around it.

What's noteworthy about the Israelites' idolatry is that it was essentially syncretic. Some might read this passage and wonder how the people could so quickly turn to an obviously false god—one constructed by their own hands—when Yahweh had just delivered them out of slavery. But they did not view the golden calf as a wholly other god; they likely believed the golden calf represented an *image* of Yahweh.[5] This is evidenced by Aaron's proclamation in verse 5b: "Tomorrow shall be a festival to the Lord."[6] The term "Lord" is a translation of the divine Hebrew name of God (יהוה), which most scholars vocalize as "Yahweh." Thus Aaron's use of the divine name Yahweh in verse 5 indicates that the calf was meant not to supplant Yahweh but to somehow relate to Yahweh. Out of their impatience, the Hebrews reverted to what they knew and mimicked the worship practices of Egypt and the surrounding areas of the ancient Near East.[7]

5. *Dictionary of the Old Testament: Pentateuch*, ed. T. Desmond Alexander and David W. Baker (Downers Grove, IL: InterVarsity, 2003), s.v. "Golden Calf" (p. 369).

6. Throughout the Old Testament, when the word "Lord" is printed in small caps, it is replacing the divine name יהוה (Yahweh).

7. Another important aspect here is the word אלים, which is translated as "gods." The expression in Exod. 32:4 ("These are your gods, O Israel, who brought you up

Ancient Egyptians worshiped tangible representations of their many gods.[8] As polytheists, they believed in multiple gods and goddesses, each associated with a different aspect of life and the natural world. These deities were considered powerful beings who could influence and control various aspects of the world. Gold and other precious materials held immense value and symbolized the eternal, indestructible nature of the gods.[9] Gold, in particular, was associated with the sun, which was seen both as a divine and life-giving force and as the creator god. As a result, gold was frequently used to create statues and images of the gods. The Egyptians believed that these statues were divine representations and served as physical manifestations of the gods on earth. They were believed to house the divine essence and power of the deity they represented.[10]

One could say that the Israelites' idolatry was not the worship of an entirely separate false god but the *false worship of the true God*. The Israelites didn't deny that Yahweh rescued them from Egyptian oppression; rather, they created a physical manifestation of Yahweh to worship, hence idolizing something that's not God. Through Aaron, the Israelites formed the image of Yahweh in their own desired likeness, thus making Yahweh in a familiar image. As Christopher J. H. Wright points out, "This is the essence of syncretism. The Israelites want to claim that they are still loyally worshiping Yahweh, the living God, and yet they are creating and submitting to idols of their own manufacture. They cannot entirely let go of the God of their history, yet they rebelliously make gods for themselves."[11] Syncretic idolatry is still idolatry because the representative idol is *not*

---

out of the land of Egypt!") is clearly a rephrasing of Yahweh's own claim in 20:2 (a historical prologue of the Sinai covenant). Thus Aaron and the people are identifying this calf as the one who delivered them from Egypt and whom they have entered into a covenant relationship with.

8. Erik Hornung, *Conceptions of God in Ancient Egypt: The One and the Many*, trans. John Baines (Ithaca: Cornell University Press, 1982), 135.

9. David Silverman, ed., *Ancient Egypt* (Oxford: Oxford University Press), 64.

10. For more on this see parts 2 and 3 of Richard H. Wilkinson, *The Complete Gods and Goddesses of Ancient Egypt* (New York: Thames & Hudson, 2003).

11. Christopher J. H. Wright, *"Here Are Your Gods": Faithful Discipleship in Idolatrous Times* (Downers Grove, IL: IVP Academic, 2020), 68–69.

God. So, even though the Israelites thought they were worshiping Yahweh, worshiping an idol of Yahweh is not worshiping Yahweh. Their idolatry was syncretic, as the golden calf represented Yahweh and another deity (their own constructed idol) at the same time.

Since the Israelites are called to be religiously and socially unique in their covenant with God (Exod. 19:5–6), their syncretic idolatry is detestable to God. In fact, this is what God prohibits at the start of the Ten Commandments (20:2–4). The first commandment concerns worshiping Yahweh alone, and the second commandment directly connects to the first by prohibiting creating images to worship other gods. The making of the golden calf violates these commands. G. K. Beale defines an idol as "whatever your heart clings to or relies on *for ultimate security*."[12] While the Israelites of Exodus 32 didn't mean to put another god before Yahweh, they placed their loyalty and reliance on a familiar image that represented Yahweh, but in doing so they violated their relationship with God.

Parallels between the Idolatry of the Israelites and the Western Church

The idolatry of the Israelites in Exodus 32 parallels the Western church's embrace of liberalism because both are syncretic. The idolatrous Western church[13] doesn't worship a different God outright but instead worships a syncretized version of God. In other words, the Western church is inclined to defy the second commandment, not the first. Violating the first commandment is, in many ways, easier to spot. We have no problem recognizing when a religious society worships a different god (i.e., Brahma) or a different religious conception of god (i.e., Allah). It's even easy to identify syncretism between religions (i.e., how Santeria blended Roman Catholicism with the Yoruba religion). It is much more difficult, however, to notice

---

12. G. K. Beale, *We Become What We Worship: A Biblical Theology of Idolatry* (Downers Grove, IL: IVP Academic, 2008), 17, emphasis original.

13. I am qualifying the term "Western church" with "idolatrous" because not all of the Western church falls into the trap of syncretism with liberal freedom. I will thus refer to only the parts of the church that *do* as the "idolatrous Western church."

when nonreligious ideologies creep into a faith tradition. This is the Western church's issue—a nonreligious ideology (liberalism) has syncretized with Christianity, creating new idolatrous versions of the faith that are *un*holy in the sense that they are not pure or unique from the dominant ideologies of our day. Instead of a faith that is totally reliant on God, this syncretized version of the faith relies on God *and* the voluntarist, autonomous self. When this change is socially codified and adopted by the church, we see people practicing both a reliance on God *and* a reliance on the liberal nation.

In addition, the Israelites' golden calf and the Western church's golden calf of liberty are syncretic in the same two ways—one social and one economic. The Israelites' desire to dictate *how* God is worshiped speaks of a social self-sufficiency that's centered on control as people make God into their own desired image. Despite witnessing numerous miracles and the presence of God all along their journey out of Egypt, the Israelites succumb to fear and seek solace in a tangible object that they can worship. This reveals a lack of faith as they rely on their own human efforts and understanding, rather than placing their trust in Yahweh. In the same way, the idolatrous Western church shifts its focus from God and God's kingdom to a reliance on personal, cultural, or national identity. The church becomes intertwined with personal and political agendas, often prioritizing self-interest or national interests above biblical teachings and the way of the kingdom. As we'll see in chapter 1, liberalism views individuals as primarily responsible for their own success and well-being, and when this notion is mixed with a Christian perspective, we get *un*biblical sentiments like "God helps those who help themselves."[14] When the church becomes overly focused on personal or nationalistic objectives, it risks replacing its biblical foundation with a narrow agenda that relies on human aspirations rather than biblical wisdom and the Spirit's guidance.

The second face of the golden calf of liberty concerns economics, and it emerges in the idolatrous Western church as the idolization of free-market reasoning (a way of reasoning that relies on market

14. This phrase is often attributed to Benjamin Franklin, but its origins are unknown.

concepts such as supply and demand and competition). While Exodus does not explicitly depict the golden calf as a symbol of wealth, the use of gold for its construction does suggest material wealth, since gold was a valuable material. Aaron literally bonded the Israelites' wealth with Yahweh through the construction of the golden calf, which suggests that *their treasure* occupied their ultimate security, at least to some degree. In an ironic twist, the gold they used came from Egypt (Exod. 12:35–36), further demonstrating Yahweh's supreme power in deliverance. The Israelites were not offering their wealth to God as a tithe but making a representation of God out of their wealth. Thus their wealth, ironically, played a part in their idolatry. The Israelites invested their wealth in an idol to dictate how Yahweh would be worshiped.

Similarly, free-market reasoning can enter the Western church in an idolatrous way. While it is good for Christians to use their wealth to financially support the church's mission, problems arise when consumerism and market-driven thinking uncritically enter the church's operations and decision-making processes. A free-market mindset tends to view everything, including ministry, through the lens of consumer preference. When free-market reasoning influences Christian exhortation, sermons and teachings often emphasize personal success, self-improvement, and self-fulfillment, which align with market-driven values. This can lead to a prosperity gospel focused on individual desires rather than kingdom-oriented efforts.[15]

Finally, the syncretic idolatry of the Israelites parallels our idolatry in the Western church because it tarnishes the holiness of the community of God's people. In Exodus 19 God calls the Israelites to be holy and unique, totally distinct from all other worldly polities.[16] God's call to holiness was meant not to create a separatist movement in the world but to show the world God's holiness. God said as much

15. "Prosperity gospel" refers to Christian teachings that assert that God grants health, wealth, and success to believers in a manner commensurate to their faith. This concept is discussed further in chapters 2 and 5.

16. The call to holiness is a repeated commandment from God that can be seen in both the Old and New Testaments. See Lev. 11:45; 19:2; 20:26; Matt. 5:48; Rom. 12:1; 2 Cor. 7:1; Eph. 1:4; 1 Thess. 4:7; Heb. 12:14; 1 Pet. 1:15–16; 2:9.

through the prophet Ezekiel: "I will sanctify my great name, which has been profaned among the nations and which you have profaned among them, and the nations shall know that I am the LORD, says the Lord GOD, when through you I display my holiness before their eyes" (Ezek. 36:23). The writer of Hebrews tells us that our holiness makes the Lord visible to the world (Heb. 12:14), and Jesus echoes the sentiment that a holy people can serve as a beacon of hope to the world (Matt. 5:14–16). When the church demonstrates holiness, it becomes a faithful witness to the transformative power of God.

Syncretic idolatry sullies the church's holiness, defiling its witness. Instead of a holy church, the world sees a hypocritical church that self-righteously judges others while looking worse than those it condemns. Jesus has a question for this type of posture: "Why do you see the speck in your neighbor's eye but do not notice the log in your own eye?" (Matt. 7:3). Maintaining a good witness demonstrates the church's commitment to God's holiness. The church should strive to live in a way that brings glory to God and reflects God's character to the world. It's only when the church lives out its witness by acting in a consistently loving manner that it becomes an attractive and inviting community people are drawn to.

As we will see in chapter 3, the church can function within a liberal society without idolizing the liberal notion of freedom. In this case the church *uses* its freedoms to promote the idea that individuals have the right to worship and believe according to their consciences without coercion or interference from the state or religious authorities. It advocates for a state that does not favor any particular religion, ensuring religious freedom for all individuals. And it embraces the principles of free markets and entrepreneurship as *tools* for fostering economic prosperity and individual empowerment to help the poor and marginalized in the society. In short, it *uses* its political freedoms to ensure its separation from the state. This allows the church to maintain its own polity as part of the kingdom of God and thus stand as a public witness for the rest of the world. When the liberal notion of freedom is idolized, however, deviant versions of the Christian faith emerge. These include assimilated and nationalistic churches as well as dualistic and materialistic churches.

The Social Face of the Golden Calf: Assimilation and Nationalization

Concerning the social face of the golden calf of liberty, two extremes emerge. On one side of the continuum stands the *assimilated church* that uncritically adopts the prevailing values of liberalism, conforming its beliefs and practices to align with Western liberal norms.[17] As a result, the church's teachings, practices, and moral insight become indistinguishable from secular trends and perspectives. The church prioritizes individual freedom and personal choice over traditional biblical doctrines and moral teachings. It encourages congregants to interpret religious texts in ways that align with their own preferences—creating God in their own image. In an effort to align with a liberal notion of freedom, the church often reinterprets biblical texts to fit contemporary societal norms. David Koyzis says that an idolized liberalism offers a false salvation that's "rooted in a fundamentally religious assertion of human autonomy against external authority."[18] The emphasis on individual autonomy and personal choice leads to a moral relativism where each individual's unencumbered interpretation of their circumstances becomes their ultimate authority. All in all, the assimilated church loses its holiness and blends in with the dominant society, which diminishes its appeal as a radical alternative to the kingdoms of the world.

On the other side of this continuum stands the *nationalistic church* that upholds the values of a liberal society as God-ordained standards. A nationalist church ironically suppresses the freedoms of people in a liberal society by narrowly interpreting voluntarist

---

17. This concept aligns closely with H. Richard Niebuhr's "Christ of culture" view, which represents an optimistic approach where Christianity harmonizes with and enhances culture's values. The goal is to integrate Christian teachings and values seamlessly into the existing cultural framework. This perspective, however, can dilute the transformative power of the Christian message. If the prevailing cultural values and norms are adopted uncritically, Jesus's distinctive teachings and radical call to discipleship may be overshadowed or ignored. See H. Richard Niebuhr, *Christ and Culture* (New York: Harper & Row, 1951), chap. 3.

18. David Koyzis, *Political Visions and Illusions: A Survey and Christian Critique of Contemporary Ideologies*, 2nd ed. (Downers Grove, IL: IVP Academic, 2019), 62.

freedom (one's ability to act according to one's own preferences) as a God-given right that must be protected by the church. The assimilated church uses liberalism progressively as free people (because people are free, they can freely make decisions), whereas the nationalist church establishes liberalism as their conservative identity marker as *freed* people (because people were made free, they can live in a new national identity distinct from those who formerly oppressed them). While liberalism advocates for the separation of church and state, a nationalistic church blurs these boundaries. It seeks to exert influence on political affairs, aiming to assert its own political and religious agendas on society and limit the freedom of others. A nationalistic church often resorts to coercion, manipulation, or fear-based tactics to ensure compliance and maintain authority. It uses guilt, shame, or threats of punishment to enforce adherence to its moral convictions. Rather than emphasizing limited government intervention, a nationalistic church exhibits authoritarian tendencies, proclaiming the secular state to be a "Christian nation." While not every church has slipped into an idolatrous, nationalistic version of the faith, many influential Christian churches, communities, and authors have.[19]

The Economic Face of the Golden Calf: Dualism and Materialism

Concerning the *economic* face of the golden calf of liberty, two extremes also exist. On one side of the continuum stands the *dualistic church*. As it applies to economics, the dualistic church serves two masters: God and money. While they consult God on spiritual matters, they use free-market reasoning for material affairs. You would be hard pressed to find a church that readily admits to serving both God and wealth. This sort of syncretism is not typically explicit—it creeps into church governance unperceived. Furthermore, it is often difficult to tell if a church is merely using the market to serve its

19. See Stephen Wolfe, *The Case for Christian Nationalism* (Moscow, ID: Canon, 2022); Jarrin Jackson, *Christian Nationalism Is Inevitable . . . and That's Good News!* (self-pub., 2023); and Dominic Francese, *Prophetic Patriotism: A New Call to Action* (Tulsa: Word & Spirit, 2023).

congregation or if it's allowing the market to determine its values and motivations. Despite this, there are some signs that could suggest that a church prioritizes market rationale over congregational needs. Does the church do any of the following?

1. Prioritize high-production value to draw large crowds
2. Invest more in marketing strategies and branding than in community service and outreach
3. Engage in outreach to grow its congregation rather than serve the needs of the community
4. Sell an image of perfection rather than acknowledge its imperfections
5. Practice secrecy rather than transparency about its finances, fundraising, and allocation of funds

Although these examples can help us get a sense of a church's implicit economic philosophy, we should note that detecting whether a church is relying more on market reasoning than on covenantal provision can be complex and may involve subjective judgment.

On the other side of this continuum stands the *materialistic church* that uses free-market reasoning to interpret biblical principles concerning money and possessions. This church merges market logic *into* the faith to create a materialistic understanding of biblical concepts such as blessing, provision, and abundance. A common expression of the materialistic church is the so-called prosperity gospel, which intertwines elements of the faith with a focus on personal prosperity and success. Hence, the prosperity gospel introduces market reasoning by promoting the idea that financial blessings and material abundance are indicators of spiritual well-being. As with the dualistic church, we can observe some signs that might suggest that a church is beholden to materialism. For example, we can ask whether the church does any of the following:

1. Regularly promote messages that emphasize accumulating wealth, financial success, and material possessions as a primary goal of faith

2. Constantly pressure members into giving money and tell them that greater donations produce spiritual rewards

3. Have a culture of judgment or exclusion toward those with less financial means

4. Allocate large portions of its budget to lavish facilities, extravagant decorations, or expensive technology

5. Show more concern for individual financial success than for addressing social justice issues, poverty, and outreach to the community

The best way to determine whether a church is materialistic is to analyze its teachings, practices, and values and compare them with those of a healthy church that practices Sabbath generosity, which we'll discuss in chapter 5.

Summary of Part 1

I flesh out the critical arguments from above throughout part 1 of this book, which is made up of three chapters that focus on the two faces of the golden calf of liberty and the effects of this syncretic idolatry on the church. In chapter 1, I explore the origins of the social side of the Western church's golden calf: the liberal notion of voluntarist freedom. I trace the Kantian roots of autonomous freedom, which are expressed clearly in Rawls's high liberal concept of "justice as fairness." This root, along with Locke's notion of property rights, inspired Nozick's libertarian view of "justice as entitlement." Both of these influential streams of thought rely on voluntarism, which, when idolized by the church, leads to a self-absorbed, syncretized faith. I argue that the church must embrace the biblical notion of "covenantal freedom" instead of a liberal notion of freedom.

Chapter 2 states that a theology of abundance can rightly combat the pervasive ideology of the free market in the church. When market logic enters our church polity, it quickly oversteps the boundaries of economic deliberation and redefines our principles of justice as we are guided by a "market morality." Churches that uncritically adopt free-market reasoning engage in idolatry in one of two ways: (1) they establish a dualistic outlook where God governs spiritual matters and the free market governs material matters, or (2) they subsume market reasoning into biblical norms, which forms a materialistic faith. The former church allows the market to share God's sovereign throne, and the latter church intertwines elements of the faith with a focus on personal prosperity and success. A theology of abundance, on the other hand, perpetuates a "Sabbath logic," which negates consumerism, promotes generosity, and gives us permission to rest and enjoy God's provision.

Chapter 3 explores what it means to be a citizen of God's kingdom today and what covenant fidelity to the kingdom of God looks like in the midst of "Babylon." Does membership in God's kingdom mean we must reject citizenship in our local nation? Can we hold some sort of dual citizenship? How does life in a Christian community work in a liberal society? To answer these questions, this chapter delineates how biblical covenants have functioned within national polities and how conflicting civic virtues can find common ground. It demonstrates how political persuasion in a pluralistic society entails a public witness of grace and generosity, which provides the world with a vision of the kingdom of God through the church's counternarrative of abundant love. Taken together, chapters 1–3 make up the critical arguments of this book. In them, I call out the Western church's idolatry by exposing its confused relationship to society.

The Biblical Foundations for Part 2: Constructing a Witness of Grace and Generosity

So far we've looked at the biblical foundations for this study's critical arguments against the church's embrace of liberal, voluntarist freedom, which led us to explore, primarily, Exodus 32, where God admonishes the Israelites for their idolatry. As this book's critical arguments mirror God's rebuke of the *liberated* Israelites, so should the *liberal* Western church be reproached for its syncretic idolatry. However, Exodus is not merely a book of condemnation—it also establishes for the Israelites what it looks like to be a *truly* free people in covenant with God. In the same way, a robust public theology of renewal cannot remain in the fallout of rebuke; it must also show what a truly free people in covenant with God looks like today. This is the aim of my constructive arguments throughout part 2.

Ethicist Hak Joon Lee sees covenant as the root metaphor of the Bible.[20] Although we tend to think of the Mosaic covenant as *the* pivotal moment between God and Israel, the Bible is full of covenants that lead up to it and others that come after it. While the Mosaic covenant is at the heart of the Torah and provides the most detailed ethical and ritual directives,[21] it is best understood as part of God's overarching covenantal history with humanity. As Lee writes, "Covenant is the modus operandi that God takes in interacting with humanity and the world, and God fulfills God's purpose for humanity and creation through covenant. In the Bible, covenant is central to God's reign, which is by nature ethical and manifested in the calling and formation of God's community."[22] From the beginning of Scripture, we see God drawing humanity into covenant relationship.

Covenants throughout the Bible

Genesis begins with God making an implicit covenant with creation. Although the word "covenant" doesn't appear in Genesis 1–3, we can see Genesis 1:26–28 as an implicit covenant that God makes with humanity. God creates humanity and establishes a life of peace, completeness, and holistic well-being (*shalom*) for them, and he names them stewards of the created order.[23] This covenant, often referred to as the Adamic covenant, is "foundational and normative for subsequent covenants."[24] Every other covenant aims to restore, in some way, the Adamic covenant.

---

20. Hak Joon Lee, *Christian Ethics: A New Covenant Model* (Grand Rapids: Eerdmans, 2021), 19.
21. Lee, *Christian Ethics*, 27.
22. Lee, *Christian Ethics*, 7.
23. Lee, *Christian Ethics*, 21.
24. Lee, *Christian Ethics*, 23.

The Noachian covenant occurs in Genesis 9:8–17 after the flood. Here God makes a universal covenant with all of humanity and with all living creatures. Lee sees the Noachian covenant as important for establishing the theological notion of common grace, since grace is extended to all.[25] While Noah's covenant is a promise to preserve creation, God later makes a covenant with Abraham that is intended to redeem humanity, and it includes promises of land (Gen. 15) and many descendants (Gen. 17). As Genesis 12 tells us, the Abrahamic covenant is both local and universal—Abraham, in particular, was blessed (local), but he was blessed in order to be a blessing to all nations (universal).

Next, the Mosaic covenant extends the local-universal paradigm, but instead of choosing an individual, God chooses a nation (Israel) to bring about God's blessing to the world. God forms this covenant with Israel on Mount Sinai after they are liberated from slavery in Egypt, and his instructions include details concerning ritual and moral life.[26] Through Moses, God gives the people laws and commandments that they unanimously agree to abide by (Exod. 19:8). Among the terms of the covenant are the Ten Commandments and various other statutes that cover aspects of moral and civic life in covenant with God. These commandments and laws serve as a guideline for the Israelites' relationship with God and with one another. The covenant also includes instructions for building the tabernacle, where God's presence will dwell among the people. Thus the Mosaic covenant forms the basis of Israel's religious and national identity. (For the remainder of this book, when I reference the old covenant, I am referring to the Mosaic covenant.)

For the Israelites, freedom is not mere liberation from slavery. Rather, freedom and the capacity to flourish are both found in covenant with God. As ethicist Scott Bader-Saye states, "Freedom and identity for Israel are not to be found in abstraction from the life and claims of others. This is why the narratives of Exodus (Israel's

---

25. Lee, *Christian Ethics*, 25. "Common grace" refers to God's grace that is available to all people regardless of their spiritual state.

26. Lee, *Christian Ethics*, 27.

liberation) and Sinai (the giving of the Torah) are interwoven in the Jewish Scriptures. In God's story there is no liberation without covenant, no freedom apart from the faithful service of God, no identity apart from the common life of the chosen people."[27] One cannot read the exodus account as a story of mere liberation—it is a story of liberation *out of* slavery and *into* covenant. God addresses *all* of Israel's needs, which includes the need for liberation *and* the need for a newly covenanted relationship with the living God. Covenantal obedience serves as a foundation for all subsequent covenants (i.e., the Davidic covenant and other references to covenant in the prophets) between God and people throughout the Bible, and it aligns God's people so that they can live and flourish in abundance.

To understand covenantal abundance, imagine a plant that struggles to grow in a desolate city corner bereft of rain and sunlight. The little soil that's there is compacted, lifeless, and lacks nutrients, making it a hostile environment for any aspiring life. Uprooting the plant from that poor environment is the necessary first step to help it flourish. But if the plant is *merely* uprooted, it will quickly die in the open air. Once the plant is uprooted (liberated) from the poor environment, it must be replanted into a good environment for it to live and thrive.

Now imagine a new location with fertile soil and abundant sunlight—ideal conditions for the plant to thrive. Let's assume there's a gardener who uproots and replants the plant in this better location. When the gardener replants the plant, he ensures it is perfectly aligned and at the appropriate depth, allowing its crown to rest just above the surface. He backfills the soil around the roots, ensuring that no air pockets remain. Once securely planted, the plant is watered by the gardener, providing it with the sustenance it requires. The soil, rich in nutrients, provides nourishment to the plant, enabling it to grow robustly. Season after season, the plant continues to thrive, expanding its reach and enhancing its surrounding landscape.

Likewise, covenant with God is the appropriate environment for God's people to flourish. The laws and statutes of the covenant were

27. Scott Bader-Saye, "The Freedom of Faithfulness," *Pro Ecclesia* 8, no. 4 (1999): 446.

never meant to be restrictive or oppressive. Jacqueline Grey and Edward Helmore see the exodus story as an invitation "out of slavery and into freedom, out of anxiety and towards rest, and from insufficiency to abundance."[28] Since God is creator and sustainer of all life, it makes sense that to truly flourish and find rest, one must be rooted in covenant with God.

Sabbath Principles in a Covenant of Abundance

The book of Exodus introduces the *Sabbath* as an integral part of God's covenant. The fourth commandment instructs the Israelites to "remember the Sabbath day and keep it holy" (Exod. 20:8). This commandment was given to the Israelites *and* their servants, animals, and even foreigners within their communities (v. 10). They all were to set aside the seventh day of the week as a day of rest. This pattern reflects the creation account where God rests on the seventh day after working for six. During the Sabbath, the Israelites were to abstain from their regular work in order to dwell in God's abundant provision. It was a time for physical rest, rejuvenation, and renewal. Although the Sabbath was presented as a gift from God throughout the book of Exodus, it was also a *sacrifice of obedience* since nothing was to be produced in the land. Thus obeying the Sabbath law was an act of trust in Yahweh. Even still, it was never meant to be a burden but was meant to be a day of joy, rest, and spiritual renewal.

These Sabbath principles were most fully articulated in the biblical tradition of Jubilee, detailed in Leviticus 25. In addition to the weekly Sabbath observed every seventh day, the Israelites were commanded to observe sabbatical years (vv. 3–4). A sabbatical year occurred every seventh year, during which the land was to lie fallow and rest, and the Israelites were not to cultivate their fields or vineyards. It was a time of rest for the land and a demonstration of trust in God's provision.

28. Jacqueline Grey and Edward Helmore, "Do What Is Right and Good: The Theological Foundations for the Common Good in the Old Testament Prophets," in *The Politics of the Spirit: Pentecostal Reflections on Public Responsibility and the Common Good*, ed. Daniela C. Augustine and Chris E. W. Green (Lanham, MD: Seymour, 2022), 92.

After seven cycles of the sabbatical year (forty-nine years), the fiftieth year would mark the Year of Jubilee (v. 8). The Year of Jubilee was a time of release and restoration. Several regulations were implemented during this year, including the release of slaves, a return of ancestral lands, and cancellation of debts. Although some scholars debate if the Year of Jubilee was ever actually observed,[29] the aspiration of Jubilee carries profound social and economic implications that would provide God's covenantal people opportunities to correct any imbalances or injustices that may have occurred over the years.

In the Old Testament traditions of Sabbath and Jubilee, we can see the foundations of a biblical social witness that promotes the flourishing of a society in covenant with God. We can see a covenantal basis for extending generosity and embrace toward the self and others. According to Grey and Helmore, covenantal fidelity allows for God's covenant partners to flourish in relationship with God and for people to flourish together in community. They write, "Justice is not an abstract concept but a relational priority that reflects the relational love of Yahweh and is outworked in the flourishing of all people in community. This requires each member of the covenant community to mirror the covenant-maker in extravagant care of others and to serve not their own interest but the common good."[30] We are dependent on God in covenant, but it is in this dependence that we flourish and help others to flourish.

The Gospel of Luke recounts the Last Supper, where Jesus gives the disciples bread and wine as a ritualistic foreshadowing of the cross: "Then he [Jesus] took a loaf of bread, and when he had given thanks he broke it and gave it to them, saying, 'This is my body, which is given for you. Do this in remembrance of me.' And he did the same with the cup after supper, saying, 'This cup that is poured out for you is the new covenant in my blood'" (Luke 22:19–20).[31] Jesus indicates

29. B. C. Babcock, "Jubilee, Year of," in *The Lexham Bible Dictionary*, ed. J. D. Barry and L. Wentz (Bellingham, WA: Lexham, 2012). There is no biblical report describing the observance of this law, hence the reason for debate.

30. Grey and Helmore, "Do What Is Right and Good," 91–92.

31. It should be noted that Luke is the only Gospel where the term "new covenant" is explicitly stated. Matthew says, "This is my blood of the covenant, which is poured out for many for the forgiveness of sins" (Matt. 26:28). Mark says, "This

that his sacrifice will usher in a new covenant, or at least a renewed sense of the old (Mosaic) covenant. Lee describes well how Jesus's new covenant was to be understood through the framework of the exodus tradition:

> Firmly standing within the exodus-Sinai tradition he inherited, he [Jesus] preached the reign of God and built a new community around him. The norms of justice, mercy, nonviolence, and faith, which Jesus emphasized in his parables and moral teachings, were covenantal in nature. He gave himself as the covenantal sacrifice and bond between God and humanity. The climax of Jesus's covenantal action was the cross. A new, inclusive, and egalitarian community was formed around his body as the new covenant (the church). Jesus fulfilled the covenant and has become the new covenant itself.[32]

Jesus's covenant with humanity is not just a contract but a covenant of love. Jesus's death, resurrection, and outpouring of the Spirit at Pentecost allowed for a renewal of the relationship between God and humanity, making it possible for all people to enter into this new covenant, a covenant of abundance. We should note the new covenant is not separate from the old covenant but builds on, expands, and renews the previous iterations of the old covenant.[33] In other words, we are not entering into a new covenant that's distinct from the one God made with Israel—Jesus is not starting something entirely new. Rather, Jesus is *fulfilling* and fully enacting the original intent of the old covenant.

Paul brilliantly fleshes out this idea in 2 Corinthians 3, where he differentiates the new covenant from the old. First, Paul describes the new covenant as a covenant "of the Spirit": "Such is the confidence

---

is my blood of the covenant, which is poured out for many" (Mark 14:24). John only recounts the Last Supper to give a backdrop of Judas's betrayal of Jesus and doesn't quote Jesus's mandate. When Paul quotes Jesus in 1 Cor. 11:25, he quotes the Lukan account of the Last Supper: "This cup is the new covenant in my blood. Do this, as often as you drink it, in remembrance of me."

32. Lee, *Christian Ethics*, 37.

33. Daniel Block, *Covenant: The Framework of God's Grand Plan of Redemption* (Grand Rapids: Baker Academic, 2021), 15.

that we have through Christ toward God. Not that we are qualified of ourselves to claim anything as coming from us; our qualification is from God, who has made us qualified to be ministers of a new covenant, not of letter but of spirit, for the letter kills, but the Spirit gives life" (2 Cor. 3:4–6). He then goes on to say that the old covenant law is written on stone (the Ten Commandments), whereas the new covenant law is written on our hearts (vv. 2–3, 7). While the law of the old covenant brings about condemnation and death, the new covenant brings about life in abundance by the transforming work of the Holy Spirit (vv. 7–11).

Paul also mentions an image of the veil that Moses wore when he spoke to the Israelites. While Moses's veil protected the radiance of his face after he encountered God at Mount Sinai, it also represents the Israelites' spiritual blindness as they turned solely to the law rather than to God (2 Cor. 3:12–14). In the new covenant, however, Christ removes the veil: "Indeed, to this very day whenever Moses is read, a veil lies over their minds, but when one turns to the Lord, the veil is removed. Now the Lord is the Spirit, and where the Spirit of the Lord is, there is freedom. And all of us, with unveiled faces, seeing the glory of the Lord as though reflected in a mirror, are being transformed into the same image from one degree of glory to another, for this comes from the Lord, the Spirit" (vv. 15–18). In God's new covenant, we are guided by the Spirit rather than the law for personal and communal flourishing. Therefore, as we are covenanted with Christ in the new covenant, we experience the sort of freedom God always intended for God's people.

As we outline God's covenant of abundance for the church today, we need look no further than the Acts 2 account of Pentecost. Pentecost, also known as *Shavuot*, is a Jewish holiday celebrated fifty days after Passover. While it commemorates the day God gave the Torah to the Israelites on Sinai, it also marks the end of the grain harvest in Israel. As such, Jews would bring the firstfruits of their harvest to the temple as an offering. In the book of Acts, it was on the day of Pentecost that the Holy Spirit descended on the gathered disciples, and tongues of fire appeared and rested on each of them. They were filled with the

Spirit and began speaking in different languages, enabling them to communicate with the diverse crowd of Jewish pilgrims throughout Jerusalem. This marked the birth of the church and the empowering of believers with the Spirit. While Shavuot marks the formation of the Israelite community under the Law, Pentecost marks the formation of the church united and empowered by the Spirit. Just as Shavuot celebrates the firstfruits of God's provision for the Israelites, Pentecost demonstrates the firstfruits of the Spirit manifested in believers.

Pentecost also parallels Jubilee in some significant ways, making it a type of Jubilee for God's covenant of abundance. While Pentecost took place on the fiftieth day after Passover (after seven weeks of sevens), the Year of Jubilee took place every fifty years (after seven years of sevens). They both carry themes of liberation, restoration, and renewal. Pentecost represents the liberation and empowerment of believers through the Holy Spirit, while the Year of Jubilee symbolizes the liberation and restoration of individuals and society. Thus just as the exodus account serves as a biblical foundation for a theology of covenant, the universal outpouring of the Spirit at Pentecost serves as a biblical foundation for a theology of God's covenant of abundance. It is through this lens that we can craft a public theology of renewal that promotes social efforts toward mutuality and hospitality and economic efforts toward generosity. All of this flows out of the idea that covenantal freedom promotes a theology of abundance.

Summary of Part 2

Part 2 consists of three chapters that flesh out this book's constructive arguments. The first of these chapters (chap. 4) maintains that an abundant, biblical freedom entails being subsumed into life in the Spirit. This new life happens when believers experience new spiritual and social freedoms as they move from a worldly covenant to God's covenant of abundance. To begin, this chapter examines two aspects of the liberal conception of self—namely, the idea that people are independent of their communities and societies, and the idea that liberalism promotes a commodified self that can be traded.

This chapter then contends that covenanted conceptions of self aim toward shalom and that Sabbath laws are God's way of preserving a healthy, holistic sense of self. Finally, this chapter concludes with an overview of how Pentecost can be viewed as a cosmic Jubilee—God's way of restoring all things back to shalom.

Chapter 5 determines how the church can approach economic matters in a renewal public theology. When the Sabbath principles of *gleaning* and *generosity* are applied to economic thinking today, the Western approach to social matters will shift from a liberal market morality toward a hospitable exchange of generosity that is part and parcel of God's covenant of abundance. This chapter contends that the biblical traditions of Sabbath, Jubilee, and Pentecost should root the way Western Christians deal with the monetary interests of the church in society.

Chapter 6 considers the social responsibilities that accompany God's covenant of abundance. While chapter 4 looks at a believer's personal morality and responsibilities in covenant, chapter 6 looks at the church's social morality and responsibilities within God's covenant of abundance. One major issue of the syncretic church is that it overemphasizes individualism, which disregards the social and communal aspects of our human constitution. This sort of thinking can relieve believers from a sense of communal responsibility to live out the church's purpose as a blessing to society. This chapter contends that social responsibility in God's covenant of abundance means serving the broader community in a posture of love, while advocating for the disenfranchised through Jubilee action.

Finally, the conclusion is the counterpart of this chapter—a bookend that demonstrates the promise of freedom when rightly understood in God's covenant of abundance. It draws together the main themes of both the critical and the constructive arguments, and details in outline what a renewal social ethics and public theology could look like in our Western liberal societies. As these arguments are drawn together and reasoned through, it is my hope that this study can in some small way help the Western church become the gracious and generous witness of God's abundance that's so desperately needed in our world today.

Conclusion

The church in every society is confronted by a golden calf—something that challenges God for lordship. The Spirit is universally at work, so we should expect the church in every society to be rebuked and affirmed by the Spirit in various, specific ways. While a public theology of renewal could be written from any context around the globe, this book looks specifically at the Western church. *Our* golden calf in the Western church is a dependence on the liberal notion of voluntarist freedom. This particularity reflects my own positionality as a German-born American with German and Puerto Rican roots. While my upbringing was not strictly American, it was totally Western, so this is the context I know best and can speak most authentically toward. However, nations around the world have adopted similar social and economic processes as a result of the late modern trend toward global neoliberalism. Thus, although this book is admittedly West-centric, one might find the arguments of this book translatable and helpful for thinking about the church's public witness around the world.

In this chapter we identified some biblical roots for the critical and constructive arguments made throughout this book. Critically, we looked at Exodus 32's account of the golden calf to show how the Western church is prone to syncretic idolatry as it adopts liberal notions of freedom into its ecclesial structures. Constructively, we focused primarily on Exodus 19–24 and Acts 2 to demonstrate that God intends the church's public witness to reflect a covenantal theology of abundance. Although I engage many other Scripture passages in subsequent chapters, these particular passages form the framework on which the rest of this study is based.

William Cavanaugh sums up well what's required of a public theology of renewal:

> If the church is going to call people away from idolatry and remind them of their primary allegiance to Christ, then it will have to do more than to rail against the illusions of freedom enforced by coercion. The church will have to tell a more persuasive story of liberation

than that told by the Empire. It will have to tell a more difficult and
complex story of liberation through obedience to God's will, not to
the human will. . . . And it will have to tell this story of liberation
not just in words, but in witness. The boldness of the imperial project
must be met by the boldness of Pentecost. The only way to recover
that boldness is to worship in the Holy Spirit at the shrine that is
not empty, but full of the presence of the one true God, the God of
Moses and of Jesus.[34]

As Cavanaugh states, the church's public witness must stand with
the boldness of Pentecost in our world today. Taking the church to
task when it compromises its covenantal fidelity requires critique, but
it also requires calling the church to be a holy, loving, and generous
presence in the public sphere. Both critique and construction are
needed to help the Western church realign with God in covenant.
May our realignment allow us to flourish, enhancing our surrounding landscape.

34. William Cavanaugh, "The Empire of the Empty Shrine: American Imperialism
and the Church," *Cultural Encounters* 2, no. 2 (2006): 19.

PART 1

THE CRITICAL ARGUMENTS

1

Conflicting Concepts of Social Liberty

Freedom and Covenant

In what way are Christians free in the Spirit? If we assume that a Christian community is free the same way a liberal society is free, we might read a passage like 2 Corinthians 3:17, which states, "Now the Lord is the Spirit, and where the Spirit of the Lord is, there is freedom," to mean that we, as a community of believers, are made up of individuals who enjoy autonomous freedom by the Spirit. But is this right? Does the Spirit enable in us a voluntarism that emphasizes the importance of individual freedom and choice? Does the verse uphold that we are free to interact with others in ways that *we* choose, based on mutual agreement and consent?

Paul believed that through faith in Christ, people are freed from the power of sin and death and are called to live a new life of freedom in the Spirit. This new life of freedom is not merely a license to act how we choose. Rather, it's a call to live in accordance with God's will in covenantal fidelity. As we'll see in greater detail below, the idea of voluntarism is not present in Paul. As discussed in the introduction, voluntarist freedom constitutes an individual's willful political action. Despite the absence of this concept of freedom in Scripture, much of the Western church has uncritically adopted it to form a syncretic religious identity. If we care to bear a Spirit-led witness in the world, we must adhere not to a liberal notion of voluntarist freedom but to a biblical notion of covenantal freedom.

As we'll see, covenantal freedom contrasts starkly with the voluntarist individualism that roots the liberal notion of freedom. Both the high liberal tradition and the libertarian position are concerned with the rights of the individual, the rule of law, and the nonarbitrariness of laws. These views differ on the scope and extent of personal liberty. For example, the high liberal tradition values the autonomy of the mind to make moral rules, and the libertarian position looks at individual rights as property rights. However, they agree that the government's role is to protect a person's individual freedom and to do so with as little governmental oversight as possible. My goal is not to settle any disputes between which version of liberalism is most fitting for our particular nation's political experiment. Instead, I aim to determine whether the Western notion of social liberty correlates with a biblical concept of freedom and what the ramifications are for the church if the two differ.

With that goal in mind, we will first review some of the philosophical foundations of Western liberalism and its ideal of social liberty. In particular, I consider the Kantian notion of autonomous freedom that arose out of the Enlightenment. We will then explore two concepts that were inspired by and rely on this voluntarist understanding of freedom: Rawls's high liberal concept of "justice as fairness" and Nozick's libertarian vision of "justice as entitlement" (inspired by the Lockean notion of property rights). Both Rawls's and Nozick's concepts are profoundly influential in Western civic societies.

Next, we will consider the biblical concept of covenantal freedom—a sort of freedom that is paradoxically based on a committed, divine dependency. In the end, I conclude that covenantal freedom is totally different from liberal freedom and that the church's embrace of liberal notions of freedom leads to syncretic constructions of the faith.

I will revisit the golden-calf metaphor from the introduction, and I will scrutinize the social face of the golden calf of liberty: voluntarist freedom. Assuming I'm correct that covenantal freedom is different from the liberal notion of voluntarist freedom, our central question becomes "What does it mean for Christians to be socially 'free'?"

Western Liberalism's Concept of Freedom

The Western notion of "social liberty" is *the condition that arises out of freely autonomous people living together in a society*. Social liberty ensures that individuals have the ability to make their own choices and pursue their own goals without being unduly restricted by external, governing forces.[1] Social liberty is an important component of a *democratic society* as it allows individuals to exercise their autonomous freedom and participate in decision-making processes that affect their lives. Social liberty is also essential to cultivate a diverse and vibrant *pluralistic society* as it allows for a range of perspectives and ideas to be exchanged.

During the Enlightenment, social liberty became a central tenet of Western political philosophy, with thinkers such as John Locke and Jean-Jacques Rousseau advocating for the protection of individual rights and freedoms as a necessary condition for a just and equitable society. The protection of individual rights and freedoms is now a cornerstone of democracy and human dignity, and it is enshrined in many legal and political systems throughout the Western world. For example, this emphasis on individual liberty was reflected in the founding documents of many Western democracies, including the US Constitution (1787), the French Declaration of the Rights of Man and of the Citizen (1789), the Universal Declaration of Human Rights (1948), and the European Convention on Human Rights (1950).[2]

1. It should be noted, however, that even the most radically liberal societies do not view social liberty as absolute. Freedoms must be limited by laws and regulations designed to protect the rights of others or to prevent harm to individuals or society as a whole.

2. Some consider the first Western founding document that detailed any notion of autonomous freedom to be the Magna Carta (1215). This document was signed

While the concept of social liberty has been subject to ongoing debate and reinterpretation throughout Western history, it has remained a fundamental value for many Western societies.

After the Enlightenment, modern ethics and political philosophy sought to divorce concepts of right action from religious underpinnings and social encumberments. This effort reflects the secularization that came out of the Enlightenment; the goal was to establish moral neutrality as a cornerstone for any system of social governance. Utilitarian theories were able to avoid making theo-political value judgments concerning morality by equating goodness with pleasure. But by relegating morality to mere consequences of actions, utilitarians sidestepped the goal of normative ethics, which determines what constitutes the morally good.[3] As an alternative, Immanuel Kant developed the notion of autonomous freedom, which roots the liberal notion of voluntarist freedom.

Kant's Notion of Autonomous Freedom

In keeping with the modern project of secularization, Kant responded by rooting his ethics in freedom and individual rights, rather than utility. Kant's view opposes utilitarianism on two grounds: (1) Kant believes an ethical system cannot simply be a calculus of pleasure and pain.[4] Being able to discern what one likes or dislikes does not equate to having a solid understanding of right or wrong. Rather than a moral theory, utilitarianism is merely a decision-making apparatus, so it fails to properly define morality or what morality is actually about. (2) Utilitarianism fails to respect, or even acknowledge, individual rights.[5] In the utilitarian approach, the rights of the individual are unprotected and can be trumped on the basis

---

by King John of England and established the principle that everyone, including the king, was subject to the law, and guaranteed certain basic rights and liberties to the people.

3. The extent and plausibility of liberal neutrality is discussed further in chap. 3 of this book.

4. Immanuel Kant, *Groundwork of the Metaphysics of Morals*, trans. Mary Gregor (1785; repr., Cambridge: Cambridge University Press, 1997), 29.

5. Kant, *Groundwork of the Metaphysics of Morals*, 38.

of general welfare. Kant would thus develop a modern theory that prizes freedom and individualism. What defines us as humans, according to Kant, is our capacity to reason over our desires. We have freedom insofar as we are able to manage our wills through reason. Freedom is not simply choosing what we want without any impediments or obstacles; rather, it is our ability to rationally determine our own willful actions. The word Kant used to express this concept of freedom is "autonomy." We usually see the word "autonomy" as meaning "independence," but Kant uses it to mean acting according to a law you gave yourself. This corresponds with the word's etymology, since the Greek word *autos* means "the self" and *nomos* means "the law." To make his point, Kant differentiates between autonomous and heteronymous behavior.[6] Instead of governing yourself through reason, heteronymous behavior is governed by other (*hetero*) forces. Pleasures and pains fall under inclinations (i.e., subjective preferences), so they come about heteronymously, as they are governed by the appetites.[7] The opposite of heteronymous inclination is an autonomous sense of duty.[8] This is the duty to act according to laws, which requires reasoning over laws we produce in ourselves, not a law that's found in nature or society. In other words, we produce laws so we can dictate the aims of our will. Here Kant extends a classically Western concept of freedom. Nicolas Berdyaev defines freedom similarly, calling it "self-determination in the inmost depths of being [that] is opposed to every kind of external determination which constitutes a compulsion in itself."[9] This human capacity is what constitutes free will, even as free will corresponds paradoxically with the foreknowledge of an omniscient God.[10]

6. Kant, *Groundwork of the Metaphysics of Morals*, 41.
7. Kant, *Groundwork of the Metaphysics of Morals*, 9–10.
8. Kant, *Groundwork of the Metaphysics of Morals*, 42.
9. Nicolas Berdyaev, *Freedom and the Spirit*, trans. Oliver Fielding Clarke (1935; repr., New York: Books for Library Press, 1997), 121–22.
10. There are several significant theological positions that attempt to reconcile God's sovereignty and our free will to choose. Open theists, for instance, claim that humans have the capacity to make genuine, nondetermined decisions because the universe is open and expanding. God's foreknowledge is not the knowledge of a closed, scripted reality (see Clark Pinnock, Richard Rice, John Sanders, William Hasker,

Theologically speaking, Kant's definition of freedom is not what's plaguing the Western church. What's problematic is the *assumed extent* of freedom—the idea that liberty constitutes voluntarism all the way through. What's problematic is the thought that we are perpetually free, even in covenant. As regards the *extent* of autonomy, there appears to be a difference between the political and ecclesial senses of liberty. The Western church has indiscriminately applied a political sense of liberty to a *theological* notion of freedom in the Spirit. As we'll see later in this chapter, biblical freedom is covenantal. When one enters a covenant, he or she is bound by its parameters. Even as one has autonomously chosen to enter into covenant, covenant partners relinquish those liberties that contradict their promises. This is similar to the social contract of politics, but it differs drastically in the way it's governed. To get a sense of this, we'll explore the major difference between political and ecclesial liberties.

Freedom in the High Liberal Tradition

Kant's notion of autonomous freedom animates the high liberal tradition as defined by John Rawls. Both Kant and Rawls believed that a society must start with a social contract in order to identify a clear sense of justice. Kant thought a social contract should come about through *hypothetical* consent.[11] Since the founders of any given nation lived in a different time with a different context, we cannot

---

and David Basinger, *The Openness of God: A Biblical Challenge to the Traditional Understanding of God* [Downers Grove, IL: InterVarsity, 1994]). The Molinist view of middle knowledge holds that God knows every possible outcome of every choice, but people have the ability to choose which path they want to take (see William Lane Craig, *The Only Wise God: The Compatibility of Divine Foreknowledge and Human Freedom* [Eugene, OR: Wipf & Stock, 2000]). Finally, the classical view of God's eternity understands God as standing outside of time and space, and knowing each choice and moment as it occurs from an eternal perspective (see Paul Helm, *Eternal God: A Study of God without Time* [Oxford: Oxford University Press, 1997]). There are many other ways to understand the paradoxical relationship between God's foreknowledge and human free will, but these three options are all coherent, and they all demonstrate that an answer to this paradox is possible.

11. Immanuel Kant, "On the Common Saying: That May Be Correct in Theory, but Is of No Use in Practice," in *Practical Philosophy*, ed. Allen Wood, trans. Mary Gregor, (1793; repr., Cambridge, MA: Cambridge University Press, 1996), 296.

merely adopt their initial intent as an infallible guide toward a just society. We have to ask ourselves what makes a law or statute just for our current context. What's needed, therefore, is a hypothetical social contract that helps us identify what's just. Such a social contract would need to establish the ideal of reason that obliges every legislature to frame every law as if everyone would agree and consent to it. Since a law is just only if it can be agreed to by the public as a whole, we must ask if everyone in our society would consent to the law. Kant never defines what such laws could be, but Rawls does. In fact, this is the impetus behind *A Theory of Justice*, Rawls's classic work, which has become one of the most important texts of modern political philosophy.

In step with the liberal tradition coming out of the Enlightenment, Rawls believes a just society must commence with a social contract between state and citizen. A social contract must be fair and equal, protecting the individual's intrinsic worth. As in Kant's hypothetical contract, Rawls believes we ought to aim for the "original position." The original position is "the appropriate initial status quo which insures that the fundamental agreements reached in it are fair."[12] This views "justice as fairness" and requires the conditions of true equality. The original position is not merely the vision of the original founders of a society. Because social circumstances change through the years, the founders' vision cannot adequately address unforeseen contemporary needs. What would the founding fathers say about, for instance, Artificial Intelligence or drone warfare or trans rights? Our original position must be, therefore, a *current* agreement between state and citizen. We can uncover such an agreement, suggests Rawls, by starting behind a "veil of ignorance."[13]

The veil of ignorance is a reasoning device, or thought experiment, that creates the conditions of true equality. Behind the veil of ignorance, we must become unencumbered by forgetting our unique individuality, all those things that give us advantages or disadvantages

---

12. John Rawls, *A Theory of Justice*, rev. ed. (1971; repr., Cambridge, MA: Harvard University Press, 2009), 15.
13. Rawls, *Theory of Justice*, 118.

in a society, and all those that situate us socially.[14] Now, under these conditions of fairness and neutrality, we can ask what sorts of laws and statutes everyone *would* agree to. Rawls's theory is, in a way, a modern social expansion of Kant's ethical notion of the freely autonomous individual: "Following the Kantian interpretation of justice as fairness, we can say that by acting from these principles persons are acting autonomously: they are acting from principles that they would acknowledge under conditions that best express their nature as free and equal rational beings."[15] The veil of ignorance provides individuals the opportunity to truly act autonomously, uncovering the rules to which they'd willingly submit.

Under the veil of ignorance, Rawls believes we would hold that everyone has equal rights to all basic liberties. If the free individual is the moral agent of a society, the social contract must provide individuals as many liberties as can be given to someone without harming others. Another Rawlsian principle is that there will be equality of opportunity, as the veil of ignorance eliminates discrimination. These principles locate Rawls firmly in the liberal tradition that's concerned with individual rights and the nonarbitrary rule of law. Yet it is on this second principle that Rawls's liberalism differs from libertarian notions of liberalism.

Rawls believes that the state has the responsibility to correct naturally born inequalities. Rawls calls this the "difference principle," which states that inequalities in a society should be allowed only if they benefit the least favored person in the society.[16] This is an egalitarian principle of distributive justice, which seeks to smooth out some of the inequalities in a society. Even though Rawls seeks a sense of distributive justice, his view is not indifferent in its distribution as in a strictly utilitarian approach.[17] Under the difference principle, any unequal distribution can be applied only if *both* parties benefit and if it helps the disadvantaged achieve greater social standing. In this

14. Rawls, *Theory of Justice*, 453.
15. Rawls, *Theory of Justice*, 452.
16. Rawls, *Theory of Justice*, 66.
17. Rawls, *Theory of Justice*, 67.

approach to liberalism, every member of a society must constantly correct for inequalities, leveling inequalities and disadvantages to ensure equal starting points and equal outcomes.

Freedom in the Libertarian Tradition

Another expression of liberalism is libertarianism, which grounds justice on a different conception of liberty. Not only must the state respect and protect the rights of the individual, but the state must be minimized so as to prevent any infringement on individual liberties. The just state is thus the "minimal state"—one that minimally intervenes in private lives and free markets. One major difference between this view and Rawls's view is that Rawls, like Kant, views freedom as autonomy, whereas libertarians view freedom as a right to property, which includes one's own self.[18] This latter notion is rooted in Locke, who famously states, "Every Man has a 'property' in his own 'person.' This nobody has any right to but himself. The 'labour' of his body, and the 'work' of his hands, we may say, are properly his."[19] Following suit, libertarians define individual freedom along the lines of property rights. Whereas Rawls equates justice with fairness (which makes room for distributive justice by an authority), libertarians believe that each one of us is the only rightful owner of ourselves. In other words, libertarianism is defined by a sense of *personhood as self-ownership.*

One of the best-known proponents of libertarianism, and a contemporary of Rawls, was Robert Nozick. In his book *Anarchy, State, and Utopia*, Nozick argues for the minimal state that is limited to protecting the rights of persons and property through a social contract.[20] The state has no right to shape the morality of individuals. "How one should act" is a personal, individual matter, and the state

18. I'd like to note that talking about humanity in terms of ownership seems to be a category error. The commodification of people is an ideological root of chattel slavery.

19. John Locke, *The Second Treatise of Civil Government* (1690; repr., Amherst, NY: Prometheus Books, 1986), 20.

20. Robert Nozick, *Anarchy, State, and Utopia* (1974; repr., New York: Basic Books, 2021), 26–27.

should step in only if a person violates the self-ownership of others. This concept of self-ownership is tied economically to our labors.[21] Nozick argues that if we own ourselves fully, then we must also fully own the products of our labor. By taking my earnings, the government takes my labor, and by taking my labor, the government denies that I own myself. Here libertarians see a moral continuity from taxation to forced labor and finally to slavery.

For Nozick, liberty as a property right gives *consent* a special significance. Any redistribution of wealth is justified *only* if it is consented to. Rights understood in this way are *alienable*—able to be given to new ownership if the individual gives his or her consent.[22] This is markedly different from Locke's view, which argues for a person's inalienable rights, and from Rawls's view, which sees property not as a natural presocial thing but as something that only emerges from the political realm. Nozick sees unconsented taxation as unjust precisely because it violates a person's right to self. While the high liberalism of Rawls states we must smooth out inequalities and disadvantages so we can have both an equal starting point and equal outcomes, the libertarianism of Nozick states that people are best protected when they are left alone and allowed to accumulate their own wealth without restrictions. Rather than allowing the state to correct things, we must make the economy just from the start and then leave it alone. So for the libertarian, the government must protect a citizen's economic freedom and must never infringe on a person's social and moral freedoms, so long as they respect the freedoms of others.

Voluntarism as Foundational for Freedom in Western Liberalism

Both high liberalism and libertarianism have profoundly influenced Western moral and political thought. While they differ on their conceptions of freedom as autonomy (Kant and Rawls) or property

21. Nozick, *Anarchy, State, and Utopia*, 172.
22. Nozick, *Anarchy, State, and Utopia*, 58.

rights (Locke and Nozick), in either case, the general liberal concept of freedom relies on voluntarism where the *individual will* is foundational for human action. As Scott Bader-Saye states, "The issue of what *ought* to be desired or what choices *ought* to be made is privatized in modern liberal democracies as a way of removing such volatile discussions from the public arena."[23] Morality and religion are left up to the individual, and the state has no claim to a person's moral or spiritual formation. The liberal sense of freedom is one that respects a person's autonomy with as little oversight and control as possible from governing forces. Rather than determining what sorts of virtues should be cultivated by the individuals who make up a community, liberal politics merely set up boundaries for how individuals can coexist in a community where consumer preference drives political decision-making.[24] In other words, there is a thick wall between a person's public and private life.

As stated earlier, this chapter does not set out to critique the liberal notion of freedom on political grounds; it does not argue, for instance, for the Western embrace of an illiberal autocratic or populist alternative for governance. Rather, this chapter makes the more modest assertion that the church must not equivocate a liberal notion of freedom with a biblical understanding of freedom. Bader-Saye argues that biblical freedom should not be conflated with the modern idea of abstract choice but entails faithful living in a divine covenant with God.[25] As is evident in both Rawls and Nozick, modern Western political philosophy has deemed personal choice itself as *the* fundamental good of a liberal society,[26] but should this sense of liberty be adopted by the confessing church? Rawls and Nozick never set out to produce standards of citizenship for the Western church but sought to frame the Western political experience in general. It is the task of Christian theologians and philosophers to frame the parameters of a national citizenship that corresponds with faithful citizenship in

---

23. Scott Bader-Saye, "The Freedom of Faithfulness," *Pro Ecclesia* 8, no. 4 (1999): 438.
24. Bader-Saye, "Freedom of Faithfulness," 439.
25. Bader-Saye, "Freedom of Faithfulness," 437.
26. Bader-Saye, "Freedom of Faithfulness," 439.

the kingdom of God (this is the topic of chap. 3). The question we must now ask is if the liberal notion of liberty corresponds with the biblical notion of freedom.

Biblical Concept of Freedom: Freedom, Covenant, and the Spirit

Let's return for a moment to the passage discussed at the start of this chapter: "Now the Lord is the Spirit, and where the Spirit of the Lord is, there is freedom" (2 Cor. 3:17). When taken in context, 2 Corinthians 3:17 clearly refers to a covenantal freedom, which differs markedly from any notion of liberal freedom. Paul begins chapter 3 explaining to the members of the Corinthian church that their personal witness is how Christ is represented to the world (vv. 2–3). As such, Paul calls them "ministers of a new covenant, not of letter but of spirit, for the letter kills, but the Spirit gives life" (v. 6). Moses, as representative of the old covenant, veiled his face to shield people from the full glory of God (vv. 12–13), but by the Spirit believers are freed from the veil and with unveiled faces can witness and reflect the glory of the Lord in a new covenant (vv. 15–18). Herein lies an interesting contrast between Rawls's "veil of ignorance" and Paul's "unveiled faces." For Rawls, justice can be achieved only when our social structures are determined fairly, "behind *a* veil" that obscures inequalities; for Paul, justice can be achieved only when we align our social structures around God's vision for us, "beyond *the* veil" that obscures our view of God's eternal perspective. Paul says that the Spirit of the Lord frees believers from the binds of one covenant, but not to be autonomously free. In the new covenant, Christians are no longer guided by the law but by the Spirit. In Paul's rationale, we are not simply free to be governed by our own wills, but we are freed from the burdens of one covenant as we enter into another.

The Bible uses the farming imagery of a yoke to help us make sense of freedom and responsibility in covenant. In its literal usage, a yoke is a wooden beam that is used to join animals together so they will walk together when plowing a field. The Bible contains several references to yoked animals, especially oxen (1 Sam. 6:10; 1 Kings 19:19; Job 1:3; Luke 14:19, etc.). But more often than not, the Bible uses the term figuratively to discuss being bound to others in covenant. Jeremiah, for instance, wore a yoke around his neck to tell the diasporic Jews to submit to the yoke of the Babylonian king (Jer. 27:8–12). At other times, God promises the Israelites that they will break free from the burdensome yoke of servitude (Isa. 58:6; Jer. 30:8). But breaking the yoke of a corrupt system does not mean the person is then unyoked. Rather, the way to truly break off a yoke is to be yoked to a new system. This is what Jesus means when he says, "Come to me, all you who are weary and are carrying heavy burdens, and I will give you rest. Take my yoke upon you, and learn from me, for I am gentle and humble in heart, and you will find rest for your souls. For my yoke is easy, and my burden is light" (Matt. 11:28–30). The burdens of the world's corrupt yoke are lifted when we replace it with Jesus's light yoke, which requires our being bound to him as disciples.

Likewise, we are freed from the weight of a covenant when we enter into a new covenant that bears its own freedoms and responsibilities. Biblical freedom is "faithful participation in (God's) covenant."[27] Bader-Saye states it well: "*Freedom is not doing what you want but being who you are.* This is not to be confused with the empty appeal to 'be yourself' since this generally means simply 'doing what you want.' Rather, *being* who you are is made possible by first *knowing* who you are. . . . Only after knowing 'who you are' as a covenant partner of the God of Israel can a person begin to live into this identity and thus live in freedom."[28] Covenantal freedom entails finding our identity in Christ and being led by the Spirit as faithful partners in God's covenant of abundance. We will see that this biblical sense of freedom is markedly different from any liberal sense of freedom, but let's first further delineate what is meant by covenantal freedom.

27. Bader-Saye, "Freedom of Faithfulness," 437.
28. Bader-Saye, "Freedom of Faithfulness," 445.

Covenantal Freedom Originates in God

The Bible designates three interrelated attributes of covenantal freedom. First, *any actual sense of freedom originates from and is rooted in God*. As the boundless and infinite creator, only God is truly free without restriction. All things draw their existence from God, who is existence itself (or "being-itself" to use Paul Tillich's term[29]), making God the sole determiner of everything that's absolute. All of the created order is therefore bound to God in existence. These ideas are present in Romans when Paul tells us, "For from him and through him and to him are all things" (Rom. 11:36), and again in Acts when Luke writes, "In him we live and move and have our being" (Acts 17:28). Our creaturely freedom necessarily entails a boundedness to God, who is the bedrock of our being.[30] On a foundational level, then, only God is truly autonomously free, and any freedoms we experience are those given to us by God. In other words, we are not free to experience anything with *absolute* autonomy, but we can share in God's gift of freedom. *Our* autonomy is, in a sense, a derivative freedom.

God is truly free and has the ability to freely give. God is also generous and desires to give, and it is only out of God's generosity that we come to know freedom. In his book *Free of Charge*, Miroslav Volf writes, "God is not a negotiator but a pure giver. We can give nothing to God but have received everything from God. . . . We are not independent of God but are living on a given breath."[31] Our dependence on God is absolute—we are receivers. When *we* give, we extend God's gift-giving propensity,[32] and when we freely choose, we do so in accordance with God's gift of freedom. Hence, any freedoms we enjoy are participatory and rooted in God's freedom.

---

29. Paul Tillich, *Systematic Theology* (1951; repr., Chicago: University of Chicago Press, 2012), 1:64.

30. Tillich, *Systematic Theology*, 1:118.

31. Miroslav Volf, *Free of Charge: Giving and Forgiving in a Culture Stripped of Grace* (Grand Rapids: Zondervan, 2005), 43.

32. Volf, *Free of Charge*, 79.

Covenantal Freedom Entails Our God-Given Free Will

Second, *covenantal freedom entails our God-given free will.* God has given us the ability to rationally determine our own willful actions—our autonomous freedom to choose. But, God has also set out our choices before us, so even this autonomy is guided. Adam and Eve had a delimited choice to eat from the tree of life (remaining in God's provision) or from the tree of knowledge of good and evil (rejecting God's provision). The prophets laid out two paths for the Israelites—one path remains in God's promise and brings about restoration, and the other rejects God and leads to destruction (see also Deut. 5:33). Our free will makes it so we always have a choice, but we do not decide what choices can be made. It's like when parents put out dinner for the family and the child says they don't want it. The parent replies, "You can eat this or go to bed hungry, because there's no other food here." Like the child, we do not choose what is set in front of us, but we can choose to accept or reject whatever is presented to us and bear whatever consequences follow.

Biblical free will means we can enter into covenant with God or not,[33] and we can choose to abide in covenant or not. But if we choose to not be in covenant with God, we are choosing to be in covenant with the world. Jesus says as much when he proclaims, "Whoever is not with me is against me, and whoever does not gather with me scatters" (Matt. 12:30). He reiterates this point in the Sermon on the Mount: "No one can serve two masters, for a slave will either hate the one and love the other or be devoted to the one and despise the other" (6:24). Thus covenantal freedom modifies the Kantian sense of autonomous choice by recognizing the limits of our choosing.

Covenantal Freedom Frees Us from Other Covenants

Third and finally, *covenantal freedom ensures freedom from other covenants.* The Bible frequently discusses freedom from two interrelated covenants—the covenant of flesh and the old covenant of law.

---

33. This assumes the Wesleyan-Arminian notion of prevenient grace.

The Bible talks about flesh as opposing the Spirit. In Romans 7:21–24 Paul talks about his internal struggles with sin: "So I find it to be a law that, when I want to do what is good, evil lies close at hand. For I delight in the law of God in my inmost self, but I see in my members another law at war with the law of my mind, making me captive to the law of sin that dwells in my members. Wretched person that I am! Who will rescue me from this body of death?" Paul sees that his sinful flesh nature is at war with the aspirations of his mind. Later in verse 25 Paul states that Jesus rescues him from this covenant of flesh: "Thanks be to God through Jesus Christ our Lord! So then, with my mind I am enslaved to the law of God, but with my flesh I am enslaved to the law of sin." Paul's language of enslavement shows that he's bound in each scenario. Paul is bound either to God's law or to the law of sin. He's either a covenant partner with God or in covenant with himself, therefore being against God. As Bob Dylan so aptly put it,

> Well, it may be the devil or it may be the Lord
> But you're gonna have to serve somebody.[34]

Similarly, Berdyaev states that when people believe they are totally free, they live in an egotistical and self-affirming way that eventually causes them to become slaves to their own "lower elements."[35] The passions they believe they're free to enjoy end up controlling their thoughts and actions, thereby subjugating them.[36] We shouldn't live ascetically and outright deny our fleshly desires, but we cannot be driven by them. Freedom in the Spirit means freedom from being totally steered by fleshly desires. The Spirit helps us rightly guide our desires.

Marriage as an Illustration of Covenantal Freedom

In marriage, we see all three elements of covenantal freedom mentioned above. Marriage is first and foremost a gift from God

34. Bob Dylan, "Gotta Serve Somebody," copyright © 1979 by Special Rider Music.
35. Berdyaev, *Freedom and the Spirit*, 132.
36. Berdyaev, *Freedom and the Spirit*, 132.

established in the garden of Eden. In Genesis 2:18 God saw that man should not be alone, so he gave him woman—"a helper as his partner." What's more is that the woman came from the very flesh of the man, so as they join again in marriage, they once more become one flesh (2:24). God's gift of marriage to humanity is a free gift that's not achieved or earned. Second, God gives us the free will to choose our partner in marriage.[37] We freely choose who we will marry, and we choose to abide in our marriage covenant. Third, in the marriage covenant we are freed from a life of solitude, and our fleshly desires can be rightly directed. The freedoms of marriage come at a cost. Spouses can no longer freely date who they want, and they are now accountable to each other. In a marriage covenant two people freely give up their autonomy to join each other. Freedoms are given up in covenant, and new freedoms are gained. In the same way, covenantal freedom requires that we freely give our autonomy to God as we gain new freedoms in the Spirit.

Idolatrous Constructions of the Faith

Having discussed the tenets of covenantal freedom, we see that a biblical notion of covenantal freedom is simply not what Western liberalism perpetuates. When Paul calls himself a slave or bond servant of Christ (Rom. 1), he is aware that the new covenant comes with loyalty clauses, so he is not simply free to do whatever he wants. Genuine biblical freedom is covenantal—a person freely chooses, without compulsion, to love and submit to God.[38] As Ronald Sider writes, "Genuine freedom is the freedom to say yes to God's will and design."[39] Modern liberal societies want to stretch autonomous choice beyond what covenantal freedom permits. Those influenced by the high liberal tradition do not want a government to restrict an

37. This example assumes free-choice marriage. It also is merely demonstrating the nature of covenant and is in no way admonishing singlehood.
38. Ronald Sider, *The Scandal of Evangelical Politics: Why Are Christians Missing the Chance to Really Change the World?* (Grand Rapids: Baker Books, 2008), 171–72.
39. Sider, *Scandal of Evangelical Politics*, 171.

individual's personal and moral decisions. They want each individual to be able to decide who or what they'll be socially. Those influenced by the libertarian tradition do not want a government to interfere with an individual's property. They believe they do not bear social responsibility to share their labor or distribute their wealth. They believe they are legally entitled (Nozick's term) to their possessions and choices, and no governmental system should tell them what to give up, even if it benefits others. In both cases, voluntarist freedom is the ultimate ideal.

Idolatry occurs whenever Christians prefer voluntarist freedom over covenant fidelity. Christopher Wright believes that Adam and Eve's temptation to eat fruit from the tree of knowledge of good and evil was not merely to know the difference between good and evil but to be able to *determine for themselves* what is good and evil. Thus they were tempted to attain moral autonomy—a noncovenantal, voluntarist deliberation of right and wrong. As Wright points out, this displaces God as sovereign: "Humans . . . in choosing to decide for ourselves what *we* will deem good or evil, usurp the prerogative of God in rebellious moral autonomy."[40] By championing personal autonomy, we attempt to dethrone God as our moral authority. To be clear, there's nothing wrong with holding a liberal government to a voluntarist standard of freedom, but we must realize that covenant is impossible for the church when a liberal notion of freedom enters its polity.

Instead of practicing covenantal freedom within a liberal society, the syncretic church preserves voluntarist freedom as an ultimate ideal *within the church*. Last chapter, I mentioned a continuum of what the syncretic church looks like. On one side of the continuum stands the assimilated church, and on the other side stands the nationalistic church. While both churches merge Christian and liberal ideologies, they can be differentiated by how they understand the church's relation to voluntarist freedom and how they view liberalism in a pluralist

---

40. Christopher J. H. Wright, *"Here Are Your Gods": Faithful Discipleship in Idolatrous Times* (Downers Grove, IL: IVP Academic, 2020), 33.

society. These two issues frame how the varying ends of the spectrum handle voluntarist freedom.

Can There Be a Voluntarist Biblical Foundation for Freedom?

Rather than looking to the exodus account as a biblical foundation for covenantal freedom, the syncretic church looks to other passages to establish a biblical foundation for voluntarist, autonomous freedom. Consider, for instance, how Lisa Sharon Harper ties her conception of liberty to the biblical concept of "dominion." She says that in Genesis 1 God made humanity in the image of God and gave them "the free exercise of dominion" over the fish of the sea, the birds of the air, and every other living creature (Gen. 1:28, Harper's trans.). For Harper, biblical freedom constitutes a free, unencumbered agency. She writes, "The closest thing we have to dominion in today's language is the concept of 'agency'—the ability to make choices that impact one's world. So, dominion is exercised in all of the choices one makes, large and small. Dominion requires liberty. To diminish liberty is to diminish dominion. To diminish dominion is to threaten the image of God on earth."[41] Thus for Harper, liberty is the freedom to wield dominion. It's a "basic need and right of humanity,"[42] which is integral to being an image-bearing person.

While Harper's "dominion as agency" concept is a befitting liberal reading of Genesis, it's not without faults. The first issue with this view is that it regards God's command of dominion as a *right* rather than a *responsibility*. Taking the command as a right seems to be reading Locke's theory of natural rights into the biblical text— something foreign to the ancient Israelite worldview. Subduing the earth has to do with cultivating, maintaining, and caring for the earth, not exerting control over it. Second, God commanded humans to fill and subdue the earth, not to have *free agency* over it. When farmers prune fruiting plants, they cut away fringe branches or shoots

41. Lisa Sharon Harper, in Lisa Sharon Harper and D. C. Innes, *Left, Right & Christ: Evangelical Faith in Politics* (Boise: Elevate Faith, 2016), 52.

42. Harper, *Left, Right & Christ*, 52.

to regulate growth and to optimize plant health and productivity. Pruning is a process of agricultural subdual, which ultimately leads to a more bountiful yield. Here subdual implies a sense of stewardship, acknowledging the responsibility of humans to protect and preserve the environment. This agricultural metaphor would have been familiar to ancient Israelites. Given this, Genesis 1:28's connection to liberal freedom is dubious at best. Nevertheless, this is the sort of reasoning Christians rely on when attempting to establish a biblical basis for voluntarist, autonomous freedom.

Distorting Public Witness: "Dominion as Agency"

As it concerns liberalism, Harper's concept of "dominion as agency" can be taken two ways: First, through a Kantian lens, it could be interpreted as the ability to govern the will autonomously. In this sense, a person has autonomous agency as a basic human right. This reading corresponds with the assimilated church that values personal autonomy on moral and social issues, even within the church. Here freedom might be understood as a person's total right to act in a way that he or she chooses. The assimilated church embraces a truly liberal sense of freedom but in so doing renders covenant fidelity with God impossible. As discussed last section, covenantal freedom requires the relinquishing of certain freedoms of autonomy in order to be bound to God in covenant.

Second, through a Lockean lens, Harper's concept of dominion as agency could be interpreted as having sovereign control over property. Just as a person has a right over his or her own property, God has given humans the freedom to wield dominion over land and social spaces. In this way, Christian nationalists believe they have a God-given mandate to lay claim to the nation. The nationalistic church values the protection of property, viewing the autonomous self, values, and tradition as fortified property.

The nationalistic church is, ironically, *il*liberal in at least the classical sense of liberty. Rather than viewing freedom as a person's autonomous right, and the free society as autonomous people living together in community, nationalists view freedom as protection against government impositions,[43] and they believe they bear social responsibility to preserve their national identity against foreign intrusion. Thus nationalists do not have a concept of a *perpetually free society*—a society that preserves voluntarist, autonomous freedom for its citizens through liberal rights. Rather, nationalists view their liberal society as a society that *has been freed* and thus adopts the notion of freedom in its national identity. Their liberal rights are protections *against* the government to preserve their identities as freed people. It is thus possible to see, for instance, an American nationalist who insists that being American means being free while holding on to illiberal, exclusionary identity politics. The Christian nationalist's notion of freedom concerns power when citizens utilize their God-given right to impose a particular national identity onto a society.[44] The nationalistic church thus deifies freedom as a marker of its own human pride. Its idol is a human construct—one that reflects its own national identity. What they have made embodies "their own pride, greed, and aggression."[45]

Since these churches are on opposite ends of the syncretic church spectrum, they are socially hazardous in different ways. Both offer distortions of the gospel, but the assimilated church's distortion leads to a corruption of biblical confession and to social conformity, whereas the nationalistic church's distortion leads to a corruption of biblical confession and to unjust social dynamics. The witness of the assimilated church is weak and ineffectual, whereas the witness of the nationalist church is dangerous and potentially oppressive.[46]

43. This is why Christian nationalists stood so vehemently against mask mandates and lockdowns during the COVID-19 pandemic. For more on this, see Samuel Perry, Andrew Whitehead, and Joshua Grubbs, "Save the Economy, Liberty, and Yourself: Christian Nationalism and Americans' Views on Government COVID-19 Restrictions," *Sociology of Religion* 82, no. 4 (2021): 429.

44. Paul Miller, *The Religion of American Greatness: What's Wrong with Christian Nationalism* (Downers Grove, IL: IVP Academic, 2022), 73.

45. C. Wright, *"Here Are Your Gods,"* 22.

46. For example, many individuals who participated in the storming of the United States Capitol on January 6, 2021, identified as Christian nationalists. During the attack on the Capitol, some participants were seen carrying Christian symbols, banners,

Public Witness in Pluralist Societies

In addition to differing views on voluntarist freedom, assimilated and nationalistic churches also diverge in their understanding of liberalism in pluralist societies and their participation in identity politics.[47] The range of a church's public witness will vary depending on how the church views diversity in pluralist societies. Pluralism refers to the coexistence and interaction of various cultural, religious, social, and ideological groups within a single society. Groups that view liberal societies as inherently pluralistic would likely advocate for tolerance and inclusivity, viewing cultural, religious, and ethnic diversity as admirable qualities. Here liberalism emphasizes the reality of pluralism *positively*, believing a diverse society enriches the exchange of ideas and fosters social progress. Freedom of expression, in this reading, enables a wide range of perspectives to be heard and debated in the public arena, and freedom of religion promotes religious tolerance, ensuring that no particular religious belief is imposed on society as a whole. By embracing pluralism, liberalism acknowledges that no single viewpoint or set of beliefs should dominate society. Instead, it encourages an environment where diverse perspectives coexist and inform each other, which contributes to the ongoing development of society.

Philosopher Charles Taylor maintains that today's Western secularity is marked by a religious pluralism that is characterized by a high degree of diversity, in terms of both demographics and ideas. He writes that our secular age "is marked by an unheard of pluralism of outlooks, religious and non- and anti-religious, in which the number of possible positions seems to be increasing without end. It is marked in consequence by a great deal of mutual fragilization, and hence movement between different outlooks. It naturally depends on

---

and signs, and there were reports of individuals explicitly invoking Christian language and beliefs to justify their actions.

47. For a variety of views on how liberal societies should deal with pluralist religious accommodation, see Monica Mookherjee, ed., *Democracy, Religious Pluralism and the Liberal Dilemma of Accommodation* (London: Springer, 2011).

one's milieu, but it is harder and harder to find a niche where either belief or unbelief go without saying."[48] Recognizing that we live in a pluralist society merely confirms the facts of our present reality. What is at issue is how groups respond to the reality of pluralism. Sider maintains that a healthy liberal outlook on pluralism recognizes religious freedom as a right and respects a person's freedom to accept or reject God. Because religious freedom is protected, liberals "insist that the state must protect the freedom of each person to embrace, practice, and share whatever religious beliefs they choose."[49] A liberal pluralist outlook is thus tolerant, respecting and not imposing upon the beliefs of others.

In addition to accepting the present reality of pluralism, the assimilated church *endorses* it in attempts to foster a tolerant, accommodating Christian witness. In some cases, religious pluralism leads to a shallow spirituality where biblical instruction and confessional proclamation are downplayed so as not to appear sectarian or intolerant. Without careful discernment, however, pluralism can lead to a church losing its distinctive identity and mission. In its pursuit of inclusivity and tolerance, the assimilated church loses sight of its mandate to be holy and set apart (1 Pet. 3:15–17) and of its mission to proclaim the gospel to all nations (Matt. 28:16–20).

The nationalistic church, on the other hand, sees pluralism not as a blessing but as a threat to one's way of life. Nationalists view pluralism as a potential challenge to dominant culture, fearing that diverse cultural expressions or practices might erode national identity. It is incoherent, however, for nationalists to frame liberal freedom in a way that rejects pluralism. An American nationalist, for instance, champions the idea that to be American means to be free. It is thus our civic duty as Americans, and our political duty as a liberal society, to cherish and protect our freedoms. Yet nationalists also carry a sectarian (and narrow) notion of what it means to be American. Nationalists emphasize the preservation and promotion of their *own*

---

48. Charles Taylor, *A Secular Age* (Cambridge, MA: Harvard University Press, 2007), 437.
49. Sider, *Scandal of Evangelical Politics*, 172.

culture, traditions, language, and values, viewing cultural homogeneity and shared national identity as crucial for maintaining social cohesion. As such, nationalists prioritize the protection of national borders and advocate for strict immigration policies. They fear the potential loss of national identity, values, and culture through significant demographic changes. In short, nationalists believe they are free by identity, not by praxis. For all their talk about freedom, nationalists do not actually aim to preserve liberalism in a pluralist society but aim to protect national identity in a pluralist society.

Public Witness That Is Covenantally Faithful

A church that adheres to covenantal freedom opposes both of these idolatrous constructions of the faith. By refusing to allow voluntarism to shape its ecclesial identity, the faithful church remains true to its identity as a community assembled around and built on the proclamation of Christ as king. Resisting the embrace of liberal notions of freedom is vital for the Western church to remain holy and set apart in the world. But because the church is called to be a light in the world, it must learn what it means to be "in the world, but not of the world"—to use the popular evangelical slogan. In our Western context, we must ask what it means to be the church in a liberal society that has no official religion. While some countries have historical or cultural ties to a particular religion, liberal societies typically do not establish an official religion or give preferential treatment to any specific faith. For instance, the founding fathers of the United States were careful to use language in the Constitution that preserves religious freedom: "Congress shall make no law respecting an establishment of religion, or prohibiting the free exercise thereof."[50] Since the US is a liberal nation, the fact that some of the founding fathers were either Deists or professing Christians is incidental.

Religious freedom *benefits* the church because the church is free to establish its own structures of worship, provided they do not

---

50. See the First Amendment to the US Constitution (https://constitution.congress .gov/constitution/amendment-1/).

infringe on the rights or freedoms of other citizens. Several illiberal societies around the world impose restrictions on religious freedom that can limit religious activities, practices, or speech. The Chinese government, for instance, tightly controls religious activities, including Christian gatherings outside state-sanctioned churches. Underground house churches, which operate outside government control, constantly face harassment, arrests, and closure.[51] Other illiberal governments control religious institutions, requiring registrations or even banning certain religious groups altogether. The North Korean regime, for instance, severely restricts religious freedom and considers Christianity a threat to its ideology.[52] Some illiberal societies have a dominant state religion, so Christians and other minoritized religious groups are oppressed. This is the case for countries like Afghanistan, Somalia, Syria, and Iraq, where Islamic extremist groups hold political influence.[53] Contrastingly, liberalism tries to maintain order by making societies fair and equal, and part of this effort includes freedom of religion. This is a noble pursuit, and perhaps it is what's needed for a pluralist society.

In a liberal nation, the church can exist as a community with minimal government interference. Thus our burdens are social and ideological, not political. The task of the church today is, as it always has been, to become a witness of God's abundant love to the world. We must let our polity become a testimony of generosity and grace in a pluralist society. Social and ideological persuasion come not by political force but by demonstrating how our Christian ideals are spiritually transformative and represent a common good for all. These pivotal topics will be picked up and expanded on in chapter 3 of this

51. "10 Things to Know about China's Policies on Religion," Pew Research Center, October 23, 2023, https://www.pewresearch.org/short-reads/2023/10/23/10-things-to-know-about-chinas-policies-on-religion/.

52. "2022 Report on International Religious Freedom: North Korea," U.S. Department of State, accessed July 4, 2024, https://www.state.gov/reports/2022-report-on-international-religious-freedom/north-korea/.

53. As of this writing in 2023, Afghanistan is led by the Taliban, Somalia is heavily influenced by Al-Shabaab, and Syria and Iraq are still influenced by ISIS, which continues to operate as an insurgency.

book. For now, it is sufficient to say that when the church truly reflects the kingdom of God, the church can point to itself as evidence of the Spirit's work in the world. If this happens, the church's polity of abundance will be so attractive to a justice-starved society that the gospel might actually look like good news to the world.

Conclusion

As we differentiate ecclesial and political concepts of freedom, we cannot condemn a secular society for endorsing a notion of freedom that defies a biblical covenant, but we can and must condemn ourselves as the church when we uncritically adopt a liberal sense of freedom to govern our ecclesial structures. Both versions of liberalism (Rawls's and Nozick's) extend concepts of freedom that contradict biblical freedom, so these notions must not enter our church polities. Throughout this chapter we reviewed two versions of liberal voluntarism. We looked specifically at Rawls's high liberal concept of autonomous freedom and Nozick's libertarian vision of freedom as property as influential expressions of modern liberalism. We then outlined the biblical notion of covenantal freedom to show how it is markedly different from voluntarist freedom. Finally, we demonstrated two ways the church is corrupted by adopting and venerating voluntarist freedom—particularly through assimilation or nationalism. This discussion was meant to nuance the claim that voluntarist, autonomous freedom is the social face of the golden calf of liberty.

To close this chapter, let's revisit our question from the introduction: In what way are Christians "free" socially, and what does this mean for the church? Freedom in the Spirit is fundamentally a covenantal freedom that sees us being integrated, communally, into God's family, with all the rights and responsibilities that follow. While this question is addressed in much greater detail in chapter 4, for now we can see that in covenant we are bound to God and to others (1 Cor. 12). Bayder-Saye states it well: "It is not a *freedom from* others, as modern individualistic accounts would have it, but is a *freedom with* others. Thus, one is free just to the extent that one belongs to God and thus to God's people."[54] When the state's polity enters the church's ecclesial structures, the church syncretizes and becomes an idolatrous religion that is alien to the kingdom of God. The political task of the church is to show society a different polity, one animated by abundant love in covenant. It is only then that the church's witness can help transform society at large.

54. Bader-Saye, "Freedom of Faithfulness," 452.

2

Moral Conflict
by Consumer Choice

Freedom from the Free Market

During the Sermon on the Mount, Jesus famously proclaims, "No one can serve two masters, for a slave will either hate the one and love the other or be devoted to the one and despise the other. You cannot serve God and wealth" (Matt. 6:24). Here Jesus situates money in a covenantal framework in which God and wealth are opposing masters. In the passage's immediate context, Jesus establishes how finances should be viewed in God's covenant of abundance. In verses 19–21, believers are told not to store up treasures on earth because they will eventually rot and decay; rather, they should store up treasures in heaven, which will last forever. We see two covenants pitted against each other: a temporary worldly covenant that is motivated by material wealth and an everlasting heavenly covenant that is under God's authority.

Furthermore, a person's covenantal allegiance is made evident by his or her vested interests. As Matthew 6:21 states, "For where your treasure is, there your heart will be also." Verses 22–23 expand on this idea by evoking the imagery of an eye as the lamp of the body or the window to the soul. What one allows into the mind through the eye produces desire, which in turn leads to action, and a person's actions reveal the person's true character.

The verses following verse 24 (vv. 25–34), emphasize the importance of not worrying about worldly securities in light of God's provision. As divine provision even reaches nature and all living things, God will certainly care for and sustain believers. Earlier in the same chapter, Jesus recounts the Lord's Prayer, in which he teaches his followers to ask for God's *daily* provision: "Give us today our daily bread" (v. 11). Just as God provided manna from heaven daily for the Israelites (Exod. 16), so will God provide every need for those who are in covenant with God. Unlike worldly covenants that reduce people to mere operatives of material transaction, God's covenant of abundance commits people to an infinite and generous God who meets every need (Phil. 4:19).

In keeping with the ideas presented throughout Matthew 6:19–34, I am resuming the critical arguments I began last chapter, but I am shifting focus to the church's relationship with money. As discussed in chapter 1, the Western church's "golden calf" is the liberal notion of freedom, which has two faces: *voluntarist freedom* (social) and *free-market reasoning* (economic). While we discussed the social face of the golden calf in the prior chapter, we will now look at the economic face of the idol. We can see the church's uncritical adoption of free-market reasoning as leading to two forms of syncretic idolatry mentioned in the introduction of this book: (1) the church only allows God to govern spiritual matters, thereby allowing the market to govern all material facets of Christian living, and (2) the church completely assumes market reasoning for its financial operations, thereby allowing the market to distort biblical principles of stewardship. We'll call churches that adopt the first form of idolatry "dualistic churches," and we'll use the term "materialistic churches" for those that adopt the second. While these churches syncretize free-market reasoning differently, they both have jeopardized God's sovereign rule over the church, giving God and the market shared custody over their financial affairs. To guard against these forms of idolatry we must understand the important yet limited role money plays in God's covenant of abundance.

In this chapter, we'll first look at how market reasoning disregards biblical warnings against coveting and how it leads to a *market morality* that determines a person's values and promotes social injustices. We will then consider what becomes of churches when they rely on free-market reasoning to guide their financial operations. These churches adopt either a dualistic or a materialistic interpretation of the biblical witness regarding money, both of which enable covetous lifestyles of consumption. The final section of this chapter looks at how Christians should regard money when viewing themselves as covenant partners with God. God's covenantal freedom frees us from yearning and from the insatiable desire to consume. In covenant we are given permission to rest and enjoy God's provisions according to a "Sabbath logic" that negates consumerism and views everything as belonging to God.

Market Logic and Covetous Living

Old Testament scholar Walter Brueggemann says that the Bible is "relentlessly material in its focus and concern."[1] The Bible is concerned with both the spiritual *and* the bodily (material) existence of people as they relate to God. It avoids the modern dualism that sees God as governing spiritual matters and natural forces as governing everything else in life. In this dualistic view, God has dominion over the spiritual realm, while *we*, through hard work and ingenuity, have dominion over the physical realm.[2] Rather, the Bible shows God as

---

1. Walter Brueggemann, *Money and Possessions*, Interpretation (Louisville: Westminster John Knox, 2016), 11.
2. Brian Fikkert and Kelly Kapic, *Becoming Whole: Why the Opposite of Poverty Isn't the American Dream* (Chicago: Moody, 2019), 96. Fikkert and Kapic call this concept "Evangelical Gnosticism" (93–96).

sovereign over *all* things and us as covenant partners who share in God's estate (Luke 15:31). God provides holistically for those who faithfully remain in God's will (Phil. 4:19). Since what we have is given to us by a generous God, we are responsible to steward the gifts well (Matt. 25:14–30).

Furthermore, saying the Bible promotes a material faith does not mean that the Bible endorses a *materialistic* faith, where significant emphasis is placed on material possessions and physical wealth. Rather, the Bible challenges people to examine how their faith informs their engagement with material possessions, economic systems, and social structures. Whereas a materialistic faith uses a market logic that prioritizes individual success, consumerism, and the accumulation of material goods as central values, a material faith recognizes that human corporal subsistence is good and that economic matters must be rightly understood in light of God's covenant with humanity. On the one hand, materiality gives a good account of our creatureliness—we are composed of spirit *and* matter, so we must care for our spiritual *and* our physical circumstances. Consumer materialism, on the other hand, is an excessive focus on material possessions.[3] It regards the gathering of possessions as an ultimate aim.

Consumeristic Desire

The Bible spends a lot of time talking about money and possessions but not to promote a way of life that's driven by consumption. The Bible reorders its readers' thinking so we might understand money and possessions rightly as provisions, or gifts, from a generous God. As we'll see below and in the final section, viewing money and possessions as gifts relieves us from the burdens of consumeristic desire, which leads to self-sufficiency and greed. This shift in thinking constitutes the necessary first step to rebuff the dualistic or materialistic faiths that emerge from an idolization of market reasoning. But

---

3. I qualified "materialism" with "consumer" to evoke the colloquial sense of the word. Philosophical materialism is a type of monism that asserts that everything is explained by material interactions, including consciousness and thought.

before we determine how markets should be viewed in a covenantal framework, we must discuss the social dangers of consumeristic desire and unregulated freedom in markets. To do this we'll look back at how Exodus frames the way we should think about money and then forward to how market economies influence a person's relationship to money.

Scripture Warns against Consumeristic Desire

The Ten Commandments provide a moral framework for how God's people should live as a covenant community with God. They provide a road map for a just and harmonious society, reinforcing the idea that covenantal fidelity leads to abundance. The first four commandments directly concern the people's covenantal relationship with God: they are to honor God, not make idols, respect God's name, and keep the Sabbath. The fifth still deals with right relationships but addresses honoring one's parents, which when rightly practiced "conditions us in our relationship toward God."[4] The final five commandments deal with right relationships with others, as they prohibit murder, adultery, theft, lying, and coveting.[5] Important for this chapter's discussion is the tenth commandment, which concerns unmitigated desire: "You shall not covet your neighbor's house; you shall not covet your neighbor's wife, male or female slave, ox, donkey, or anything that belongs to your neighbor" (Exod. 20:17). This prohibition is against *coveting*—the intense desire for something that belongs to someone else. In particular, the tenth commandment addresses coveting the belongings and entitlements of a neighbor.

Some have argued that the tenth commandment is unique because it is the only commandment that is internally focused on personal

---

4. Craig Keener, "Thoughts about the First Five Commandments—Exodus 20:1–12," Journeyonline.org, accessed August 5, 2023, https://journeyonline.org/thoughts-about-the-first-five-commandments-exodus-201-12/.

5. It is interesting to note that the Ten Commandments preconfigure Christ's greatest commandment in Matt. 22:37–39 to love God (the first five commandments) and to love others (the second five).

attitudes whereas all other commandments detail action.[6] Brueggemann argues, however, that the tenth commandment also deals with
action. The Hebrew word for "covet" is *hamad*, which concerns an
attitude of *wanting* but also the action of *taking*.[7] Brueggemann
writes, "The combination of *wanting* (*desiring*) and *seizing* (*acquir-
ing*) produces an acquisitive system of money and possessions that
is self-propelled until it becomes an addiction that skews viable social relationships, so that no one is safe from predatory eagerness."[8]
Coveting is thus desire that leads to the action of taking. Instead of
being consumed by a desire for what belongs to others, God's people
are encouraged in the tenth commandment to appreciate what they
have, cultivating a sense of responsibility and stewardship over what
has been entrusted to them.

Free-Market Reasoning Fuels Consumeristic Desire

Exodus shows us that life should not consist of the pursuit of
commodities. Yet one of the major functions of a free-market economy is to *increase desire* for consumption. In a free market, goods
and services are exchanged with minimal government regulation so
the invisible forces of supply and demand determine what resources
are allocated for production and how the goods and services will
be priced and distributed. Consumers determine what goods and
services are available for society based on their spending decisions.
Markets, therefore, determine trends through consumption.

Markets also *shape* desire through advertising. Advertising exists not
only to raise brand awareness but to motivate consumers to purchase
a company's goods or services. In a competitive market, companies

---

6. See John H. Sailhamer, Walter C. Kaiser Jr., and Richard S. Hess, *Genesis–
Leviticus*, rev. ed., The Expositor's Bible Commentary, ed. Tremper Longman III
and David Garland (Grand Rapids: Zondervan, 2008), 483; Lee Haines, "Genesis
and Exodus," in *The Wesleyan Bible Commentary*, vol. 1, part 1 (Grand Rapids:
Eerdmans, 1967), 234.

7. Brueggemann, *Money and Possessions*, 17. Peter Enns argues similarly, stating
that *hamad* refers to an inward desire that, when fanned, leads to action. Peter Enns,
Exodus, The NIV Application Commentary (Grand Rapids: Zondervan, 2000), 424.

8. Brueggemann, *Money and Possessions*, 17.

compete with each other to sell their goods or services to consumers; advertising helps companies gain an edge over their competitors. To win the consumer's choice, marketers aim to *persuade* the public by appealing to affections. They strive to make emotional connections between consumers and the products or services that are being sold. Markets employ many other strategies to increase consumer desire: generating subconscious longings for goods through media product placement, hyping up a product's demand and exclusivity by making limited editions, fabricating a sense of urgency through exclusive deals or limited-time offers, creating reward systems, such as loyalty programs, to incentivize consumer engagement, and so on.

Not only do competitive markets shape desire, but they perpetuate yearning. Markets succeed when they lead people into a cycle of continuous consumption and desire for new products and experiences. As long as we have a desire for something else, we have a motivation to go on. Yet consumerism keeps people in a state of perpetual yearning and desiring without *true* fulfillment. Consumerism generates desire, which fuels ambition, but ambition to what end? These aspirations are met with a hollow outcome—mere material possessions. The accumulation of material capital does not, and cannot, satisfy the cycles of desire perpetuated by consumption. As Miroslav Volf writes, "The bottomless pit of our hollow core will never be satiated. No matter how much we have, we remain 'not-enough' people. The gratification of our desires will then know only outer obstacles but no inner restraint. No matter how much we have, we will still hunger and thirst, railing against the obstacles others place in the path of the satisfaction of our insatiable desires."[9] Consumeristic desire is never fulfilled but only grows, spiraling toward greedy ambition and narcissism. It's not water that is poured on the fire but gasoline. Consumerism teaches us to want what we do not have and to desire the *pursuit* of fulfillment rather than the real satisfaction that's found in the God who exceeds our desires.

---

9. Miroslav Volf, *Free of Charge: Giving and Forgiving in a Culture Stripped of Grace* (Grand Rapids: Zondervan, 2005), 109.

Exchanging God's Provision for the Market's Clutter

When we consider the tenth commandment, we can see that consumerism promotes a covetous lifestyle that perpetuates unsatisfied desire. This sort of covetous lifestyle exists when markets are unregulated and free to shape desire and perpetuate yearning for the sake of capital. When markets are granted such influence over our lives, they will inevitably determine what we must possess to lead a good life. Accordingly, if a market helps us determine our values, then it cannot be seen as a morally neutral tool. Markets are supposed to serve us as we organize productive activity, but we begin serving markets when we allow them to shape our desires and determine our values. Similarly, Brueggemann says that the biblical narrative does not see money and possessions as neutral, inanimate objects. Rather, they are seductions that lead to idolatry, which compels devotion and eventually leads to servitude.[10] This point should make us "reconsider the quasireligious passion of a consumer economy that is propelled by insatiable desire, in which we never have enough money or enough of the possessions that money makes possible."[11] When consumers venerate the second face of the golden calf, they exchange God's provision for the market's clutter.

The West's "quasireligious passion" for consumption is plainly on display when we consider market capitalism's effect on Western holidays. Christmas and Easter have long been supplanted by extensive marketing, seasonal merchandising, and a culture of materialism that drives sales. As observations of Christ's birth and death are overshadowed by holiday consumerism, Santa Claus and the Easter Bunny become patron saints of the market. Consumption even overtakes the attitudes of gratitude and generosity that these holidays are supposed to instill.

Yet perhaps the clearest example of consumerism's encroachment on an American holiday is Black Friday—the holiest day of

10. Brueggemann, *Money and Possessions*, 8.
11. Brueggemann, *Money and Possessions*, 10.

capitalism's liturgical calendar.[12] Black Friday takes place the day after Thanksgiving, a national holiday dedicated to giving thanks for the blessings of the past year. Black Friday, conversely, is a day that marks the beginning of the holiday shopping season, so retailers all across the US offer major sales and discounts to stimulate consumer spending. It's common for stores to open early on Black Friday, for shoppers to form lines outside before the stores even open, and for shoppers to camp outside the night before. Black Friday sales are so strong that in recent years some stores began starting their sales as early as the afternoon of Thanksgiving. So in a sad and ironic turn, Thanksgiving, the day our society set aside to give thanks and to rest in abundance, has been entirely co-opted by consumeristic messaging that says, "You do not have enough." Consumers have no rest, no contentment, no Sabbath. The market gives us full houses but empty homes.

While the Bible implores us to trust God's provisions and rest in God's abundance, market logic says we must strive for a better life—one that only comes about through consumption. We cannot serve both God and wealth because wealth is an unjust master that keeps us wanting more, knowing full well that nothing it offers will ever satisfy. Because consumption never allows us to achieve satisfaction, we remain perpetually stuck in the failure of never reaching the goal of fulfillment.[13] God, on the other hand, is a good master who offers both future fulfillment in the eschaton *and* present fulfillment through Sabbath. While the market keeps people perpetually yearning, God perpetually meets our needs and longings. The key is to desire what God has for us, not what the market tells us we should want.

12. While there are several conflicting stories regarding the origins of Black Friday, it is generally believed that the term "black" is used because retailers move from operating at a loss (red) to making profits (black) as a result of the massive spike in sales Black Friday brings. Sarah Pruitt, "What's the Real History of Black Friday?," History.com, updated November 17, 2023, https://www.history.com/news/black-friday-thanksgiving-origins-history.

13. Nimi Wariboko, *The Split Economy: Saint Paul Goes to Wall Street* (Albany: SUNY Press, 2020), 73.

The Scope and Dangers of Free-Market Reasoning

Market reasoning has infiltrated not only parts of the Western church but every facet of society. David George argues that while private ownership of production was the hallmark economic advancement of the nineteenth century, the prevalence of market capitalism defines our late modern era.[14] Market capitalism shapes the way societies organize their economies, allocate resources, and pursue social progress. Today nearly every vocation in the West carries consumeristic demands. We even see, for instance, public servants and workers in the helping professions viewing themselves as market participants who service customers.[15] Market capitalism's pervasiveness is also global. Although it originated in the West, market capitalism's influence is now global as multinational corporations, interconnected financial markets, and international supply chains have expanded beyond Western borders, allowing nations around the world to exchange goods, services, and capital. Market reasoning, thus, has helped our late modern era globalize, making its presence universal and inescapable. When market reasoning speaks into every sector of life, it implements an entire worldview that eschews biblical concepts like covenant, abundance, and grace.

Transactional Value versus the Value of Gift

Market reasoning assumes value is only monetary, crowding out moral definitions of what constitutes value and worth, such as gifts that are not transactional. Pentecostal ethicist and theologian Nimi Wariboko states that even the accounting equation (assets = liabilities + equity), which informs thinking in accountancy, has theological implications. The equation is an "enactment of a totalizing will" that functions as a universalizing will to truth.[16] It implies a concept of truth

---

14. David George, *Preference Pollution: How Markets Create the Desires We Dislike* (Ann Arbor: University of Michigan Press, 2001), 1.

15. George, *Preference Pollution*, 1.

16. Nimi Wariboko, *Economics in Spirit and Truth: A Moral Philosophy of Finance* (New York: Palgrave Macmillan, 2014), 41.

because truth extends as written records of facts, and what's reported on a ledger is meant to correspond to reality. The aim of accountancy is to attain equilibrium as debits match credits. In this way, the accounting equation sets up a worldview akin to Rawls's notion of "justice as fairness," which leaves little room for grace. Wariboko writes, "With this watertight notion of truth, with every credit matched to a debit, every giving corresponding to a taking, there is no logic of gift or grace that exceeds the circuit of compensation; nor can there be any transaction that can transcend the very measure of exchange or escape return."[17] How then can the accounting equation make sense of a covenantal notion of provision that sees wealth as given and not earned, where we are stewards of God's abundance and not merchants of fairness?

Transaction is a zero-sum game. The net effects of economic operations should always be zero; one person's loss is another's gain. Conversely, *gift giving* is *not* a zero-sum game. Sociologist Marcel Mauss has shown us that gift exchange does indeed engage reciprocity, but it does so in terms of social relations, not economics.[18] Gift giving involves giving or receiving items without the expectation of a direct or equal economic return. For instance, no one expects the host of a birthday party to repay guests for their gifts with goods or services of equal monetary value. Imagine a child feeling pressure to pay for his or her birthday presents! Rather, an appropriate social reciprocation might entail the birthday boy or girl showing gratitude by smiling, offering a word of thanks, or giving a hug to the gift giver. Reciprocity is not equivalent to market exchange, but it points to a different dynamic of human interaction.[19] In other words, the primary focus of gift giving is not to exchange things of equal economic value but to exchange things that have social and symbolic meaning.

In *Scroogenomics*, economist Joel Waldfogel makes a case that gift giving during the holiday season, particularly around Christmas,

17. Wariboko, *Economics in Spirit and Truth*, 41.
18. Marcel Mauss, *The Gift: The Form and Reason for Exchange in Archaic Societies* (London: Routledge, 2010), 25.
19. Mark Sampson, *The Promise of Social Enterprise: A Theological Exploration of Faithful Economic Practice* (Eugene, OR: Cascade Books, 2022), 92.

leads to wasteful resource allocations and economic waste, citing, among other things, that American Christmas shoppers create an annual deadweight loss of $12 billion.[20] "Deadweight loss" refers to the difference between the amount spent on gifts and the value received, which is often much lower. Thinking of gift giving along these economic terms misses the point that gift giving isn't merely about satisfying preference. Gifts are often "expressive of relationships that engage, challenge, and reinterpret our identities."[21] In other words, gift giving creates a space where friendships can be fostered. Political philosopher Michael Sandel argues that viewing gift giving as preference satisfaction implies a moral, utilitarian posture toward friendship. He writes, "To insist that the purpose of all gifts is to maximize utility is to assume, without argument, that the utility-maximizing conception of friendship is morally the most appropriate one, and that the right way to treat friends is to satisfy their preferences—not to challenge or deepen or complicate them."[22] This point implies two things: (1) economic reasoning does not appropriately account for the social exchange of gift giving, and (2) economic reasoning can imply a moral grounding. In this case, the economist viewed gift giving through a utilitarian framework. This latter inference suggests that markets are not always morally neutral, a topic we'll explore next.

Market Reasoning Devalues Human Dignity and Commodifies Human Life

We've already discussed above how market reasoning *influences* our moral deliberations by determining trends through consumption and by shaping our desires through advertising. Sandel additionally suggests that because markets lead to commodification, they "crowd out" the moral norms that should otherwise govern our nonmarket values. Market reasoning determines the value of things only according to

20. Joel Waldfogel, *Scroogenomics: Why You Shouldn't Buy Presents for the Holidays* (Princeton: Princeton University Press, 2009), 69.

21. Michael Sandel, *What Money Can't Buy: The Moral Limits of Markets* (New York: Farrar, Straus and Giroux, 2012), 102.

22. Sandel, *What Money Can't Buy*, 103.

the laws of supply and demand. This, according to Sandel, empties the public life of moral argument because it does not determine what public goods or services *should* be commodified. In its supposed moral neutrality, it renders a judgment that everything has a price.

Therefore, a morality built on market logic fails to respect human dignity and the full, incalculable value of a person's life. For example, Sandel considers "death pools"—a controversial form of entertainment and gambling. In a death pool, participants make a list of individuals (usually celebrities, public figures, and other well-known people) they believe will die within a certain time frame, usually within a year. A portion of the pooled money can be won if one of the people on the list dies within the specified time frame.[23] Sandel argues that it is morally objectionable to profit from death by betting on when someone will die because it eschews human dignity, making light of life and human mortality.[24] One might argue that it is morally permissible because betting on the date someone will die does not hurt the person or aid in their death. But just because someone is not actively killing or hurting someone does not mean the activity he or she is participating in is morally justified. What is immoral about a death pool is not the fact that a person is physically harmed but that the person's life and death are commodified.

Commodifying human life for fun or for financial gain is treating a person like a discardable object. One might respond that because the death pool person is typically a *public* figure, he or she is fair game for commodification. The public owns certain rights over public figures and has a right to treat them as public goods for consumption. While some laws might protect the use of public images, the moral matter at hand concerns if a person should, for any reason, be degradable. As a response, we can appeal to the Kantian notion of human dignity that states people have *inherent worth*,[25] so it is wrong to commodify a person, even if he or she is famous.

---

23. Sandel, *What Money Can't Buy*, 141–43.
24. Sandel, *What Money Can't Buy*, 142.
25. Michael Sandel, *Justice: What's the Right Thing to Do?* (New York: Farrar, Straus and Giroux, 2009), 111.

Market Reasoning Creates Social Injustices

Another significant reason for limiting markets is because market reasoning can create social injustices. Whenever market forces and economic activities produce unequal distributions of resources, opportunities, and outcomes or marginalize or disadvantage certain groups or individuals, they perpetuate social injustices. The zero-sum game of accounting does not pay attention to the inequalities that exist in a society. As Wariboko writes, "The dynamism of money is about the dynamism of human interactions. Accounting is about the record of the sediments and deposits of such interactions and encounters. But often then structures and ethics that guide the production and distribution of money in the whole economy are not life-giving enough to the collective economic existence of all classes in society. The monetary structures and general market system create crushing inequalities and other forms of injustice that limit the participation of the poor in the economy."[26]

If someone, by no choice of their own, is raised in stressed financial circumstances, the chances of him or her succeeding are drastically reduced. Studies show that a child who has test scores in the bottom half of their class but who comes from a wealthy family has a 40 percent greater chance of achieving financial success than a child who has test scores in the top half of their class but who comes from a low-income family.[27] Markets create inequalities because they favor the greatest consumers of a society, which happen to be the wealthiest members.

Unregulated markets can lead to low wages, poor working conditions, and a lack of job security for workers. This can lead to exploitation and can perpetuate cycles of poverty. In a market economy, basic services such as health care, education, and clean water are often

26. Wariboko, *Economics in Spirit and Truth*, 52.

27. Anthony P. Carnevale, Megan L. Fasules, Michael C. Quinn, and Kathryn Peltier Campbell, "Born to Win, Schooled to Lose: Why Equally Talented Students Don't Get Equal Chances to Be All They Can Be," Georgetown University Center on Education and the Workforce, accessed August 22, 2023, https://cew.georgetown.edu/cew-reports/schooled2lose/.

treated as commodities subject to market forces. When this happens, those with greater purchasing power are able to access better services, while others are denied access. Essential goods and services become unaffordable for marginalized groups. Thus a free-market economy can create economic injustices that could last generations. In the US, for instance, the African American population still faces significant financial and social inequalities due to slavery and Jim Crow laws.

Even with a totalizing will toward fair exchange, markets in themselves cannot create parameters of justice and fairness; these parameters must be set through sufficient moral reasoning. Because markets favor the greatest consumers, they inevitably create inequalities, which lead to injustices. While one might say capitalism is egalitarian (anyone can get rich if they have grit and ingenuity), in reality it creates a caste system based not on birth, race, or gender but on talent, grit, and economic circumstances. We've already mentioned how economic circumstances crucially affect a person's chances for success, but even the idea that talent and grit are all that are needed to succeed is flawed. Our natural talents aren't totally up to us; we were born with certain abilities and aptitudes. And what if we happen to be talented in an area that's not valued by the society we live in? Particular talents that are valuable in our specific time and era might be highlighted over other talents that are not socially valuable.[28] For instance, a woman may be the best painter in her country, but if her country does not allow free artistic expression, then her artistic talent is not valued. A great artist will be impoverished, not because she lacks talent or grit, but because she has a talent that is not valued in that particular economy.

Talents that are valued in a market economy are typically those that can produce more wealth, so what about those talents that are unquantifiable in monetary terms? How can a market measure a person's talent for empathy, humor, creativity, or resiliency? A person can have many talents or traits that help communities thrive, but because such talents lack calculable outcomes, that person may be

28. Michael Sandel, *The Tyranny of Merit: Can We Find the Common Good?* (New York: Farrar, Straus and Giroux, 2020), 123.

overlooked or discarded by a consumer-driven culture. Market capitalism promotes the meritocratic promise that anyone can rise as far as their efforts and talents take them.[29] The subtext of this promise, however, is that our talents must be those that are easily monetized and that can create a direct monetary impact. Markets are used as a tool to bring about or perpetuate a predetermined logic. But as we've discussed above, if the logic is zero-sum and graceless, it will perpetuate consumeristic desire and create inequalities.

I'd like to reiterate that this book does not aim to create a *general* political theory, nor does it provide counsel to Babylon for how it should govern itself. Any assertions this book makes concern the *church's relation* to the world. In this vein we can say the church must not allow free-market reasoning to determine anything about its polity—it must come to know what God says about money in Scripture and be bound by those principles. Before discussing what God's economy entails, we will profile the dualistic and materialistic church to demonstrate what happens when churches are guided by free-market reasoning.

How Free-Market Reasoning Distorts the Faith

As mentioned in chapter 1, there are two common ways that the Western church embraces free-market reasoning. First, the dualistic church separates spiritual and financial matters; so while God governs spiritual matters, market logic governs material matters. Second, the materialistic church *attempts* to offer a holistic view of Christian living, but it does so by blending free-market reasoning with biblical values. Both churches commit idolatry but in different ways. The former props up money to be enthroned next to God, and the latter syncretizes money into God. We will look at both of these distortions in turn.

The Dualistic Church

Brian Fikkert and Kelly Kapic call the dualistic approach "Evangelical Gnosticism." Evangelical Gnosticism, as they define it, occurs

29. Sandel, *Tyranny of Merit*, 24.

when the church adopts elements of naturalism, the philosophical belief that only natural forces govern the universe.[30] A naturalist opposes spiritual explanations of natural phenomena, arguing that all experiences can be explained empirically. Evangelical Gnostics view the world through a dualistic frame where God determines spiritual matters and the laws of nature determine everything else. This sort of dualism plays out when material matters are seen as distinctly nonspiritual and when spiritual matters are seen as nonmaterial. This is what happens, for instance, when someone seeks medical treatment multiple times before ever praying for healing.[31] They believe, often implicitly, that since the ailment is a physical issue, it belongs to the order of nature. This reasoning is problematic though, because if God can only act on spiritual matters, then God is not actually sovereign. God and nature would share the throne.

We should note that a holistic, nondualistic view of God's sovereignty does not reduce every issue to the spiritual realm. Instead it posits that God is sovereign over all matters, whether they are spiritual or physical. In fact, a truly holistic view of life imagines physical matters as always having a spiritual component and spiritual matters as always having a material component. Just as dualism makes the mistake of separating the spiritual and the material, it is also a mistake to view everything as exclusively spiritual or entirely physical. In this regard, a refusal to visit a doctor on the basis that it is a sign of unbelief would be misguided. When a sickness is considered only physical, there's no need to pray for healing, and when it's considered only spiritual, there's no reason to visit a doctor. A holistic view of health and illness requires us to recognize *both* the material *and* the spiritual realities involved. God has blessed physicians with brilliance and medical aptitude to heal people through medical means, but God also heals people miraculously through spiritual means.[32]

---

30. Fikkert and Kapic, *Becoming Whole*, 93.
31. Fikkert and Kapic, *Becoming Whole*, 95.
32. Whether supernatural healing is the suspending of natural forces or the emergence of unknown natural forces is irrelevant to this point. The point I'm making is that prayer as an act of faith can somehow catalyze a divine healing to occur.

Thus a nondualistic approach to sickness and health prays *and* seeks medical counsel. It trusts in God and in those whom God has gifted to be physicians.

The dualistic church seems disingenuous to the public because it serves two masters. With its devotion split between God and the market, its witness is tainted and thus appears inauthentic. A dualistic church claims to be a holy witness to the world but then conforms to the world to gain its acceptance. As we noted in the previous section, unregulated markets lead to a market morality. Thus when a church functions dualistically, it promotes *both* biblical values *and* market morality, which creates a conflict. Congregants are told to be content with what God has provided *and* to strive for greater consumption. They're told to trust God in all manners of life *and* to yearn for what the market dictates as valuable. Hence church members are taught to love God *and* money, to simultaneously be grateful *yet* covetous. The dualistic church nurtures congregants to be split against themselves—to stand with one foot in the kingdom of God and one foot in the kingdom of the world.

The Materialistic Church

While the dualistic church is common, the materialistic church might be even more prevalent. The materialistic church integrates its love for God and for money to form a singular warped version of God and the Christian faith. The clearest examples of materialistic churches are those that preach the so-called prosperity gospel. Theologian and political scientist Andreas Heuser describes the prosperity gospel as teachings that focus on the individual's material success as a sign of divine grace.[33] Prosperity preachers use contemporary marketplace language to teach what they believe are biblical principles of faith, prosperity, stewardship, and healing.

While all prosperity teachings emphasize faith, wealth, health, and victory, historian Kate Bowler makes a helpful distinction between

---

33. Andreas Heuser, "Prosperity Theology: Material Abundance and Praxis of Transformation," in *The Routledge Handbook of Pentecostal Theology*, ed. Wolfgang Vondey (London: Routledge, 2020), 410.

hard and *soft* prosperity teaching.[34] According to hard prosperity teaching, God's will is for believers to succeed, so a Christian who is not prosperous must have a weak faith.[35] In contrast, soft prosperity adheres to the principles of abundant living, but it does not view these principles as formulaic in the way that hard prosperity does.[36] Many mainstream churches around the world have adopted the optimism of soft prosperity as foundational for their economic thinking.[37] Bowler's distinction allows us to differentiate between the soft prosperity teaching that emphasizes biblical concepts of material abundance and the hard prosperity teaching that interprets biblical concepts through the lens of market capitalism.

The prosperity gospel is usually traced back to the "Word of Faith" movement popularized by Kenneth Hagin and others throughout the second half of the twentieth century.[38] Many renditions of the prosperity gospel can be found among Charismatic, Pentecostal, and evangelical circles, but there are some general concepts that consistently emerge in both hard and soft prosperity teachings: (1) material blessings on earth are seen as foretastes of what is to come; (2) God desires believers to be prosperous in all areas of life, which includes finances; (3) health and wealth are signs of God's favor and blessings on the lives of believers; and (4) believers should speak positively and claim God's blessings on their lives. These four elements depict a this-worldly realized eschatology that recognizes God's abundance in the material realm today.

The Marketization of Divine Abundance

Although using market-driven language to discuss biblical concepts can be dangerous, the four themes above *can* be understood through a covenantal framework of God's abundance. The Bible

---

34. Kate Bowler, *Blessed: A History of the American Prosperity Gospel* (Oxford: Oxford University Press, 2013), 97.
35. Bowler, *Blessed*, 8.
36. Bowler, *Blessed*, 8.
37. Bowler, *Blessed*, 237.
38. Heuser, "Prosperity Theology," 411.

does say, after all, that "all things work together for good for those
who love God, who are called according to his purpose" (Rom. 8:28).
Yet prosperity preachers often go beyond these themes and preach
a marketization of divine abundance. For instance, some prosperity teachers claim there is a causal link between a person's positive
confession of faith and the blessings they receive. Some teachers
may be as crude as to say poverty is a sign that a person lacks faith.
Some also teach a concept called "seed faith," the idea that donations made to pastors, evangelists, and ministries are "seeds" of offering that, when sown with faith, will produce a bountiful harvest.
Although these preachers typically evoke the principles of sowing
and reaping that can be found in Galatians 6:7–9, they, in effect,
imagine God as a nonrelational, cosmic bank. A person deposits
money (in faith) to later withdraw funds that have accrued interest
that was multiplied by faith. Here even God is subservient to the
will of the market.

This sort of blasphemy is clearly exemplified in televangelist Gloria
Copeland's statement "You give $1 for the Gospel's sake and $100
belongs to you; give $10 and receive $1,000; give $1,000 and receive
$100,000. . . . In short, Mark 10:30 is a very good deal."[39] This line
of reasoning is idolatrous because Copeland reduces God to a financial system, and with enough faith *you* can conquer the system. It's
like walking up to a slot machine at a casino and feeling a mix of
nervousness and anticipation at the chance of winning. But instead
of leaving it to chance, by faith you *will* the three golden sevens to
perfectly line up. By faith you've conquered the system. In this scenario, *you*, and not God, are in control. God is bound by the rules of
the market, and you, by faith, can cash in your winnings. If God is
subject to the rules of the market, then God is not sovereign. And by
gaining power over the system, *you* are sovereign. At its worst, then,
the materialistic church teaches congregants to idolize themselves.

39. Gloria Copeland, *God's Will Is Prosperity* (Tulsa: Harrison House, 1978),
54. I should note that while Copeland seems to indicate that believers are making a
deal with God, the passage she evokes, Mark 10, makes no such claim. Rather, Peter
explains how even though following Jesus is costly, the blessings outweigh the losses.

Transactional and Predictable Gifts

As is the case for the dualistic church, the liberal notion of free-market reasoning is also normative for the materialistic church, and this is especially evident in the prosperity gospel. In *Economics in Spirit and Truth*, Wariboko traces the logic of the prosperity gospel, contending that it is deeply indebted to neoclassical economics. In particular, the prosperity gospel is based on a linear understanding of the world that treks along a normal distribution curve.[40] "Normal distribution" follows a symmetrical curve, which suggests that data near the mean are more likely to occur than data far from the mean. Because this model is predictable with few variances, one can assume that returns unfold proportionately against what's offered. Thus, prosperity preachers imply in their rhetoric that "returns from giving are normally distributed in the sense that those who get higher returns (blessings) have given more, taken higher risks of faith by giving more."[41] This same logic undergirds modern finance theory.

One major theological concern that arises from adopting a linear understanding of the world is that it renders superfluous the Spirit's role in gift giving.[42] Normal distribution is transactional and predictable, but the biblical witness sees the Holy Spirit as giver of blessings. The linear model thus "reveals a pneumatology that presents the Spirit as a wind (pneuma) that does not really move to where it wishes to go."[43] Because linearity constricts and boxes in the movement of the Spirit, it also wildly distorts the biblical concept of faith.

Redeeming the Prosperity Gospel?

A potentially positive implication of prosperity logic is that it is fundamentally egalitarian. The spread of blessing is not based on class, race, gender, status, or education but is totally commensurate

---

40. Wariboko, *Economics in Spirit and Truth*, 91–92.
41. Wariboko, *Economics in Spirit and Truth*, 92.
42. Wariboko, *Economics in Spirit and Truth*, 97.
43. Wariboko, *Economics in Spirit and Truth*, 97.

to an individual's faith when they give an offering.[44] Prosperity is available to anyone with enough genuine faith. Yet along with a skewed view on faith, prosperity logic has two additional pitfalls. First, it gives the preacher an airtight alibi for when prosperity does not come about—the unprosperous person is viewed as lacking genuine faith. Second, it is radically individualistic and does not look at the prosperity of an economy as a whole, which would benefit the whole community. This sort of individualism can lead to selfish ambitions.

While the prosperity gospel's individualism can lead to selfishness or, at worst, self-idolization, we must contend with the undeniable fact that prosperity teaching has profoundly influenced social uplift (improved living standards and well-being) for impoverished people around the world. Theologian Edward Suh contends that we must be mindful of the sociological dynamics that are at play in the prosperity gospel movement, even as we critique the exploitative elements that exist within the movement.[45] Opposing the narratives of victimization that emerge from circumstances of poverty, the prosperity gospel offers an inherent message of empowerment. Although the prosperity gospel uses the language of financial blessing, as Suh states, "It is not the promise of financial blessings that is transforming lives in the Prosperity movement. Rather, it is the invitation to freedom from being defined and limited by the narratives of our past that is the true transformative factor in Prosperity theologies that then manifests in flourishing life."[46] Thus there is a liberative dimension of the prosperity message that empowers individuals trapped in cycles of poverty to take control of their circumstances. Prosperity teachings can help people focus on personal transformation "that results in new patterns of life that promote flourishing in themselves, their families, and their communities."[47]

---

44. Wariboko, *Economics in Spirit and Truth*, 93.
45. Edward Suh, *The Empowering God: Redeeming the Prosperity Movement and Overcoming Victim Trauma in the Poor* (Eugene, OR: Pickwick, 2018), 3.
46. Suh, *Empowering God*, 4–5.
47. Suh, *Empowering God*, 88.

While liberation theology addresses poverty on systemic, social levels, the prosperity gospel deals with poverty on an individual level, which offers believers graspable methods for personal social uplift.[48] This could be one of the reasons why Pentecostalism, a movement that tends to embrace prosperity teaching, is growing so much in impoverished parts of the world. This sentiment echoes what one commentator told Donald Miller and Tetsunao Yamamori during their research on global Pentecostalism: "While Liberation Theology opted for the poor, the poor opted for Pentecostalism."[49] Perhaps prosperity teachings address the issues surrounding poverty in more tangible ways. After all, it's easier to support an individual by changing his or her outlook than it is to change systems and governments through social intervention. Both courses of action are needed, but it is the prosperity gospel's emphasis on personal social uplift that makes it so popular around the world. As theologian Frank Macchia points out, global expressions of the prosperity gospel are typically rooted in context-specific problems of poverty instead of being driven by mere materialism and the accumulation of wealth.[50]

In order to redeem the prosperity gospel from its capitalistic misgivings, Suh suggests understanding human flourishing through a framework of empowerment/liberation rather than through the narrow frame of health and prosperity.[51] The former framework still respects the material aspects of life, recognizing that empowerment and liberation often entail financial prosperity. Because this framework is broader, it deals more holistically with the whole person. The prosperity gospel would do well to affirm "the comprehensive materiality of the shalom that God desires to bring into the lives of His people."[52] Such a view respects what God is doing on earth today,

48. Suh, *Empowering God*, 88.

49. Donald Miller and Tetsunao Yamamori, *Global Pentecostalism: The New Face of Christian Social Engagement* (Berkeley: University of California Press, 2007), 12.

50. Frank Macchia, "A Call for Careful Discernment: A Theological Response to Prosperity Preaching," in *Pentecostalism and Prosperity: The Socio-Economics of the Global Charismatic Movement*, ed. Katherine Attanasi and Amos Yong (New York: Palgrave Macmillan, 2012), 226.

51. Suh, *Empowering God*, 129.

52. Suh, *Empowering God*, 172.

while rejecting an over-realized eschatology that *limits* God's action to this-worldly material blessing.[53]

With these necessary demarcations, we must ask if what Suh is envisioning as a redeemed prosperity gospel should still retain the name "prosperity gospel." When the prosperity gospel focuses on empowerment and liberation in a holistic framework, isn't this just describing a theology of abundance? I have argued elsewhere,[54] and will reiterate here, that Pentecostals and Charismatics should avoid the term "prosperity gospel" in reference to God's abundance and should instead use "theology of abundance." While a theology of abundance affirms materiality and even prosperity, it views any sense of prosperity as a gift from God, not a faith-based transaction. Perhaps the best thing to do is to leave the term "prosperity gospel" with the materialistic church as we advance a better understanding of holistic prosperity through God's abundant gift.

Market Reasoning in the Church Leads to Idolatry

There is no doubt that churches can fall into idolatry when they are guided by free-market reasoning. Using market reasoning as a tool to serve the congregation is okay when churches truly believe God is sovereign over spiritual and material matters. The problem arises when the church allows the free market to govern all nonspiritual matters. This is how an otherwise faithful church falls into dualistic idolatry. Likewise, it's okay for churches to focus on material prosperity as part of a holistic sense of empowerment. The problem arises when the church considers material prosperity as life's ultimate good. In this case, an otherwise faithful church falls into materialistic idolatry. Both of these idolatries can be avoided with a proper understanding of God's sovereignty in covenantal relationship. Once we realize that

53. As we follow this framework, we must still be critical about the problems with hard prosperity mentioned above and about the prosperity gospel's implications of triumphalism (an attitude of superiority after achieving success), which devalues the dignity of disabled people. Suh, *Empowering God*, 112.

54. Steven Félix-Jäger, *Renewal Worship: A Theology of Pentecostal Doxology* (Downers Grove, IL: IVP Academic, 2022), 79.

everything we have is a gift from God, then every other aspect of our lives falls into place. This entails adopting a Sabbath logic instead of free-market reasoning when it comes to finances.

Sabbath Logic and Covenantal Living

In the final section of this chapter, I'd like to discuss the first step toward developing a Sabbath logic in economics: viewing money and possessions as gifts from God. Chapter 5 of this book fleshes out what a Sabbath logic in God's covenant of abundance entails, but for now I'd like to focus on the necessary mindset shift we need to guard against free-market logic entering the church.

Denying Individual Ownership and Embracing God's Ownership of All

As we've stated above, market logic is rooted in consumeristic desire, but Sabbath logic is rooted in covenantal provision. As covenant partners with God, the creator of all things, we can rest assured that everything belongs to God. The notion that we are entitled to things as autonomous individuals is both biblically incorrect and epistemologically arrogant. It ignores the fact that we are *not* God but part of God's created order. Thus a covenantal approach to abundance is not individualistic like the prosperity gospel but takes into account human flourishing and God's provision for all.

Brueggemann has developed six theses to summarize the Bible's general approach to money, two of which are critical and four of which are generative and instructive. We've already addressed various aspects of Brueggemann's critical theses in the sections above, but to reiterate, one thesis says that money and possessions are seen as seductions leading to idolatry.[55] It isn't money itself that is idolatrous but the love of money (1 Tim. 6:10). The West finds itself so overwhelmed by market reasoning that wealth generation has become its central aspiration—its idol. Brueggemann writes, "It does not

---

55. Brueggemann, *Money and Possessions*, 8.

require much imagination to transpose the bull [calf] of gold to the icon of Wall Street, with its 'bullish' markets, to see the allure of money that may distort neighborly covenantal relationships."[56] This point leads to another of Brueggemann's critical theses: money and possessions can become a source of social injustice. Deuteronomy insists that money should be managed to foster justice for the good of the community (Deut. 16:20). The biblical tradition connects remembering God as owner and doing neighborly justice with the money that's provided. Conversely, forgetting God as owner results in exploitation.[57] In sum, the Bible warns against money's ability to enter every facet of life and our propensity to exploit others once money has become central.

Brueggemann also points out four generative and instructive theses: (1) money and possessions should be viewed as gifts from God; (2) money and possessions are received as rewards for covenantal obedience; (3) money and possessions belong to God and are held in trust by people in community; and (4) money and possessions are to be shared in a neighborly way.[58] These theses demonstrate that money and possessions are not in themselves evil or corrupting; rather, they are gifts from God. And if they truly are gifts from God, then money and possessions are not merely neutral but good. Money isn't the problem; idolatry is. Idolatry can be avoided when we recognize that everything is borrowed from God. This simple notion can help us move from the graceless, zero-sum game of "economic justice as fairness" to the countercultural way of life encouraged by Sabbath generosity. As Volf states,

> If we believe that God has given us everything, then giving will be our way of living. We'll still work to earn, because the gift of work is the primary means by which God gives what we have. But earning and possessing will become folded into giving. . . . Earning and possessing are not just a bridge between our desires and their satisfaction. They

56. Brueggemann, *Money and Possessions*, 8.
57. Brueggemann, *Money and Possessions*, 5.
58. Brueggemann, *Money and Possessions*, 1–6.

are a *midpoint* in the flow of gifts: from God to us, and through us to others. We give because we have been given to; we don't let others simply fend for themselves because we haven't been left to fend for ourselves.[59]

This generative frame of thinking demonstrates what an appropriate relationship with money looks like.

Rejecting the Scarcity Mindset and Embracing the Abundance Mindset

Considering the Lord's Prayer again (Matt. 6:9–13), we can see that verses 11–12 succinctly outline what economic justice looks like in God's covenant of abundance: "Give us today our daily bread. And forgive us our debts, as we also have forgiven our debtors." It would be wrong, and dualistic, to spiritualize this passage as if it's only talking about spiritual matters and the forgiveness of sins. Rather, Jesus addresses the holistic self, both spiritual and material. Because our ledger is wiped clean, we should wipe clean the ledger of those who have wronged us. This seemingly refers to wrongdoing, but might it also be talking about monetary debts? As ethicist Hak Joon Lee points out, "Far from being a mere liturgical chant, the petition of daily bread and forgiveness of debts had real existential meaning and resonance with the people's desperately impoverished economic condition."[60] As discussed in the introduction to this chapter, verse 11 talks about God's daily provisions, but verse 12 is joined with it, meaning that God's provisions have to do with debt cancellation. Thus the "daily bread" provisions are spiritual *and* material—we also thank God for health and nourishment.

Trusting in God's provision frees us from a scarcity mindset, where we worry about not having enough.[61] We are no longer burdened by

---

59. Volf, *Free of Charge*, 107–8.

60. Hak Joon Lee, *Christian Ethics: A New Covenant Model* (Grand Rapids: Eerdmans, 2021), 313.

61. Chapter 5 of this book distinguishes the difference between "economic scarcity" and the "scarcity mindset." For now it is sufficient to say that economic scarcity

the anxieties that accompany lack. In the same way, releasing some-one's debt demonstrates our willingness to alleviate another's burden. Relying on daily bread means trusting God for *every* provision. The basis of this trust is the belief that God knows what everybody needs and provides accordingly. The act of releasing a person's debt can be viewed as an extension of this trust. Forgiving a debt demonstrates a belief that God will take care of both our own and others' needs.

As Scott Bader-Saye puts it, trusting in God's provision is the antidote to our fears of insecurity:

> In the Lord's Prayer, Jesus teaches his followers to pray "Give us this day our daily bread" (Matt. 6:11). Jesus does not encourage us to pray for tomorrow or the next day or for enough money to secure a grand retirement. Rather, he calls us to be content with God's provision for the day. Just a few verses later Jesus tells his followers, "Do not store up for yourselves treasures on earth" (v. 19). These teachings indicate that following Jesus will involve releasing our "stored-up" goods to those who have needs now so that we might be the means by which God gives to them their daily bread. Excessive fear closes us off from such vulnerability and from welcoming the daily gift of God's provision.[62]

In other words, storing up treasures on earth indicates a lack of trust in God. When you store up earthly provisions, you are saying, in effect, that you do not believe God will provide for you tomorrow. Sabbath logic says that God, who is in control of everything, *will* provide. Our fear of lack is, therefore, demonstrating that we're not abiding by a Sabbath logic. When we're concerned about tomorrow, it's impossible to dwell in the blessings of Sabbath.

This is not to say that we will not have times of need. In response to Pharaoh's vision of impending famine, God instructs Pharaoh to store up grain. This is one instance in which God instructs someone

---

is a mere indicator that resources are lower than the relative standard of a society's wants and desires, whereas the scarcity mindset is the state of mind that there are not enough resources to go around.

62. Scott Bader-Saye, *Following Jesus in a Culture of Fear: Choosing Trust over Safety in an Anxious Age* (Grand Rapids: Brazos, 2020), 47.

to store up treasure during times of plenty, because God knows this time will be followed by a time of scarcity. God's instruction, if followed, would mean that Egypt and all the surrounding countries would be provided for through the famine. Though these resources are supposed to be shared and used to help others, Pharaoh instead, in his wickedness, hoards and profits from them. The point is this: a mindset of abundance that views God as provider does not deny the possibility that there will be times of need. It relies on the promise, rather, that God will provide even when times of need arise, and if we trust in God's abundance, we will all make it through.

People often quote Philippians 4:13 ("I can do all things through him who strengthens me") out of context. The passage is actually about trusting God in times of need. Consider the verse in its immediate context with the verses right before it and you'll see how the passage shows Paul's faith in God through any sort of financial situation: "I have learned to be content with whatever I have. I know what it is to have little, and I know what it is to have plenty. In any and all circumstances I have learned the secret of being well-fed and of going hungry, of having plenty and of being in need. I can do all things through him who strengthens me" (Phil. 4:11–13). As Paul demonstrates, faith means trusting God in every situation, allowing the Spirit to guide us through seasons of fortune *and* famine. Anytime people die because of a lack of resources, someone else in their community has hoarded and taken on a Pharaonic mindset of scarcity. We are called to share our resources, which are God's anyway, to help others who are in need. Sabbath logic produces this shift in mindset.

Conclusion

While one may wish to consider the social harms that free-market reasoning brings to a society, as Michael Sandel has, this chapter focused on the church's idolatrous embrace of market logic. Our Western society relies so heavily on market logic that many Christians simply accept capitalism as the natural method for dealing with money and possessions. Consequently, the church adopts market logic uncritically, without ever examining whether what the Bible says about wealth and provision is at odds with market logic. When free-market reasoning enters the doors of the church, the market and not God begins to determine the church's values and motivations.

As we have seen throughout this chapter, the Bible promotes a Sabbath logic in which God is the provider and people are stewards. Therefore, since everything belongs to our generous God, the church should view matters of wealth through a covenantal framework based on generosity and grace, not on zero-sum entitlements. Market-driven churches fall into either dualism or materialism. In both cases, wealth is viewed idolatrously. Dualistic and materialistic churches, like the assimilated and nationalistic churches profiled in the prior chapter, are distortions of the faith—syncretic versions of Christianity that broadcast a tainted witness to the world. Throughout chapters 1 and 2 we have covered the social and economic faces of the West's golden calf of liberty. The next chapter will discuss what it means to be a citizen of God's kingdom while also participating in our national polity. We'll see how assimilated, nationalistic, dualistic, and materialistic churches *all* fail to respect the church's holiness and why a covenantal view of freedom promotes a genuine witness of the kingdom of God.

3

Conflicting Citizenships and the Kingdom

Living in a Free Country

John 18 recounts Jesus's trial before Pontius Pilate. When Jesus arrives at the Roman headquarters, Pilate asks, "Are you the King of the Jews?" (v. 33). Pilate asks this because Jewish priests and elders accused Jesus of inciting a rebellion against Rome and claiming to be their king. The Jewish leaders deceptively portrayed Jesus as a cunning rebel—a national threat against Rome. Jesus responds promptly, "My kingdom does not belong to this world. If my kingdom belonged to this world, my followers would be fighting to keep me from being handed over to the Jews" (v. 36). Jesus communicates he is *not* establishing a worldly kingdom to forcefully displace other worldly kingdoms. Jesus's response convinces Pilate to try releasing Jesus, saying that the Jewish leaders' charges have no basis (v. 38), but, as we know, Pilate later cedes to the demands of the Jewish leaders and sends Jesus to the cross.

Among other things, this passage demonstrates that Jesus imagined the kingdom of God not as a worldly kingdom but as a spiritual reality that affects the world. As a spiritual reality, the kingdom of God reverses the present conditions of the world through the Spirit-filled witness of the kingdom's citizens. According to Luke's Gospel, the kingdom of God involves proclaiming good news to the poor, releasing captives, healing the blind, and freeing the oppressed (Luke 4:18–21, 33–35; 6:20; 7:20–22). These are tangible, real-world effects of God's holistic kingdom. Jesus seems to describe the kingdom of God as a message that needs to be received and embodied, rather than a worldly rule that needs to be governed. Thus the message of the kingdom of God often calls for a radical change of relationship toward others (Mark 4:11–20; 9:43–48; Luke 4:43–44; 8:10–15; 9:60–62; 18:28–30). Jesus's actions exemplify how to *live out* the kingdom of God, and his words are meant to encourage us to do the same.

Considering Jesus's descriptions of the kingdom of God, we can assert that a public theology of renewal calls the church to be a Spirit-led witness that reflects and reveals God's kingdom. This assertion, however, leaves open the question of how far the church should be aligned with the state. Should the church oppose the state in its civic dealings or become one of its institutions? Perhaps the answer eschews both of these two poles. Nevertheless, it is integral for any public theology to determine how the church relates to the world. Hence this chapter addresses what it means to be a citizen in God's kingdom while also being a citizen of a particular nation.

To begin with, this chapter offers a clear distinction between the nature and requirements of the two opposing kingdoms. It profiles the kingdom of God and the kingdom of the world, showing how any part of the kingdom of the world is, to use the eschatological imagery of Revelation, Babylon. The best state of the kingdom of the world is *still* Babylon, and it is still fundamentally opposed to God's kingdom. This realization leads to the final section, which looks at the church's priestly task of mediating between the world and God's kingdom. Political persuasion in a pluralist society requires the church to offer a counternarrative of abundant love, to lead a public witness of grace and generosity that helps the world envision the kingdom of God today. By living in a reality of abundance, the church can help the world see God's kingdom as a spiritual reality that is not just a system of beliefs but a kingdom that is tangible and already present.

Citizenship in Two Kingdoms

As we consider what it means to be covenanted with God while also being socially contracted with a nation, we must begin by exploring the compatibility, or lack thereof, between the kingdom of God and the kingdom of the world. For our purposes here, we will consider only one particular faction of the kingdom of the world: the liberal state. Does the kingdom of God oppose the liberal state? Or are they somehow in allegiance with one another through the church? Can the church relate to the state without falling into the syncretism described in the previous chapters? Can Christians establish a sort of dual citizenship with the kingdom of God and the kingdom of the world? To begin answering these questions we must look at what sort of allegiances both the kingdom of God and the liberal state require of their citizens.

Defining and Differentiating the Two Kingdoms

The Bible references both the kingdom of God and the kingdom of the world. The *kingdom of God* is a spiritual reality inaugurated by Christ, where god reigns as king (Ps. 103:19; Mark 1:15; Rom. 14:17). During the eschaton, this fully redeemed spiritual reality is consummated. Currently, the church exists in a proleptic reality (acting as if a future event has already happened) where the kingdom of God is inaugurated but has not yet come to fruition. The *kingdom of the world*, on the other hand, is led by Satan and is morally opposed to God's desire to reconcile everything (John 14:30; Col. 1:13; Rev. 11:15). As a result of this opposition, systems of oppression, poverty, and injustice have emerged all over the world today.

The church should not be equated with the kingdom of God, nor should the state be equated with the kingdom of the world. Rather, the church should be seen as a *reflection* of the kingdom of God. Through its public witness, the church can make the kingdom of God visible to the world.[1] In the same way, the state is not the kingdom of the world but a created institution that materializes as an expression of the kingdom of the world. This is akin to how the book of Revelation depicts Rome as an institutional expression of Babylon (Rev. 17:5–18). The state is God's agent to maintain justice and order on earth. Conversely, the church is God's agent to bring about the kingdom of God on earth. The state is an extension of a political kingdom, and the church is an extension of a holistic kingdom. While the state is motivated by justice and correction, the church is motivated by love and reconciliation (2 Cor. 5:11–21). In other words, the state is a secular entity that has been given power to protect its citizens and promote social cohesion. While the state is not the kingdom of the world in its entirety, it is related to it and is thus subject to the same moral decay as the kingdom of the world. The church is in a state of anticipation, living as if the kingdom has already come in its fullness, while the world lives as if the kingdom will never come. The eschaton is the moment in time when the kingdom is fully realized, when God's kingdom reigns and Satan's kingdom is defeated once and for all.

Now that we have defined the public functions of the church and the state, we must ask how Christians can engage in both by first considering the different type of allegiances each requires. Every Christian voluntarily joins the kingdom of God through the church in covenant. Citizenship in the kingdom of God constitutes a covenantal relationship between God and creation. Since the creator of all things is the Lord of the covenant, a covenant with God is all consuming and affects every aspect of life. As covenant partners with God, Christians are totally dependent on God (the provider) and relate interdependently to each other (the stewards) in God's kingdom.

---

1. Stanley Hauerwas, *The Peaceable Kingdom: A Primer in Christian Ethics* (Notre Dame, IN: University of Notre Dame Press, 1983), 97.

Covenant requires a two-way relationship that is both dependent and interdependent. Covenanted Christians are obligated to serve God, rely on God, and be accountable to God. They are also obligated to serve and rely on each other and to be accountable to each other. The liberal state, conversely, *seems* to require very little from its citizens as far as allegiance is concerned. Citizens are not required to be in covenant with the state, but they involuntarily enter a social contract. The liberal state is founded on the idea that its citizens have certain inalienable rights, such as life, liberty, and the pursuit of happiness (as quoted from the Declaration of Independence). It does not require its citizens to swear an oath to any specific leader or government, nor should it demand that they sacrifice their personal interests for the interests of the state. Instead, citizens are expected to abide by the laws of the state and to participate in the democratic process. A foundational claim of liberalism is that it is neutral on matters of religion and morality. This means that the state does not impose any particular religious or moral code on its citizens but, rather, allows people to live in accordance with their own beliefs and values. If the liberal state *is* neutral on these matters, then covenanted Christians should be able to live with minimal governmental interference. However, as we'll explore in the next section, this may not be the case.

The Major Conflict of Citizenship in Two Kingdoms: The Myth of Neutrality

Some sort of dual citizenship is inevitable, and some consider liberal state citizenship to be ideal for the church to flourish. For instance, theologian Theo Hobson argues that the liberal state is the proper modern context for Christianity.[2] Hobson concurs with our general critical thesis that the church betrays its covenantal fidelity when liberal freedom dictates the church's moral and religious sensibilities. Yet he argues that the church should look at liberalism not

---

2. Theo Hobson, *Reinventing Liberal Christianity* (Grand Rapids: Eerdmans, 2013), 11.

as a pervasive enemy but as an ally.[3] Hobson goes so far as to say that liberalism is the "best possible context in which the ecclesial vision can exist."[4] In other words, the church best thrives in a liberal society not because liberalism is some sort of new Christendom but because it gives the church freedom to express itself how it will.

This is certainly an advantage for Western Christians but only if the liberal state is truly neutral and requires its citizens to adhere to an unencumbered (free from external restraints) social contract. If liberal neutrality exists, then there should be no conflict between the church and the state. However, as we've been arguing throughout this book and as we'll see below, the secular state is *not* neutral. Rather, it instills social and economic values into its citizens. If the liberal state is in fact not neutral, then the church has to battle the state's pervasive ideologies and has to safeguard against those ideologies. If liberalism's claim to neutrality fails, then a congenial dual citizenship between the kingdom of God and the liberal state also collapses. The matter of dual citizenship thus entails either rejecting some or part of one of the kingdoms or merging their ideologies (syncretism). Throughout this chapter, we will discuss rejecting some or part of one of the kingdoms, as we've already laid out the dangers of syncretic idolatry in the previous chapters. But before we consider the various facets of this dilemma, we must define what it means to live in a pluralist society.

The word "pluralism" typically refers either to *the plurality of human cultures*, where varied cultures exist together in near proximity, or to *religious pluralism*, where varied religious traditions are not only in proximity but are viewed relativistically as equally valid. These distinctions can get a little messy, since we know that religion is part of culture, and religious beliefs always influence culture. Nevertheless, a pluralist society recognizes the importance of accommodating multiple perspectives while appreciating the prominence of religion in culture. Pluralism is considered an essential characteristic

---

3. Hobson, *Reinventing Liberal Christianity*, 244.
4. Hobson, *Reinventing Liberal Christianity*, 296.

of a secular society because there is no officially sanctioned religious or moral authority.[5] Throughout this book, when I refer to a "pluralist society," I am referring to the former sense of cultural plurality, which also accounts for religious influence on culture. This sense of plurality maintains that liberal societies are pluralist by fact but not by principle. It does not affirm the equal validity of every religious tradition but recognizes the fact that different cultures and religions coexist in a society.

Liberal Societies Privatize and Demote Religious Faiths in Their Efforts Toward Neutrality

Liberals claim that a pluralist society aspires to uphold the rights and freedoms of all its citizens, regardless of their cultural and religious beliefs. The government's role is thus to ensure that these rights and freedoms are respected and protected. The church shapes the moral lives of its constituents, and the state simply creates the parameters where it and other social groups can coexist. Therefore, a liberal government must find some way to meet the needs of its religious citizens while still protecting religious freedom.

To help safeguard this pluralism, liberal governments maintain policies of religious neutrality. Consider again, for instance, the First Amendment of the United States Constitution: "Congress shall make no law respecting an establishment of religion, or prohibiting the free exercise thereof."[6] This right is enshrined in the Constitution to prevent governmental interference, to ensure the government cannot force its citizens to practice or prevent them from practicing any particular religion. This means, therefore, that it is inappropriate to consider the United States a "Christian" nation. The US does not have a state-sanctioned religion, nor does it prevent anyone from

---

5. Lesslie Newbigin, *The Gospel in a Pluralist Society* (Grand Rapids: Eerdmans, 1989), 1.

6. "The Bill of Rights: A Transcription," National Archives, accessed October 14, 2023, https://www.archives.gov/founding-docs/bill-of-rights-transcript#:~:text=Bill%20of%20Rights.%22-,Amendment%20I,for%20a%20redress%20of%20grievances.

practicing their own religion as long as the religion's practices do not harm or violate another American's individual rights.[7] While many of the American forefathers were Christians,[8] they resolutely established a liberal standard of religious freedom.

Newbigin points out that one way liberal societies accommodate competing faith claims is by relegating them to matters of private opinion. If Christians make objectivist claims, for instance, a pluralist society will view such claims as opinions they are entitled to hold but not as matters of public truth. This view is embedded in the fabric of American governance and was even given as a rationale for the idea of separation of church and state by Thomas Jefferson. Consider what Jefferson wrote to the Danbury Baptist Association in 1802: "Believing with you that religion is a matter which lies solely between Man & his God, that he owes account to none other for his faith or his worship, that the legitimate powers of government reach actions only, & not opinions, I contemplate with sovereign reverence that act of the whole American people which declared that their legislature should 'make no law respecting an establishment of religion, or prohibiting the free exercise thereof,' thus building a wall of separation between Church & State."[9] While Jefferson calls for a "wall of separation" so the church can be protected from government interference, he also calls religious beliefs matters of private opinion. Calling religious belief "opinion" delegitimizes its weight in public discourse. So while the sciences are seen as making claims of factual knowledge for public use, religions do not. Newbigin states, "If Christians . . . appeal to the authority of Scripture or of the Church, they know that others will regard this appeal as simply the expression of a personal choice."[10]

7. For instance, it would be illegal to practice human sacrifice, child marriage, or polygamy, even if it is a religious tradition.

8. We should note that several prominent forefathers, such as Benjamin Franklin, George Washington, and Thomas Jefferson, were not orthodox Christians but deists. See David Holmes, *The Faiths of the Founding Fathers* (Oxford: Oxford University Press, 2006), 163.

9. Thomas Jefferson, "V. To the Danbury Baptist Association, 1 January 1802," National Archives, accessed October 15, 2023, https://founders.archives.gov/documents/Jefferson/01-36-02-0152-0006.

10. Newbigin, *Gospel in a Pluralist Society*, 40.

This divide is based on the idea that religion is subjective and based on faith, while the sciences are neutral and based on empirical evidence. Even though empirical evidence is construed inductively, the "facts" of science are seen as being neutral. Religious beliefs are seen as personal matters of faith—not neutral but encumbered.

Miroslav Volf and Matthew Croasmun point out, however, that a sharp contrast between scientific truth and arbitrary religious belief is untenable.[11] Science and religion answer different types of questions and contribute to different types of knowledge. As Volf and Croasmun write, "Scientific research, a fantastic tool, is *driven by* purposes and value, but it is *about* facts and explanations and cannot set purposes and define values. It can tell us a lot, for instance, about what humans tend to desire and why and how to achieve their goals more effectively but not much about what they ought to desire and why or what kind of life is worth desiring."[12] Science can provide information about the costs and benefits of different options, but it cannot provide moral or spiritual guidance on which is better or worse in the way religion does.

Liberal Societies Promote Overarching Goods and Communal Norms

So how *can* a society deliberate on values in a way that is neutral? As discussed briefly in chapter 1, utilitarians equate goodness with pleasure in order to avoid making theo-political value judgments concerning public action. Thus, the utilitarian approach appeals to a pluralist society because it does not rely on religious insight for moral or political deliberation. But does this really determine which values are good for a society or does it only reveal a consensus of opinions? We must ask, Is our Western aspiration for neutrality merely a guise for governing by the will of a majority? While it is true that utilitarianism can provide a useful mode of decision-making, it does

---

11. Miroslav Volf and Matthew Croasmun, *For the Life of the World: Theology That Makes a Difference* (Grand Rapids: Brazos, 2019), 81.
12. Volf and Croasmun, *For the Life of the World*, 81.

not necessarily guarantee that the majority will be right in its decisions. This is especially true in situations where minority groups are systematically disadvantaged by the majority. Consider, for example, how enslaved African Americans might have viewed white America's utilitarian governance. In an effort to achieve neutrality, a liberal society may give way to the ill will of a majority. Might is a poor judge of what is right. In reality, those in power inevitably use their influence to ensure that their interests are put first and that "justice" is always skewed in their favor. Thus not only is the possibility of liberal neutrality unlikely, but its application is problematic.

Philosopher Alasdair MacIntyre points out that a liberal society claims to promote a pluralistic "range of goods" that are pursued in a "range of compartmentalized spheres."[13] Liberalism claims not to promote any "overarching goods" in a society, in order to maintain neutrality. Instead, a liberal society recognizes various goods[14] in different spheres of value. MacIntyre writes, "So it is within a variety of distinct groups that each individual pursues his or her good, and the preferences which he or she expresses will express this variety of social relationships."[15] In other words, liberals are part of several communities (political, economic, familial, religious, cultural, etc.), and each community has its own standards and values. Thus a liberal person comes away with a range of goods particular to him or her. Liberal neutrality allows for these varying collections of goods to coexist in a pluralist society.

MacIntyre sees three possible levels of debate concerning the good. The first level is a public deliberation of what the good life means for a society. It deals with what might be considered the overarching good of a society—the particular *telos* the citizens aim to achieve. The second level of debate tallies and weighs the preferences of a nation's citizens. This level of debate tallies preferences through

13. Alasdair MacIntyre, *Whose Justice? Which Rationality?* (Notre Dame, IN: University of Notre Dame Press, 1988), 337.
14. Here MacIntyre does not use the term "goods" in an economic sense (i.e., goods and services), but uses the term to mean values that associate with *the* good or highest virtue of a society.
15. MacIntyre, *Whose Justice? Which Rationality?*, 337.

empirical means such as counting votes, surveying public opinion, or responding to market-driven consumer choice. Finally, the third level of debate concerns the rules and procedures used to tally preferences. This level of debate looks to justify why the society tallied preferences the way it did. It strives to use reason to come up with the parameters of deliberation (i.e., Rawls's veil of ignorance that's used to determine the "original position" of a hypothetical contract).[16] According to MacIntyre, the first level of debate is avoided by a liberal society because of its insistence on plurality.[17] By advancing tolerance, a liberal society cannot aim to determine any overarching good. A liberal society limits, therefore, its moral and social deliberations to tallying preferences and then justifying its methods. Instead of allowing for a first-level public discourse to deliberate the common good, liberalism relies on the legal system to determine what is just. As MacIntyre writes, "The lawyers, not the philosophers, are the clergy of liberalism."[18] This, for MacIntyre, misses the point of being a moral agent within a society. He suggests that in order to be a moral agent, one must be willing to engage in meaningful dialogue about the common good and take responsibility for it.

Avoiding the first level of debate does not mean there are, in fact, no overarching goods in the society. It means the society is simply not acknowledging the overarching goods that are operant (implicitly) in its public discourse. Whether a liberal society wants to admit it or not, it unavoidably shapes people's values and morals toward something. In order to maintain liberal neutrality, governments refrain from taking sides in conflicts between interests. Yet we have laws that reflect *judgments* of right and wrong. How did those judgments come about? Furthermore, schools teach students to believe in one thing and not another.[19] No matter how neutral a society aims to be, there is inevitably a communal screening of what is socially permissible and what is taboo. Somewhere along

---

16. MacIntyre, *Whose Justice? Which Rationality?*, 343–44.
17. MacIntyre, *Whose Justice? Which Rationality?*, 343.
18. MacIntyre, *Whose Justice? Which Rationality?*, 344.
19. Newbigin, *Gospel in a Pluralist Society*, 224.

the way, judgments of value *were* made. What is the basis of these judgments? Are they merely an aggregate of majority opinions, or are they rooted in a pre-established set of communal values? If the former is true, then the society is foundationally neutral but susceptible to tyranny of the majority. Experience says, however, that the former is not the case. Laws against littering imply a moral judgment that littering is wrong and that we should take care of our environment. We do not think of those laws as "most people prefer it if we do not litter." When American schoolchildren learn about "Honest Abe" in their history lessons, they are implicitly taught the value of honesty as a moral good. It seems that liberal societies, whether they like to admit it or not, are indeed rooted in a pre-established set of communal values.

While MacIntyre believes liberalism is by far the strongest claimant to provide a ground for neutrality, it still fails to deliver a *truly* neutral state.[20] The ideals of liberalism inevitably, and unavoidably, formed a liberal tradition with its own overarching goods. *The* essential good of a liberal society is the "liberal terms of debate." MacIntyre writes, "The overriding good of liberalism is no more and no less than the continued sustenance of the liberal social and political order."[21] While liberalism does not *claim* a predetermined set of goals or values, it *enacts* certain predetermined values, such as individual autonomy, free choice, and equality, in order to maintain a liberal society. These values, according to MacIntyre, belong to the social and political order of liberalism. Thus, by *being* liberal, a liberal society imposes overarching values onto its citizens and then seeks to protect those values through the rule of law. This has led MacIntyre to write, "Like other traditions, liberalism has internal to it its own standards of rational justification. . . . Like other traditions, liberalism expresses itself socially through a particular kind of hierarchy."[22] In short, liberalism is not neutral but has become a tradition with its own set of values and concepts of justice.

20. MacIntyre, *Whose Justice? Which Rationality?*, 346.
21. MacIntyre, *Whose Justice? Which Rationality?*, 345.
22. MacIntyre, *Whose Justice? Which Rationality?*, 345.

The Overarching Values and Norms of Liberalism

To claim that liberal neutrality is impossible is not to condemn Western values—it's merely to assert that Western values inevitably exist, which renders incoherent the push for pluralist tolerance on the grounds of neutrality. The general point of pluralist tolerance, that one *must* tolerate other religious expressions of ultimacy, is itself intolerant and thus self-defeating. It implies that no religious belief should be considered superior to any other, regardless of its truth or falsehood. It assumes religion is only a matter of personal opinion, so it should not be considered in civic discourse. But these justifications are made *because* pluralism is seen as a foundational value of a liberal society. Liberalism has given Westerners a set of values that have shaped their worldviews—liberalism, in other words, alters, defines, and projects moral and cultural norms onto a society. It is not neutral but carries its own norms and establishes its own encumbered way of life.

What then are the norms of a liberal society? While there are no definitive lists of norms to draw from, we can imagine a few implicit values that emerge from Western social commitments to liberalism, pluralism, democracy, and the free market: liberty, industriousness, fairness, and diversity. *Liberty* entails a posture of respect for civil liberties as citizens attempt to balance individual and social responsibilities. As a free-market society, the West values creativity and productivity in the arts, enterprises, and scholarship as a sign of Western *industriousness*. Western societies by and large adhere to the Rawlsian principle of "justice as *fairness*," which promotes equal opportunities for all its citizens. The "American Dream," for instance, is based on the idea that anyone can achieve their life goals through hard work and determination because a liberal society is a free and fair society. The last implicit value, *diversity*, is more aspirational than the others and is not held by all in Western societies. In fact, heated public debates occur frequently around the topic of diversity. Yet, in its most positive formulation, one might see a pluralist liberal society as a melting pot—as a bridge builder and peacemaker that celebrates diversity. These implicit values are viewed as inherently good in Western societies—they are not neutral values but might be considered the virtues of a liberal tradition. Societies shape their citizens by setting certain standards and by establishing a shared commitment to the common good. The common good is defined by a society, explicitly or implicitly, and is enacted by training in those virtues.

The Kingdom of God and Babylon

The argument of neutrality says that liberalism, by its nature, is tolerant of different opinions, religious beliefs, and other values, thus making it an impartial platform for any religious ideology, including Christianity. But, if the liberal state is not neutral, as we've determined above, then the idea that the Western church is positioned within a context of neutrality is also false. Rather, it is positioned within a *competing* narrative—one that is based on the idea that individuals should be free to pursue their own happiness in their own way. Hence, we've spent chapters 1 and 2 highlighting many ways the narrative of liberalism competes with the biblical narrative of covenant. But as we problematize the Western claim of liberal neutrality, does that mean that liberalism, in all its encumbered variety, is *not* a good earthly backdrop for the kingdom of God? Or can it be that of all the imperfect options available, the liberal state is still the best context for Christianity to flourish? In other words, is the liberal state the best Babylon? We know that on this side of the eschaton the church *must* exist within an earthly political context, but should the church oppose this political context or embrace it? Should the church seek to change it or avoid interacting with it? To answer these questions we must first determine what it means to simultaneously be a citizen of God's kingdom and of the liberal state.

Belonging to the Kingdom of God While Living in Babylon

Augustine's *City of God* was the first book to introduce the concept of "dual citizenship" into theological literature.[23] To describe

---

23. The book, which claimed that the church did not harm Rome, was written as an apologetic for the church.

Christianity's relationship with Rome, Augustine used an image of two cities: the City of God and the City of Man. For Augustine these two cities demonstrate two different motivations: "Two cities have been formed by two loves: the earthly by the love of self, even to the contempt of God; the heavenly by the love of God, even to the contempt of self. The former, in a word, glories in itself, the latter in the Lord."[24] As Greg Forster describes it, the essential contrast between these two cities is a psychological difference. God is prioritized in the City of God, but humanity is prioritized in the City of Man.[25] Christians are dual citizens of both cities, but Christians must *belong* to the City of God even as they *live in* the City of Man. Forster describes Augustine's position well: "The City of God must perform a delicate balancing act, exercising citizenship in the earthly city but ultimately loyal to its higher citizenship in heaven."[26] Loyalty to the City of God takes priority over allegiance to the City of Man, but Christians must still strive to live peaceably in the world. So what does it mean to live peaceably in a liberal state while prioritizing allegiance to God?

Christians Are Contracted Residents, Not Covenant Partners, of the State

Applied to the biblical concept of the kingdom, we might say Christians can live in the kingdom of the world as *contracted residents*, but they must belong to the kingdom of God as *covenant partners*. This major distinction between the two citizenships demonstrates a difference in allegiance. While the kingdom of the world (the liberal state in our case) requires commitment to a social contract, the kingdom of God requires covenantal fidelity. The kingdom of the world requires adherence to laws in order to govern a pluralist society. To preserve as much freedom (liberty) as possible, there should be a minimal set of rules that citizens are contractually bound

24. Augustine, *The City of God*, trans. Marcus Dods (Moscow, ID: Roman Roads Media, 2015), 385.
25. Greg Forster, *The Contested Public Square: The Crisis of Christianity and Politics* (Downers Grove, IL: IVP Academic, 2008), 71.
26. Forster, *Contested Public Square*, 64.

to follow. The kingdom of God, on the other hand, requires total allegiance from its citizens. God's kingdom is based on covenantal loyalty where its citizens are entirely dependent on God as they give their whole selves over to God's sovereign rule. In the kingdom of the world, citizens are incentivized to abide by the law through promises of fairness, security, and the protection of their rights. In the kingdom of God, however, citizens are incentivized to remain in the kingdom by their commitment to covenant as members of God's family. God's kingdom does not merely set rules for ordered cohabitation but promises life in abundance. As covenant partners, we are children adopted into the kingdom by the king—our promised inheritance is the kingdom itself (Rev. 5:10).

If our ultimate allegiance is to the kingdom of God, then to what extent should we be involved in the state's polity? In *A Pentecostal Political Theology for American Renewal*, theologian Steven Studebaker considers the kingdom of God through an eschatological lens, arguing that the Spirit of Pentecost is at work in our present age. The eschatological Spirit is working through *every* aspect of life to lay a foundation for a fully redeemed reality.[27] Christians are caught between two times and two worlds. Our "time" is between the *already* and the *not yet*. The kingdom of God has already been inaugurated by Christ through his earthly ministry, yet we await its consummation upon Christ's return. We are also caught between two "worlds"—the kingdom of the world, which is realized through the empowered state, and the kingdom of God, which is governed by God. A kingdom ruled by God embodies a world of peace and goodwill—a reconciled reality where all people, including the poor, marginalized, and dispossessed, equally share in God's provision (Matt. 5; Luke 6). Nationalistic expressions of Christianity arise whenever the kingdom of God and the kingdom of the world are conflated.[28] As mentioned in chapter 1, Christian nationalism creates a reality where God is not sovereign but shares the throne with a national polity.

27. Steven Studebaker, *A Pentecostal Political Theology for American Renewal: Spirit of the Kingdoms, Citizens of the Cities* (New York: Palgrave Macmillan, 2016), 142.
28. Studebaker, *Pentecostal Political Theology*, 4.

According to Studebaker, the kingdom of God is not reflected in any earthly political system. Rather, life in this world is life in Babylon, characterized by economic success and political ambition. Babylon represents "corrupt life in and of this world,"[29] thus symbolizing a society that's focused on the things of the world—namely, wealth, consumption, power, and self-gratification. Thus the state is not amenable to the ways of the kingdom of God. The state is concerned about its own goals and polities, not about God's everlasting reign. Even if a state does not ostensibly oppose the kingdom of God, it is in no way its covenantal partner. God's kingdom does not have allies. God is a jealous God (Exod. 34:14), and being God's covenant partner requires full submission and full allegiance. Thus Christians can adhere to the social contract and laws of a liberal state, but they cannot go beyond that basic social contract and give the state their allegiance or even partner with the state since they are exclusive covenantal partners with God.

Christians Are Witnesses to, Not Advocates for, Any Liberal State

Recall Hobson's line of reasoning that says the church can flourish in a liberal state because such a state is free. This point implies that Christians should advocate for a liberal state because it makes Christian life and community more tenable. The liberal state, he argues, should be viewed as an ally to the kingdom of God.[30] We must remember, however, that the liberal state is still a Babylonian state. It may not be as oppressive as other states in Babylon, but it's *still* Babylon. The church should not be asking which state is easier to thrive in but should be asking, How can the church be a witness in *this* given context? The church's witness of the kingdom is indispensable, regardless of the earthly political context it finds itself in. Even if the liberal state is more virtuous than other political states, it still encourages many vices (inequality, selfishness, consumeristic

---

29. Studebaker, *Pentecostal Political Theology*, 9–10.
30. Hobson, *Reinventing Liberal Christianity*, 244.

desire, etc.). The church should not, therefore, advocate for any sort
of political regime but must advocate only for the things of the kingdom. Advocating for a political regime is advocating for both its good
elements and its bad ones.

Theologian Preston Sprinkle says that Christians should imagine
themselves as exiles in Babylon.[31] Because our true citizenship is in the
kingdom of God, we should see ourselves as foreigners in the country
we live in. Just as it is impossible to imagine Christ holding allegiance
to the kingdom of God while also waving around a Roman flag, so
too should it seem bizarre for a Christian to be a devoted follower
of Christ on Sunday and then to proselytize their national ideologies
from Monday through Saturday.[32] Rather, Christians should take their
cue from the Israelites in exile during the Babylonian captivity who
were good, law-abiding citizens but only if the laws of the state did
not conflict with God's laws. In the book of Daniel, for instance,
we read about Shadrach, Meshach, and Abednego being punished
in Babylon because they would not bow down to a golden image set
up by King Nebuchadnezzar (Dan. 3). We also read about Daniel
refusing to eat the king's food because it violated Jewish dietary
laws (1:8–16) and later being thrown into a lion's den as punishment
for publicly praying to Yahweh (Dan. 6). Even in exile the Israelites
continued to worship God in synagogues. In the same way, Christians must set their true allegiances to God alone and persist as law-
abiding citizens (so long as the laws do not conflict with God's laws)
in whatever Babylonian state they find themselves in.

Furthermore, because the church is global, there is *no singular
political theology* that is normative for all Christian political thought.
There is a multiplicity of political structures through which Christians have borne witness to the kingdom of God.[33] Christian political
thought is unavoidably diverse and shaped by many different contexts.

---

31. Preston Sprinkle, *Exiles: The Church in the Shadow of Empire* (Colorado
Springs: David C. Cook, 2024), 20.
32. Sprinkle, *Exiles*, 138.
33. Amos Yong, *In the Days of Caesar: Pentecostalism and Political Theology*
(Grand Rapids: Eerdmans, 2010), 110.

Arguing for one normative political theology disregards the specific political situations that various tribes and tongues experience.[34] Yet because local theologies in our pluralist present have global reach and impact, they must recognize Christianity's effect on other traditions around the world. We live in a global tapestry of cultures and politics that blend together. Local cultural and political expressions might best be understood as "glocal," engaging global matters through local positionality.[35] Even as this current volume is an attempt at a Western public theology, I recognize that many of the issues brought about by liberalism are also global issues.

Advocating for kingdom principles, despite whatever political regime we are in, keeps us politically engaged but not partisan or politically sectarian. The right approach, in other words, is for the church to advocate for love, justice, generosity, and reconciliation in *any* political context, not to advocate for a particular kind of political context or regime. Denying Babylon's allyship does not mean the church should be a separatist community. It means the church must place its trust in God alone and not in the state. Yet the church should be active as a public witness in the world. To this point, Studebaker sees the active Spirit as inspiring the church to create a culture that nurtures life and manifests the Spirit-breathed divine image.[36]

As the Spirit is constantly working toward renewal, we must be aware of what God is doing in our world. The key is to join in the Spirit's work, not to fight against God with our own political agendas. There is no ideal state in which the kingdom of God can flourish—God's kingdom mission is always sanctioned, regardless

34. Yong constructs what he calls his "many tongues" thesis, which posits that any reflection on political theology can be summarized with the phrase "many tongues, many political practices." As the Spirit is poured out on the whole world, the people of God are opened up to a multiplicity of political stances, practices, and theologies. Yong recognizes that political theologies *already exist* in a variety of local expressions. Arguing for one normative political theology disregards the specific political situations that various tribes and tongues experience. Yong, *In the Days of Caesar*, 109–10.

35. For more on this topic, see chaps. 3–4 of Steven Félix-Jäger, *Art Theory for a Global Pluralistic Age: The Glocal Artist* (New York: Palgrave Macmillan, 2020).

36. Studebaker, *Pentecostal Political Theology*, 170.

of the national context. The church must be obedient to God's call in any given circumstance.

Christians Can Be Socially Contracted Patriots but Not Deeply Allegiant Nationalists

There is also a problem with the liberal state when it starts demanding more from its citizens than what has been contracted. The foundation of any social contract is mutual consent, where members of a society consent to a governing authority, and the government agrees to protect its citizens' rights and uphold the rule of law. The government assures that its citizens' freedoms are protected and not contravened unless a person violates the rights and freedoms of another citizen. While this is technically what it means to be socially contracted with a state, there is often social pressure to conform to a nation's social ideals. This is what occurs when patriotism, the love of one's country, turns into nationalism, a passionate sense of loyalty to a narrow view of one's country coupled with the belief of the nation's superiority over other nations.

Patriotism, in its best form, inclusively respects differences among its citizens while promoting a collective sense of unity. Nationalism, on the other hand, looks to conform its citizens to an ideal of citizenship. Citizens in the liberal tradition might see patriotism as a vice, believing a person has to lose his or her individualism and ability for rational criticism in favor of a national agenda,[37] but this reasoning flows from the premise that a liberal state is neutral. Since every state is actually encumbered, it inevitably defines and extends social values. Patriotism, then, can be seen as a way of honoring the values that the state represents. The extension of social values should be viewed not as a bad thing but as something expected from any nation. Our argument against liberalism's claim to neutrality is meant not to condemn liberalism's principal values but to demonstrate that these values do exist and, in many ways, compete with the values of the kingdom

---

37. Alasdair MacIntyre, "Is Patriotism a Virtue?," March 26, 1984, the Lindley Lecture, University of Kansas, https://mirror.explodie.org/Is%20Patriotism%20a%20Virtue-1984.pdf, 18.

of God. When the values conflict, Christians, as covenant partners, must choose to follow God's values over those of the state. Conflicts often arise when the state goes beyond the minimal requirements of the social contract and calls for deeper allegiance.

As we've noted above, liberty, industriousness, fairness, and diversity are some of the principal values of the liberal state. A liberal patriot, then, is proud of his or her nation's ideals but respects the freedoms of other citizens as they determine what liberty, industriousness, fairness, and diversity look like in their particular contexts. A nationalist, on the other hand, predetermines what each ideal means and then calls for nationwide conformity to *their* definitions of each ideal. Furthermore, nationalists tend to add moral and religious ideals to the characterization of what it means to be a citizen. When patriotism melds into nationalism, what emerges is social pressure for national conformity—an allegiance to the state that requires more than what is contracted. Nationalists extend totalizing calls to national loyalty akin to covenantal fidelity. Nationalists claim that to be American, for instance, is to live in a particular way and to take on a specific, totalized identity. But, as mentioned, God is a jealous God and refuses to share the throne with any nation. Christians must find their totalized identity as children of God in Christ alone (John 1:12). Consider how Paul describes total allegiance to Christ to the church in Colossae: "Watch out that no one takes you captive through philosophy and empty deceit, according to human tradition, according to the elemental principles of the world, and not according to Christ. For in him the whole fullness of deity dwells bodily, and you have come to fullness in him, who is the head of every ruler and authority" (Col. 2:8–10). Our fullness is in Christ, as we call him Lord. The liberal tradition is a human tradition, and Paul warns us not to be taken captive by it.

Christians Can Be Conscientious Objectors but Not Violent Revolutionaries

The conflict of values between the kingdom of God and the state leads to another question: If we are to choose God's values over those of the state, how do we make sense of Paul's command in Romans 13 to submit to the governing authorities? Must we submit to unjust governments? Paul famously exhorts the church in Rome to obey the governing authorities, saying that all authority comes from God:

> Let every person be subject to the governing authorities, for there is no authority except from God, and those authorities that exist have been instituted by God. Therefore whoever resists authority resists what God has appointed, and those who resist will incur judgment. For rulers are not a terror to good conduct but to bad. Do you wish to have no fear of the authority? Then do what is good, and you will receive its approval, for it is God's agent for your good. But if you do what is wrong, you should be afraid, for the authority does not bear the sword in vain! It is the agent of God to execute wrath on the wrongdoer. Therefore one must be subject, not only because of wrath but also because of conscience. For the same reason you also pay taxes, for the authorities are God's agents, busy with this very thing. Pay to all what is due to them: taxes to whom taxes are due, revenue to whom revenue is due, respect to whom respect is due, honor to whom honor is due. (Rom. 13:1–7)

After contentious elections, this passage has been used by Christians from varying political parties to urge other Christians to fall in line under the newly elected leadership. Adherents of the victorious party often say something like, "Romans 13 tells us that all governing authorities are instituted by God, so we must believe that this president was chosen by God." Amusingly, those partisan Christians use this logic as a defense only when *their* party is elected. Nevertheless, do these Christians have a point? If God institutes all governing authorities, and God knows what the leaders' positions are, doesn't it follow that God also supports those positions? Otherwise, wouldn't God have instituted someone else to lead?

When looking at the context of this passage, we see that Paul was writing to the Roman church when the Roman Empire was in power. Paul was calling Christians, a minority group in Rome, to live peaceably under Roman rule. Christians were not to take up arms or revolt against Rome but to contribute positively to the communities they lived in. Although Rome had the ability to enforce certain laws, its ultimate authority came from God, and its purpose was to serve humanity. Forster sees Paul as emphasizing three principles in his command to obey worldly governments: "Government's authority is for the purpose of promoting justice (v. 3); government exists to serve the community (v. 4); and obedience to government is based on conscience (v. 5)."[38] As we consider these principles, we notice that Paul's claim that all authority comes from God is not to promote a *particular* government but to show that the world, generally speaking, has been empowered to govern itself. God has given governments the authority to enforce law and order, provide guidance, and protect people from harm. Therefore, obedience to worldly governments is an act of obedience to God. To this point Newbigin says, "There has to be some kind of ordered structure of power. Without it, human life would dissolve into anarchy. These structural elements are necessary to guide and protect human life. They serve God's purpose."[39] We should, therefore, respect governments, as God has appointed them to serve a function.

Newbigin also points out, however, that a state's God-given authority can be abused and used for tyranny.[40] Thus, even though authority in general is God-given, we are not called to blindly follow governments in their corruption. When governments fail to act justly, they are acting against God's divine purposes, so people are warranted in challenging the government, so long as they abide by the rule and consequence of the law. This is evidenced, for instance, by the many times Paul himself wound up imprisoned during his missionary journeys. He and Silas were imprisoned in Philippi (Acts 16:16–30), he was arrested and held in custody in Jerusalem (Acts 21), he was held in custody in Caesarea (Acts 24), he was under house arrest in Rome (Acts 28), and he might have been imprisoned a second time in Rome (2 Timothy). How can the same man who said

38. Forster, *Contested Public Square*, 32.
39. Newbigin, *Gospel in a Pluralist Society*, 205.
40. Newbigin, *Gospel in a Pluralist Society*, 206.

to obey authorities also be arrested and imprisoned so many times? Certainly Paul chose to obey God instead of human authorities when the worldly law conflicted with God's law, but even in his arrests, he never failed to respect the law.

As contrary as it may sound, conscientious objection and civil disobedience are forms of submission to the law. The law states that a person should follow a rule or suffer particular consequences, so if a citizen purposefully and conscientiously disobeys the law and willingly submits to punishment, then the citizen has still respected the rule of law. Paul did not try to fight back when he was arrested, nor did he try to cause a revolt against the governing authorities. He submitted to the consequences of breaking the law, thereby living by the rule of law. The same can be said of Esther, who willingly risked being imprisoned for her unsolicited approach of the king to advocate for her people (Esther 4). The same can be said of Shadrach, Meshach, and Abednego, who willingly went into the fire after refusing to bow down to a statue of Nebuchadnezzar (Dan. 3). The same can be said of Jesus when he did not fight back against authorities during his arrest, trial, and crucifixion (Matt. 26; Mark 14; Luke 22; John 18). And the same can be said of the first-century martyrs and of anyone who accepted the consequences of refusing to bow down to the Caesars of their day. In our modern era, both Martin Luther King Jr. and Gandhi demonstrated nonviolent resistance to corrupt governmental authorities. Their civil disobedience landed them in prison, but it ended up bringing about major social change in the US and India, respectively. Both demonstrated submission to the rule of law even as they resisted the government's corruption.

Does submission to the rule of law mean there is never a place for revolution? Liberalism was, after all, a major influence on both the American Revolution and the French Revolution. In both cases political factions fought against governing monarchies for independence, claiming the British Loyalists and the coalition forces, respectively, oppressed citizens through antiliberal rule. Liberalism was, at the time, a revolutionary idea that challenged existing power structures and established principles of government. However, it was also based on the idea that individuals should be free to pursue their own interests and that the government should be limited in its power. Thus while revolutions were initially necessary to establish liberal states, liberalism has since provided a basis for a peaceful transfer of power.

Similarly, the Bible and the Apocrypha recount the liberation of Israel from Egyptian slavery (Exodus), the conquest of Canaan (Joshua), and the Maccabean Revolt (1 and 2 Maccabees). There are also instances in the Bible where individuals are commended for disobeying unjust or immoral commands (Exod. 1:17; Acts 5:29). Is it possible to reconcile Paul's command to obey authorities with these biblical examples of revolution or defiant resistance? While there may be other reasons to justify a revolution, we cannot find such reasons in Paul or in the rest of the New Testament, for that matter. Throughout the New Testament, Paul and Jesus seem to emphasize the principles of nonviolence and submission to authority in peaceful ways consistent with their new covenant understanding of God's kingdom.[41] Paul, for instance, calls us to live peacefully and to pray for our leaders (1 Tim. 2:1–2), and he also reminds us that "our struggle is not against blood and flesh" (Eph. 6:12). Moreover, Jesus said to render to Caesar what is Caesar's (Matt. 22:15–22; Mark 12:13–17; Luke 20:20–26) and to turn the other cheek, go the extra mile, and give to those who ask (Matt. 5:38–42). He even rebuked Peter's violence at his arrest (Matt. 26:52). When Jesus seemed to act violently, like when he flipped over the tables in the outer court of the temple (Matt. 21:12–13; Mark 11:15–18; Luke 19:45–46; John 2:14–17), he did so as a prophetic act to condemn the temple's practices of atonement, ushering in a new era where forgiveness comes through him (Mark 11:22–25). As will be discussed further below, this was a violent, prophetic demonstration against systems, not people.

41. Kaitlyn Schiess writes about how during the Revolutionary War, Patriot and Loyalist preachers both used Scripture to defend their stances on the war. While the Patriots used Old Testament passages of revolution, the Loyalists used Romans 13. See chap. 2 of Kaitlyn Schiess, *The Ballot and the Bible: How Scripture Has Been Used and Abused in American Politics and Where to Go from Here* (Grand Rapids: Brazos, 2023).

We might say, nevertheless, that the American and French Revolutions were morally justified because they led to greater goods. This sort of utilitarian reasoning is acceptable for a secular society, but we cannot act as if the Bible sanctions this reasoning. For Christians to justify revolutions, they must take on a Christian realist approach and leave Scripture out of their reasoning. They might say, for instance, "The Bible doesn't sanction my act of revolution, but it doesn't condemn it either." There is no clear guidance here; you will either have to be satisfied with the idea that you justified your revolution by extrabiblical reasoning or have to be contented to remain under the oppressive rule you're seeking liberation from. God's covenant of abundance does not sanction efforts of force. Rather, it emphasizes God's sovereign reign over all people and nations, and God's desire for all of creation to be unified in peace and harmony (shalom). Hence, as mentioned in this chapter's introduction, Jesus taught that his kingdom is not of this world but a holistic kingdom that transcends the material realm (John 18:36). The kingdom of God affects the world, but it does not do so through force.

Concluding Thoughts on Living as Dual Citizens in Babylon and the Kingdom

In this section, I've argued that living in Babylon does not mean we are allies, partners, or advocates for our particular state of Babylon, regardless of how tolerant that state is of Christianity. As Christians, we cannot be nationalists with deep loyalty or allegiance to any liberal state. Nor can we be violent revolutionaries if our state is corrupt or perpetuating injustices. Instead, we are to live in Babylon as politically engaged resident aliens and foreigners who advocate for and bear witness to the kingdom that holds our ultimate allegiance. We are to maintain social contact with the state as we devote our full allegiance and loyalty to the kingdom of God, which shapes our identity. When our state is corrupt or in opposition to the principles of God's kingdom, we are to conscientiously object to their corruption and then willingly submit ourselves to the rule of law, regardless of the consequences.

With this in mind, we can now explore in more depth how all this relates to the concept of covenant and how the church can engage in public life to expand God's kingdom while fulfilling rather than compromising its covenant partnership and obligations.

Covenantal Ambassadors of God's Priestly Kingdom

We've established above that the kingdom of God's polity is one that is universal and not of this world. The kingdom of God does not seek earthly, national power but seeks to transform hearts and minds all over the world by the power of the Holy Spirit. We also established that the kingdom of God affects our lives entirely and thus affects how Christians engage the world. Christopher Wright suggests that Christians should be involved in public discourse but should not use force, political or otherwise, to advance a social agenda.[42] Politically coercive efforts are not only futile but can actually lead to a compromise in covenant as Christians rely on the false gods of whatever political system they seek to engage. Yet the church *must* be active in its public witness—it cannot sit idly by in the face of Christ's mandate to make disciples of all nations (Matt. 28:19–20). Christians must find a way to engage the world that is neither nationalist nor separatist. The church cannot seek to expand God's kingdom by force, nor can it shy away from public witness.

Fulfilling Our Covenant Obligation to Bring Light to the World

To understand what Christian engagement in a pluralist society entails, we must revisit what it means to be covenanted with God. Throughout the Bible, covenant has been God's method for bringing about salvation and reconciliation to the whole world. According to Wright, we live in a cursed earth since Adam and in a covenanted

---

42. Christopher J. H. Wright, *"Here Are Your Gods": Faithful Discipleship in Idolatrous Times* (Downers Grove, IL: IVP Academic, 2020), 128–29.

earth since Noah.[43] In the introduction, we saw that God established a way of life with Adam and Eve that was, essentially, covenantal. God gave humans dominion over creation and blessed them to flourish. Eating from the tree of life symbolized dependence on God (the source of life) and obedience to God's will. When they ate from the tree of knowledge of good and evil, they broke their covenant with God, turning their backs on God's promises and provisions. Hence, humanity lived in a state of rebellion after the fall until the time of Noah. The Noachian covenant was the first explicit covenant God laid out with humanity. It was a way to reestablish relationship with humanity in a constrained way, outlining responsibilities, blessings, and consequences. Faithfulness to the covenant would lead to flourishing, but infidelity would lead to hardship and ruin.

Even through these rigorous parameters, the Old Testament covenants were meant to bring redemption to the whole world. As Wright states, "Israel, according to many texts, was created by God not only to be the vehicle by which his redemptive blessing and covenant relationship would spread to people from all nations on earth but also to be shaped through its Torah to be a model of what a society governed by the character and demands of Yahweh God should look like."[44] Thus God's covenant with Israel was not meant to be exclusive but was meant to be a sign of commitment to all of humanity. While a message of universal blessing was already present in the Abrahamic covenant (Gen. 12:2), God chose Israel in particular to bring about redemption.[45]

At Mount Sinai, God chose Israel to draw the rest of creation back into right relation with God. In Exodus 19 God called Israel a "treasured possession" that will be a "priestly kingdom" (vv. 5–6). The role of the priest was to mediate between God and the people. Priests interceded on behalf of the people before God. Thus calling Israel a "priestly kingdom" meant that Israel was chosen by God

---

43. Christopher J. H. Wright, *The Mission of God: Unlocking the Bible's Grand Narrative* (Downers Grove, IL: IVP Academic, 2006), 433.

44. C. Wright, *"Here Are Your Gods,"* 106.

45. C. Wright, *Mission of God*, 447.

to serve as a mediating channel through which God's blessings and salvation would flow to the rest of the world.[46] Israel was called to be holy and set apart—entirely unique. As such, Israel would represent God's character and values to every surrounding nation. The people of Israel were meant to be a living testimony of the righteousness and holiness of God. By obeying God's law, Israel would flourish and attract other nations to come to know the living God.

As discussed above, prior to his arrest and crucifixion, Jesus performed a provocative prophetic act that condemned Israel for not living out its priestly duties. Jesus's actions were a form of protest against the commercial activities happening in the temple courts. In order to provide travelers with pure animals to sacrifice, money changers and sellers of sacrificial doves set up shop in the outer court of the temple. Jesus entered the temple courts and turned over the money changers' tables along with the benches of the dove salesmen (Matt. 21:12–13; Mark 11:15–19; Luke 19:45–46; John 2:13–22). This act rendered the temple's sacrificial system inoperable, which symbolized its covenantal bankruptcy.

During his demonstration, Jesus condemned the temple for corrupt practices, but he also condemned Israel for not being a priestly nation. Israel was supposed to be a light to the nations (Isa. 42:6) but reduced its priestly calling down to mere insular sin-management through a marketized system of atonement. Mark's account of this prophetic act is interposed in the story of the cursed fig tree. This "Markan sandwich" indicates that the temple no longer bore fruit because it, like the cursed fig tree, was out of season (Mark 11:24–25).[47] Consequently, Jesus's prophetic act meant that he would subvert the old covenant's system of atonement, which had become inward-looking and legalistic, and establish a new covenant system of atonement that made salvation available to all through Christ's own sacrifice. This is evidenced by the Johannine account of this story, where Jesus

---

46. C. Wright, *Mission of God*, 330.
47. For in-depth exegesis of this passage, see Robby Waddell, "Prophecy Then and Now: The Role of Prophecy in the Pentecostal Church," in *Transformational Leadership: A Tribute to Dr. Mark Rutland* (Lakeland, FL: Small Dogma, 2008), 129–44.

said, "Destroy this temple, and in three days I will raise it up" (John 2:19). Jesus replaced the old system of atonement, which was based on temple sacrifices, with a new system of salvation made possible by his own death. This new system ensures that salvation is available to all nations. In this way Jesus fulfilled the Israelites' covenantal duties on their behalf—where the nation of Israel failed, Jesus succeeded. Through his own sacrifice, Jesus fulfilled the old covenant's system, allowing what was meant to happen all along to come to fruition: incorporation of the rest of the world into the covenant promises. Hence Jesus is the true high priest (Heb. 4:14–16) and the true light of the world (John 8:12).

According to 2 Corinthians 5:20, our role is to represent the kingdom of God to the world as ambassadors of Christ. Just as an embassy houses representatives of a sovereign nation, so should the church represent God's kingdom while inhabiting a state. As ambassadors, Christians fulfill a priestly role when they reflect the kingdom of God to the world and bear witness to God's work in the church. Perhaps the best biblical instruction concerning public witness comes from Jesus's discourse about salt and light during the Sermon on the Mount. After the Beatitudes Jesus states,

> You are the salt of the earth, but if salt has lost its taste, how can its saltiness be restored? It is no longer good for anything but is thrown out and trampled under foot. You are the light of the world. A city built on a hill cannot be hid. People do not light a lamp and put it under the bushel basket; rather, they put it on the lampstand, and it gives light to all in the house. In the same way, let your light shine before others, so that they may see your good works and give glory to your Father in heaven. (Matt. 5:13–16)

The concept of "saltiness" can refer to the strength of the church's witness. Like Israel, the church is called to be holy and unique—a compelling demonstration of a better way of life. As salt, the church evinces a community of love to a world filled with hate, a community of reconciliation to a world that lacks grace, a community of generosity to a greedy world, and a community of hope in a world marked by despair. It becomes a desirable, radical alternative community in our broken world.[48] Biblical scholar Michael Bird calls this approach of social engagement "the Thessalonian Strategy." Rather than coming in with force, Paul "turned the world upside down" by offering a compelling alternate vision of what the world could be like. As Bird writes,

> The first Christians were not political activists trying to crash the system; they were not out on the streets with placards saying, "Occupy Rome," nor did they see themselves as a direct threat to Roman rule. However, they did see themselves as a clear alternative to the idolatry, injustice, and brutality of the empire. . . . The church did not overwhelm the Roman Empire by direct confrontation; rather, it held out a more compelling worldview, offered a more attractive way of life, and promised a better reward for the faithful. The church became an invisible society that soon eclipsed the visible echelons of power.[49]

In this way, the church was able to impart a vision of hope, love, and peace to an empire that seemed determined to perpetuate violence and suffering. The church's witness cannot become weak and domesticated, echoing just another part of the world's system,[50] but must be a strong and distinct voice of love, grace, generosity, and hope.

Being "light" refers to social engagement in the world. If the church is light, then it is not separatist—light illuminates dark places. While

48. Hauerwas, *Peaceable Kingdom*, 6.
49. Michael F. Bird, *Religious Freedom in a Secular Age: A Christian Case for Liberty, Equality, and Secular Government* (Grand Rapids: Zondervan, 2022), 128–29. Although Bird's thesis about the Thessalonian Strategy is sound, one major theme in his book is that the church should advocate for a secular government that secures religious freedom for all (see chaps. 3–5). It is in such a pluralistic society that Christianity can stand in greater contrast to other worldviews. I believe, however, that the message to be an alternate community is true irrespective of the governing authorities. The church must keep its witness in times of oppressive totalitarianism and in times of open pluralism. As discussed in the prologue of this book, I believe it moot to advocate for a particular type of secular government.
50. Stanley Hauerwas, "Church Matters," in *Christian Political Witness*, ed. George Kalantzis and Gregory Lee (Downers Grove, IL: IVP, 2014), 19.

the church is called to be a holy, alternate community, it is not called to be hidden or tucked away. The church's uniqueness should be ever-present, all over the world. Because the world is full of darkness, the church must enter everywhere with good works and proclamations of God's glory. This is also why there is no "ideal" Babylonian state for the church to flourish—light is needed in every dark place, regardless of the national government. While it may be *easier* to function in a liberal society, it is not ideal because the church is *on mission*. The church has a responsibility to bring the hope of Jesus to all nations, not just to those that are open to religious dialogue. This means that the church must be willing to enter whatever society it is in, no matter the political climate, and bear witness. Desiring an ideal state for the church to subsist in is like saying it is more ideal for a firefighter to put out a small kitchen fire than a large fire that has engulfed a commercial building. The small fire may be less dangerous, but the firefighter is on mission either way. The firefighter is *needed* in both situations, just as the church's witness is needed everywhere that is dark. The church is called to *be* light in dark places, not to make the environment more conducive for its light. The former approach reveals God's polity and inspires social change, whereas the latter aspires to alter social circumstances in order to reveal God. Being salt and light demands the former approach.

Persuading the World through Faithful Witness, Not Forceful Coercion

While public engagement is important for being a good witness in the world, we must note that public engagement does *not* mean forcefully coercing people into a specific way of thinking or living. A coercive witness contradicts the kingdom values of love and compassion and creates an atmosphere of fear and resentment. Furthermore, coercion violates free will by pressuring people into belief against their self-governed wills. A coercive witness leads to acceptance of a straw man version of God's kingdom, one driven by fear and fabrications of the gospel. A noncoercive Christian witness involves leading by an example of love. Rather than imposing their Christian ideals on others, Christians express their faith's transformative power through countercultural expressions of grace and generosity. This sort of witness is one of *persuasion* rather than coercion.

Public persuasion is the deliberate effort to influence the attitudes and actions of people in a general public. While the purpose of persuasion is to convince people to adopt a certain outlook, the goal is not manipulation. Manipulation is a form of persuasion that's deceptive and attempts to persuade someone toward a hidden agenda. The sort of persuasion Christians should engage in is sincere, transparent, and forthright with their evidence. Hence a Christian's actions and lived testimony are powerful forms of persuasion because they *prove* that what the Christian says is sincere. In this way, Christians can use their witness to show others that their words are motivated by a love that is genuine.

Not only are Christians called to be good witnesses in the world, but they also have the right to speak to the public as citizens of a democratically operated, liberal society. Although liberalism has mistakenly construed itself as neutral, it is nevertheless an ideology of tolerance. A liberal society says, essentially, that one can believe whatever he or she wants as long as those beliefs adhere to the state's liberal ideologies of tolerance and fairness and preserve the freedoms of others. Therefore Christians can rightfully participate in noncoercive forms of persuasion. Christians can, without fear of persecution, express their beliefs and values and encourage others to embrace them. Volf argues that Christians should engage the public in their own religious voice, communicating "that God loves all people, including the transgressors, and that religious identity is circumscribed by permeable boundaries."[51] The church's voice is needed for a robust public discourse, and our task as Christians is to show why our gospel message is good, true, and beautiful as we extend an invitation to everyone to enter the gates of God's kingdom. As such, the church must enter the public square with its own authentic voice, coupled

51. Miroslav Volf, *A Public Faith: How Followers of Christ Should Serve the Common Good* (Grand Rapids: Brazos, 2011), 133.

with a loving witness that reflects the kingdom through acts of grace and generosity.

Conclusion

This chapter considered what it means to be a citizen of the kingdom of God while simultaneously living in the world. It challenges the liberal claim of neutrality by arguing that liberalism has become a tradition with its own values that often compete with those of the kingdom of God. It also critiques both the separatist and the nationalist approaches to dual citizenship, showing that neither adequately demonstrates Christian witness as God's priestly ambassadors in the world. The church is called to reflect the kingdom of God, offering a persuasive witness of God's polity, which is marked by grace and generosity, as will be shown in part 2.

This chapter concludes the critical arguments of the book. I argued that parts of the Western church have idolized the liberal notion of freedom, which has social and economic implications. This chapter adds to those arguments, demonstrating that the liberal claim of neutrality made Westerners believe (1) that the state was not influencing the church with its values and (2) that the liberal state is the best context for the church to flourish. When both of these points are uncritically adopted, liberal ideology easily and covertly enters the church's polity, and we end up with the syncretic forms of the faith described throughout the previous chapters. This syncretism undermines the church's ability to truly reflect the kingdom of God, as its values are co-opted or merged with the state's.

As a counterpart to the critical arguments of part 1, part 2 offers constructive arguments for a public theology of renewal that's centered around God's covenant of abundance. As we conclude part 1, I'd like us to consider a quote by Christopher Wright that perfectly captures what it means to follow Christ and reflect his kingdom:

> [Jesus's disciples] were called to practice the values of *God's* kingdom, as taught and modeled by Jesus himself, even while they necessarily

had to live in Caesar's kingdom. They were to be "in the world but not of it" (see 1 John 2:15). Such practices included the things Jesus himself did or told them to do—breaking down social barriers, practicing costly forgiveness and table fellowship with those whom society despised, canceling debts, turning the other cheek, offering generosity to the poor and the outsider, loving even the enemy, welcoming the outcast. These were radical and subversive of the established order, the social boundaries, and the religious codes of their day, both Jewish and Roman. Disciples of Christ were called to a very different way of living and relating, shaped by Jesus and his kingdom, not Herod's or Caesar's.[52]

Jesus's teaching and example provided a new foundation for his followers, one that forever changed the course of history. My hope is that the church of the twenty-first century will emulate the ways of Christ, and my goal in part 2 is to provide a theological framework for how that might take place.

---

52. C. Wright, *"Here Are Your Gods,"* 127.

THE CONSTRUCTIVE ARGUMENTS

4

The Free Person

Life in God's Covenantal Community

If you are a person in covenant with God, you are part of God's people. This statement may seem obvious, but it highlights the relationship between the individual and the community in covenant. While God knows and values us individually (Ps. 139:1–6; Matt. 10:29–31), our personhood is *fully* known in God's covenant as we relate to God and others. We saw this in Exodus 19 with Israel being God's *chosen people* and prized possessions. As a "kingdom of priests," *every* member of the covenant community shared a special, direct relationship with God. As biblical scholar Carmen Imes states, "Every Israelite is a covenant member. Everyone is responsible to ensure the covenant is kept."[1] Thus individuals in covenant are part of a broader community that is holy, in close contact with God, and obedient to God's commands.

1. Carmen Imes, *Bearing God's Name: Why Sinai Still Matters* (Downers Grove, IL: IVP Academic, 2019), 64.

This covenanted conception of self is not exclusive to the Old Testament Israelites but is also important for believers today. In fact, Peter echoes Exodus 19 and describes *the church* as a "royal priesthood" chosen to "proclaim the excellence of him who called you out of darkness into his marvelous light" (1 Pet. 2:9). As a universal priesthood, the church represents God to the world, as every member bears God's name. Later, Peter makes the move to include the Gentiles in God's covenant because they are filled with the Holy Spirit. Peter recognizes the outpouring of the Spirit at Cornelius's house (Acts 10) as evidence of God expanding the "covenant community" and making it accessible to all who believe.[2] Now anyone who believes, Jew and Gentile alike, is grafted into the covenant family of God's people.

As this covenanted conception of self differs drastically from that of Western liberalism,[3] it is our task in this chapter to pick up where chapter 1 left off and explore what it means to be a person who is grafted into God's covenant of abundance. I will begin by naming, and arguing against, two facets of a liberal conception of self: (1) that people are unencumbered by communities or societies and (2) that liberalism promotes a commodified self that can be exchanged. Then I will argue that a covenanted conception of self is communal and that God established Sabbath laws to preserve a robust sense of self that is defined by rightly relating to God and others. Finally, this chapter outlines how Jubilee and its inherent liberation principles contrast with the commodified self that is ensnared by market logic, and how Pentecost can be viewed as a "cosmic Jubilee"—God's way of calling and empowering a covenant community to make disciples and promote reconciliation. We will look at what personhood entails in God's covenant of abundance and what that means for the church's public life. This chapter establishes the conceptual parameters for the constructive arguments that follow.

2. Imes, *Bearing God's Name*, 182.

3. There exists copious amounts of research tracing individualism to the Renaissance humanism that was assumed by Protestantism. Most influential of these works is Max Weber's *The Protestant Ethic and the Spirit of Capitalism*, trans. Talcott Parsons (New York: Scribner, 1958).

Liberal Conceptions of Self

In chapter 1 we discussed how the liberal notion of freedom affects the modern sense of self. In particular we noted that the autonomous freedom of the high liberal tradition envisions people as perpetually free even as they exist in some sort of social contract. We also saw that the libertarian view of personhood sees people as free because they own themselves and their labor. The former view envisions an "unencumbered self" that is free from social influences and restraints, and the latter view depicts a "commodified self" that sees people as property. As discussed in chapter 1, these two visions of the free person are based on a voluntarist understanding of freedom that is incompatible with the biblical notion of covenantal freedom. They also correlate with the two faces of the golden calf: the unencumbered self is connected with the social side of liberty, and the commodified self bears upon the economic side of liberal freedom. Ultimately, both visions of freedom contradict the covenantal view of freedom found in Scripture.

These concepts of freedom are pervasive and influence the church's view of personhood. For instance, some Christians may view the ability to control their own desires as a sign of freedom, but this may really just be another form of self-sufficiency, which leads, invariably, to an idolatry of self. These Christians cling to control as they petition the Spirit for power. Scripture suggests something different: true freedom is found in submitting to God's law in covenantal fidelity. We are not empowered to hold a self-sufficient control over sin but urged to give our whole selves over to God, who has conquered sin and death. We will stop sinning not because we've gained personal control over sin but precisely the opposite—because we *gave up* control of ourselves to God, the only one who can rightly orient us in every way. Before I offer a covenantal view of the free person, it's important for us to further delineate both the unencumbered and the commodified self. Only then can we distinguish these concepts from the covenanted self that is encumbered but free to rest from both consumption and production. As a result, we can better understand how covenantal freedom fits into the overall picture of abundant life in the Spirit.

The Unencumbered Self

The liberal notion of the self as "unencumbered" refers to being free of burdens, limitations, or hindrances. Philosophically, it denotes a person's ability to express themselves authentically without being weighed down by societal expectations, external constraints, or emotional concerns. The unencumbered self is a person who is free, autonomous, and rationally driven, not swayed consciously or subconsciously by those things that situate people in a society. Liberalism, especially the Rawlsian conception that views justice as fairness, seeks to "provide a framework within which its citizens can pursue their own values and ends, consistent with a similar liberty for others."[4] The unencumbered self is a person who can think for themselves, make their own decisions, and live a life that reflects their own values and beliefs. Thus this conception endorses a person's pure ability to make free decisions. As Michael Sandel points out, what is most essential for an unencumbered conception of personhood is not the ends one chooses but a person's capacity to choose in the first place. Thus the unencumbered self is an independent agent capable of unmitigated choice.[5]

Sandel, however, questions the premise of a truly unencumbered self because of the self's relationship to communities. This conception of an unencumbered self asserts that one can voluntarily *choose* a "cooperative" community but rejects the idea that one is unavoidably part of a "constitutive" community.[6] In other words, people can choose their associations, but a person's identity is not fundamentally determined by his or her citizenship in the chosen community. However, people in a community are not merely autonomous individuals who happen to live in close proximity. Rather, they are "fellow

4. Michael Sandel, "The Procedural Republic and the Unencumbered Self," *Political Theory* 12, no. 1 (1984): 82.
5. Sandel, "Procedural Republic and the Unencumbered Self," 86.
6. Sandel, "Procedural Republic and the Unencumbered Self," 87.

participants in a way of life with which [one's] identity is bound."[7] We are all members of families, communities, and nations, and we bear their histories as citizens. The attachments that come along with membership in these communities actually, in part, define us. As Sandel states, "Allegiances such as these are more than values I happen to have, and to hold, at a certain distance. They go beyond the obligations I voluntarily incur and the 'natural duties' I owe to human beings as such. They allow that to some I owe more than justice requires or even permits, not by reason of agreements I have made but instead in virtue of those more or less enduring attachments and commitments that, taken together, partly define the person I am."[8] Sandel says, therefore, that the unencumbered person could only exist as an attachment-less person "wholly without character."[9] In short, our attachments and commitments shape us, forming integral parts of who we are, and these factors contribute to the way we interpret our experiences and construct meaning. If we are, therefore, unavoidably encumbered, to what extent are we actually autonomously free?

Furthermore, the concept of an unencumbered self clashes with the concept of the covenantal self described in chapter 1. The covenanted self enjoys a derivative freedom of will. In other words, people have free choice in their acceptance or rejection of God, which entails a delimited choice between two covenants. Our freedom of will begins with the fact that we are given agency to reject God. Therefore, freedom of will is our ability to move from one covenant to another and to experience the covenantal freedoms therein. Thus, our autonomy, understood as the ability to make free choices, *begins and ends* with a choice between covenants. Once a covenant has been chosen, every subsequent decision is encumbered by the attachments and commitments of the covenant. It is our choice to be attached to God in the covenant of abundance or to be attached to a false god (the self, the nation, or any other worldly pursuit) in covenant with the world.

7. Sandel, "Procedural Republic and the Unencumbered Self," 90.
8. Sandel, "Procedural Republic and the Unencumbered Self," 90.
9. Sandel, "Procedural Republic and the Unencumbered Self," 90.

The Commodified Self

While covenanted personhood opposes the liberal idea that people can live unencumbered by a community or society, it also opposes the free-market instinct to commodify all things, including people. We see this tendency in business and marketing books that talk about people using trade analogies. They describe people as resources and assets that need to be managed rather than as human beings who have inherent, untraffickable worth. They might talk about relationships as investments that need good management to get a great return or connections as assets that can be leveraged to gain professional or economic advantages.[10] Perhaps using market terms analogically helps like-minded readers conceptualize effective strategies for networking or provides useful ways to make beneficial business and life decisions. But in a liberal, free-market society where everything is subject to commodification, this sort of talk is dangerous. It reinforces a conception of self that is already pervasive in a market-driven society.

Market societies not only encompass economics but also encourage market reasoning to permeate social interactions, personal relationships, and even the way people perceive worth and value. Thus folks in a market society are guided by a market morality. In a market society, folks may regard the phrase "people are assets" not as a metaphor but as an accurate portrayal of personhood. The marketization of everything breaks communal solidarity as "people of affluence and people of modest means lead increasingly separate lives."[11] As we commodify ourselves and each other, we move farther apart and away from being in community with one another.[12] In the next two chapters we'll discuss ways to overcome the marketization

---

10. Consider, for instance, how sales guru Jeffrey Gitomer refers to personal relationships as an asset base, labeling them, literally, as "human capital." Jeffrey Gitomer, *Jeffrey Gitomer's Little Black Book of Connections: 6.5 Assets for Networking Your Way to Rich Relationships* (Austin: Bard, 2006), 39.

11. Michael Sandel, *What Money Can't Buy: The Moral Limits of Markets* (New York: Farrar, Straus and Giroux, 2012), 203.

12. Paul de Neui, "From Commodification to Community: Lessons and Confessions," *The Covenant Quarterly* 81, no. 1 (2023): 41.

of persons in community, but for now I'd like to focus on how market logic negatively affects our conception of self.

We'll refer to the "commodified self" as the idea that aspects of an individual's identity and experiences can be treated as commodities—goods or products that can be bought, sold, and traded in the marketplace. Joseph E. Davis sees two meanings for the commodified self: (1) when a person's self-understanding is mediated by consumption and (2) when a person models his or her personal life and relationships on market relations.[13] The former meaning sees people valuing themselves based on the things they buy, whereas the latter meaning refers to how a person presents himself or herself through "personal branding."[14] Both of these meanings, however, use market logic to understand and evaluate personhood.

A person's self-understanding is mediated by consumption when companies position their goods and images "not simply as fulfilling desires but as meeting a felt need for connection, recognition, and values to live by."[15] Companies take advantage of these needs by creating goods that symbolize status or identity—they yearn to make their products indispensable to a person's sense of self-worth. Personal branding also follows market logic as people are forced to consider the "selling parts" of their personalities or skills.[16] Davis calls self-branding "an exercise in self-commodification, because people are asked, in essence, to relate to themselves as a commodity, a product."[17] When people think of themselves as commodities, they can be marketed as "ownable" objects. This notion reveals a major consequence of the application of market logic to personhood: if something can be owned, then it can be trafficked. Since the commodification of self can lead to the exchange of humans as capital, commodification is an ideological root of chattel slavery. This point was not lost on Khalia Williams, who sees a clear connection

13. Joseph E. Davis, "The Commodification of Self," *The Hedgehog Review* 5, no. 2 (Summer 2003): 41.
14. Davis, "Commodification of Self," 41.
15. Davis, "Commodification of Self," 46.
16. Davis, "Commodification of Self," 47.
17. Davis, "Commodification of Self," 48.

between commodification and American slavery: "An extreme case of commodification is slavery, when human beings themselves became a commodity to be sold and bought. Steeped in racism, patriarchy, exploitation, and capital gain, slavery in America objectified Black bodies, relegating them to property by which the slave owner could profit financially. Slavery was a business, one that was built on the bodies of Africans in America."[18] Thus slavery was a system based on capitalistic exploitation and dehumanization of black people, who were trafficked like objects.

As we've seen throughout this section, the commodified self is rooted in a free-market logic that is applied to personhood. However, in chapter 1's discussion on libertarianism, we noted that the libertarian sense of freedom could be seen as another ideological root for the commodified self. The libertarian sense of freedom, as defined by Nozick, is to "own one's self."[19] If a liberal society protects a person's right to property, then a person's self-ownership demonstrates that both the person and the person's labor are properly theirs. It is unjust, therefore, for governments to impose taxes on *any* properties because they do not belong to the government. To shield the person from the government, however, Nozick commodifies the person but protects him or her from unfair, unconsented exchange. The clear problem with this thinking is that persons are *still* commodified. Instead of saying people are not for sale because their worth is inherent and incalculable, libertarians say people are not for sale because their owners do not want to sell themselves. In fact, Nozick believes that one can give up their own ownership so long as he or she gives the buyer consent.[20] Thus Nozick accepts and even celebrates the tenants of the commodified self but argues for moral limits on exchange that are based on consent.

Only a liberal sense of self could justify viewing people as human capital. It is a graceless conception of self that is stripped of personal

---

18. Khalia J. Williams, "Liturgical Undoing: Christ, Communion, and Commodified Bodies," *Review and Expositor* 115, no. 3 (2018): 352.

19. Robert Nozick, *Anarchy, State, and Utopia* (1974; repr., New York: Basic Books, 2021), 172.

20. Nozick, *Anarchy, State, and Utopia*, 58.

dignity and communal solidarity. Theologian Paul Louis Metzger argues that Christians should adopt a "personalist ethics"—an ethical framework that emphasizes the intrinsic value and dignity of each person. This is necessary because personhood, for Metzger, involves "human freedom for communion with God and other humans as mysterious, embodied beings."[21] A personalist perspective on ethical reasoning protects against social forces that reduce humans to consumer appetites.[22] Our next task is to outline a conception of personhood that, like personalism, dignifies people and rejects the liberal concepts of both the unencumbered and the commodified selves. The conception of personhood we'll argue for is rooted in God's covenant of abundance.

A Covenanted Conception of Personhood

The body is the location in which one is thrust into the world. We perceive the world as bodies, and we are perceived *by* the world, which establishes our "being-in-the-world" (a term in philosophy that refers to the way humans exist in relation to the world). We are aware of things as they relate to us, and we become aware of our place and presence in the world of perception. We are also born into a community. By perceiving our relatedness to all that surrounds us, we notice other people and appreciate the community that cultivates our being.[23] In short, our community plays a crucial role in our perception of the world, both in terms of language and in terms of our

---

21. Paul Louis Metzger, *More Than Things: A Personalist Ethics for a Throwaway Culture* (Downers Grove, IL: IVP Academic, 2023), 5.

22. Metzger's theological reason people should be valued is that they are made in the image of the triune God who is worthy. God exists in an eternal loving relationship between the Father, Son, and Spirit, and this relationship captures both ends of reciprocated love. Proclamations and affirmations of God's worthiness are poured in and out of God's very being. Because people are made in the image of the worthy, relational God, they too have an inherent worth that should be respected and dignified by virtue of merely being human. Metzger, *More Than Things*, 20–26.

23. This sense of human constitution is influenced by George Lindbeck, *The Nature of Doctrine: Religion and Theology in a Postliberal Age* (Louisville: Westminster John Knox, 1984), and Paul Ricoeur, *From Text to Action: Essays in Hermeneutics II*,

individual and collective histories. As we move forward, we'll see how being a member of God's chosen, covenantal community shapes the believer's individual sense of self and how Sabbath laws support a holistic sense of personhood. As we attempt to see how the biblical concept of covenant shapes both our conception of self and our relations to others, we will see how such a conception determines our actions as moral agents.

The Covenantal Self Is Shaped by Community

The community with which we are aligned provides us with a sense of belonging and a shared identity, which helps us develop a sense of who we are and what our values should be. Alasdair MacIntyre calls humans "story-telling animals"—that is, beings that make sense of their lives by constructing narratives that provide coherence and meaning.[24] Our identities, values, and moral frameworks are developed within the context of stories. Moral concepts and virtues are embedded in the narratives we tell about our lives and the communities to which we belong. Basically, being story-telling animals means that our lives are not a disconnected series of events but narratives with beginnings, middles, and eventual ends.[25]

MacIntyre's narrative conception of personhood is a powerful alternative to the voluntarist conception of self. The narrative self is encumbered by its context, existing in relation to other people and things in a temporal community. Since the community shapes our sense of and capacity for right and wrong, people are only truly capable of morality in a community. MacIntyre offers a response to an extreme form of individualism that separates the moral agent from reality. In his view, people have a wider sense of moral responsibility and accountability that is reflective of not just the choices we make but also the communities we inhabit. This encumbered sense of self

trans. Kathleen Blamey and John Thompson (Evanston, IL: Northwestern University Press, 2007).

24. Alasdair MacIntyre, *After Virtue: A Study in Moral Theory* (London: Bloomsbury, 2013), 250.

25. MacIntyre, *After Virtue*, 258.

is congruent to our renewal public theology because we understand Christians as part of a greater religious narrative rooted in Scripture.

Because we are in covenant with God, we are wrapped up in God's story. As such, our sense of self is not individualistic or unencumbered but totally dependent on a guiding biblical narrative. We are not merely individuals who stand in proximity with other individuals in a similar context but children of God in God's covenant. Other members of this kingdom are not strangers but brothers and sisters. Our entire identity is rooted in this proclamation: as God's children we are members of God's kingdom. This is a crucial point for understanding our own agency in God's covenant of abundance. By our own volition, we freely choose to give ourselves over to God, and henceforth we are saturated by the Spirit in every aspect of our lives. We are at once filled and led by the gracious and generous Spirit of God. Public life in the Spirit thus entails being fully encumbered by the easy yoke of Christ. We should note, however, that although Christ's yoke is easy, our commitment to it is not shallow. Covenant requires full allegiance.

The Covenantal Self Is Fully Devoted

Jesus references many times when half-hearted discipleship simply will not do. For instance, in Matthew 12, after curing a demoniac, Jesus states, "No city or house divided against itself will stand" (v. 25), and "Whoever is not with me is against me" (v. 30). This signals that discipleship requires total allegiance to God, just as Christ demonstrates complete solidarity with God when he casts out demons. Later while Jesus is teaching, some from the crowd inform him that his mother and brothers want to speak to him. Jesus responds, saying, "Who is my mother, and who are my brothers?" He then points to his disciples and says, "Here are my mother and my brothers! For whoever does the will of my Father in heaven is my brother and sister and mother" (vv. 48–50). Jesus is not downplaying his love of his family but demonstrating that membership in the kingdom of God requires full, and first, allegiance.

Some of the most perplexing passages of Scripture concern the cost of discipleship. Consider, for instance, what Jesus says we must do to follow him: "Whoever comes to me and does not hate father and mother, wife and children, brothers and sisters, yes, and even life itself, cannot be my disciple" (Luke 14:26–27). Did Jesus really say we have to *hate* our families (and life itself!) to follow him? This seems both heartless and contradictory to Jesus's constant commands to love everyone—our neighbors (Matt. 22:39; Mark 12:31; Luke 10:27; John 15:12) and our enemies (Matt. 5:43–44; Luke 6:27). In fact, Jesus even tells us to honor our mothers and fathers (Matt. 19:19). Understanding Luke 14:26–27 through the lens of covenant helps us reconcile what Jesus says here in Luke with his many commands to love throughout the Gospels. Full allegiance to God's covenant means we cannot make the kingdom of God secondary to anything, including ourselves or our families. What's not acceptable, therefore, is allowing special exceptions on kingdom matters to accommodate those we're close with. Jesus uses hyperbole to say that our love and allegiance to God must be so complete that our greatest earthly love (our love of family and our own lives) looks like hatred. By using hyperbole, Jesus describes something that is, in certain ways, ineffable—our love for God is without limit, and discipleship costs us more than we can grasp.

The Covenantal Self Values Self and Others Equally

Membership in God's kingdom is costly and requires being encumbered by Christ's yoke. While the self and others are to be valued greatly, they will only be rightly regarded in a kingdom context where Jesus is Lord. Furthermore, when Jesus is respected as Lord, our moral deliberations will be rightly situated as God intends them. In contrast, modern consequentialist conceptions of moral judgment put the individual in the position of deciding what is right and wrong.[26]

---

26. This is especially true of consequentialist theories that do not practice the benevolence principle of utilitarianism. This principle states that actions should aim to maximize overall happiness or well-being for the greatest number of individuals.

In both egoism and altruism, for instance, the subject's interests take center stage, as they concern moral deliberation. Egoism prioritizes a person's self-interest over the interests of others, and altruism prioritizes the well-being of others above their own. Both of these miss the mark, however, because they view the self as an unencumbered agent who freely determines ethical action. An excessive emphasis on either individual self-interest (egoism) or the interests of others (altruism) fails to adequately account for the complex interdependencies and mutual responsibilities that exist within a community.

Because a covenantal approach to moral agency views people as beings-in-community, individuals must promote *both* personal *and* communal flourishing. Central to a renewal public theology is, therefore, an ethics of mutuality. Mutuality calls for an equitable system of reciprocity where individuals share benefits *and* obligations. It recognizes that the well-being of one individual is intrinsically tied to the well-being of others. Thus rather than promoting competition and personal interests, mutuality promotes the idea that collaborating and sharing resources lead to better outcomes for everyone in a community.

Mutuality also shapes one's conception of self. Jesus did say, after all, that the second commandment is to "love your neighbor as yourself" (Matt. 22:39). This passage is significant in a few ways: First, loving your neighbor as yourself implies that we must first *love ourselves*. Because we are in covenant with God, we must position our self-worth in the fact that we are God's beloved children. We cannot loathe ourselves and simultaneously believe what God believes about us. Self-hatred makes light of God's unconditional love for us. Second, we cannot give what we do not have, so in order to love others, we must first be loved. The good news is that we are first loved by God, and abundantly so. Our love for others should flow out of the abundance of love we receive from God. Third and finally, Jesus says that the second commandment is *like* the first, which states: "You shall love the Lord your God with all your heart and with all your soul and with all your mind" (v. 37). This means that our love for others is *of the same sort* as our love for God. It is not a different kind of love—if you love God, then you should also love God's children. I would not be amenable to someone telling me that they loved me but hated my daughter. In the same way, it is impossible for us to *really* love God if we do not love God's children. Hence, Jesus calls these the greatest commandments on which "hang all the Law and the Prophets" (v. 40). In other words, if we follow these two commandments perfectly, we'll follow all of God's laws perfectly. We'll live a life of total covenantal fidelity.

God's Covenant Community Is Characterized by Shalom

If Jesus is Lord of the covenant, and if our personhood is determined by God and shaped by God's covenantal community, then it follows that we should also observe what God *intends* for humanity. What does it look like to be in right relationship with God and others? For philosopher Nicholas Wolterstorff, the biblical concept of shalom presents a comprehensive vision of God's intention for humanity. In other words, the free covenantal self lives in a community characterized by shalom.

"Shalom," Wolterstorff writes, "is the human being dwelling at peace in all his or her relationships: with God, with self, with fellows, with nature."[27] Shalom, a Hebrew word often translated as "peace," entails more than the mere absence of conflict; it encompasses spiritual, relational, societal, and environmental well-being. Shalom demonstrates God's plan for humanity as one of restoration, redemption, and reconciliation, which aims to bring about holistic well-being, harmony, and flourishing in all aspects of life. Shalom invites humanity to live in right relationship with God, with one another, and with the created world now and in the future.

We see traces of shalom throughout the entire biblical narrative. First, in Genesis, God's original intention for humanity is depicted as dwelling in harmony with God and the created order. This is

---

27. Nicholas Wolterstorff, *Until Justice and Peace Embrace* (Grand Rapids: Eerdmans, 1983), 69.

evident when God steps back, witnesses the perfect harmony of creation, and calls it "very good" (Gen. 1:31).[28] Humanity was thus in a state of shalom before sin entered the world (Gen. 3). Henceforth, throughout the Bible, God's plan is portrayed as one of redemption; God works to restore all things back to shalom. For instance, we see in Colossians that Paul advocates for a renewal toward shalom in Christ: "Do not lie to one another, seeing that you have stripped off the old self with its practices and have clothed yourselves with the new self, which is being renewed in knowledge according to the image of its creator. In that renewal there is no longer Greek and Jew, circumcised and uncircumcised, barbarian, Scythian, enslaved and free, but Christ is all and in all!" (Col. 3:9–11). By bringing people together in unity, God transcends national and ethnic barriers and restores shalom. Ultimately, God's plan for humanity is fulfilled by consummating the kingdom of God, where shalom reigns forever. This includes the permanent eradication of sin, suffering, and death, as well as the establishment of the New Jerusalem that is characterized by God's perfect shalom. Thus, as God's definitive promise for humanity, shalom constructs a fitting ethical vision for our public theology of renewal.

For Wolterstorff, shalom not only means being in right relationships but also constitutes *enjoying* one's relationships.[29] Wolterstorff writes, "To dwell in shalom is to *enjoy* living before God, to *enjoy* living in one's physical surroundings, to *enjoy* living with one's fellows, to *enjoy* life with oneself."[30] God's plan for humanity includes the restoration of broken hearts, minds, and bodies, bringing about inner peace, well-being, and, ultimately, joy. It is fundamentally about human flourishing, where impediments are eliminated and life can be enjoyed fully.[31] God does not merely demand our obedience but

28. Hugh Whelchel, "'And It Was Very Good': God's Original Vision of Shalom," Institute for Faith, Work & Economics, September 13, 2021, https://tifwe.org/and-it-was-very-good-gods-original-vision-of-shalom/.

29. Wolterstorff, *Until Justice and Peace Embrace*, 69.

30. Wolterstorff, *Until Justice and Peace Embrace*, 70.

31. Nathan Shannon, *Shalom and the Ethics of Belief: Nicholas Wolterstorff's Theory of Situated Rationality* (Cambridge: James Clarke & Co, 2015), 90.

desires for us to flourish in all things.[32] We should, therefore, strive to live a life that expresses this truth and to experience the fullness of joy that God desires for us.

As the vision of shalom helps situate us as covenanted people, it also helps us restore relationships with others. Wolterstorff demonstrates how an ethical vision of shalom promotes justice and righteousness as it incorporates "right harmonious relationships to other *human beings* and delight in human community."[33] Wolterstorff draws from Psalm 85:10 to show justice as being intrinsically tied to shalom.[34] But perhaps more pointedly, he quotes Isaiah 32:16–17, which explicitly ties justice to shalom:

> Then justice will dwell in the wilderness,
>   and righteousness abide in the fruitful field.
> The effect of righteousness will be peace [shalom],
>   and the result of righteousness, quietness and trust
>   forever.

This passage shows that justice reigns when shalom is restored.[35] What Wolterstorff leaves out, interestingly, is verse 15—the verse immediately preceding this passage—which states that an outpouring of the Spirit enables justice and shalom:

> . . . until the Spirit is poured upon us from on high,
>   and the wilderness becomes a fruitful field,
>   and the fruitful field is deemed a forest. (v. 15 ESV)[36]

These three verses *must* be read together because they create a conditional statement: "Until the Spirit is poured out . . . then justice will

---

32. Edward Suh, *The Empowering God: Redeeming the Prosperity Movement and Overcoming Victim Trauma in the Poor* (Eugene, OR: Pickwick, 2018), 38.

33. Wolterstorff, *Until Justice and Peace Embrace*, 70.

34. Wolterstorff, *Until Justice and Peace Embrace*, 70.

35. Wolterstorff, *Until Justice and Peace Embrace*, 70.

36. The ESV is used here because it translates *ruah* in a way that demonstrates the outpouring of the Spirit as a divine act.

dwell . . ." This is of particular significance to our public theology of renewal because it prefigures the role of Pentecost in bringing about shalom. Just as an outpouring of the Spirit enabled shalom for the Jews in Isaiah, so does the universal outpouring of the Spirit at Pentecost enable shalom for all. The vision of shalom as applied to God's covenant of abundance holds, therefore, that covenantal freedom entails being subsumed into *life in the Spirit*, where we are freed from worldly pressures and led toward a life of harmony with God, others, and nature.

The Sabbath Helps Us Attain and Maintain Shalom

Scripture also shows us how to work toward attaining and maintaining shalom in our lives. Throughout the Bible, the observance of Sabbath (*shabbat* in Hebrew) is understood as contributing to shalom. The fourth commandment says to "remember the Sabbath day and keep it holy" (Exod. 20:8), and although it doesn't explicitly use the word "shalom," the idea that we will find peace and restfulness by observing the Sabbath is inherent in the commandment. The Sabbath provides a time for rest and reflection, which allows God's people to spiritually realign themselves with God for a sense of harmony, completeness, and peace (shalom). To this day on the Sabbath, Jews often greet each other with the phrase "Shabbat Shalom," wishing peace and wholeness upon one another. By keeping the Sabbath in our present day, we create rhythms of rest, play, and work that help us properly organize our lives for flourishing.

Theologian A. J. Swoboda, in his masterful book *Subversive Sabbath*, contends that resting in God's abundance is our *first* order of business. When we read Genesis 1, we might think that the precedent of Sabbath means to work for six days and rest on the seventh, just as God did. However, Genesis 1 tells us that humans were created on the sixth day, the day before God rested. Our first full day on earth was the seventh day. Thus human existence *began* with rest. God rested after six days of work, but *our* precedent is to begin the week enjoying God's work. As Swoboda states, "Humanity had only God's goodness to celebrate, nothing more. Work had not even begun. The Sabbath teaches us that we do not work to please God. Rather, we rest because God is already pleased with the work he has accomplished in us."[37] As we position Sabbath at the forefront of our weekly rhythms, we reorient our thoughts and activities to appreciate our lives as gifts from God; we dwell in shalom. As we recognize God as the source of all our blessings, we orient our time around God. The Sabbath reminds us that even our time belongs to God, so we should steward it well.[38]

Two Sabbath principles are particularly poignant to understanding personhood in our public theology of renewal: Sabbath rest and Sabbath play. Since God built rest into "the DNA of creation," all of creation must rest in order to flourish.[39] As we take breaks from work, commerce, and productivity, we allow our minds, bodies, and souls to rest. Thus our Sabbath rest is holistic. As an artist, theologian, and philosopher, I am constantly thinking of ways to solve the world's problems. I use an interdisciplinary approach to gain insight into societal issues from multiple angles. I hope to use this understanding to raise awareness and create solutions that bring about positive change. One day in prayer, I felt the Lord convicting me that because I was externally focused on problem solving, I wasn't really resting my mind or my heart on the Sabbath. I sensed God telling me that resting on the Sabbath entails rejoicing in the goodness of creation. After all, there are six more days of the week to fix the world!

The second essential principle of Sabbath is play. Cultural theorist Johan Huizinga argues that play, though an "irrational activity," is one of the hallmarks of civilization.[40] Play is older than recorded history, predating the formation of societies.[41] Although play serves no functionality in itself, it seems to be a fundamental facet of life as even animals engage in it.[42] It is a foundational structure of civilization

---

37. A. J. Swoboda, *Subversive Sabbath: The Surprising Power of Rest in a Nonstop World* (Grand Rapids: Brazos, 2018), 7.

38. Swoboda, *Subversive Sabbath*, 8.

39. Swoboda, *Subversive Sabbath*, 11.

40. Johan Huizinga, *Homo Ludens* (London: Routledge, 1949), 5.

41. Huizinga, *Homo Ludens*, 1.

42. Huizinga, *Homo Ludens*, 4.

that somehow supports human flourishing. Perhaps the reason play is so essential to human flourishing is because it is *purposeful without purpose*. In play humans simply exist, full of agency, without any burden to produce. Play, in other words, helps us recognize our inherent value as we let go of any values we assign to ourselves based on our productivity. Theologian Jürgen Moltmann states it well: "We too are evidently supposed to be busy with something, as if our existence were justified or rendered beautiful by this. The opposite is true: Our existence is justified and made beautiful before we are able to do or fail to do anything."[43] Moltmann's statement underscores the idea that play is an act of self-affirmation—our innate worth shines through as we exist free of worldly constraints.

Sabbath can be thought of as a mandate to play. In the same way that Sabbath helps us situate our lives in light of God's providence, Sabbath reminds us that we are God's children, intrinsically valuable and loved by God. In Sabbath play, we are free from any expectations or obligations that are associated with productivity. We are able to exist in a state of pure joy, free from striving or comparison. In such a state, we can recognize our intrinsic value, regardless of our past achievements or failures. Sabbath reorients our sense of self as we step away from the world of productivity and commodity to play.

Swoboda writes, "As the church enters Sabbath, it is embodying the rest of God for the world. And it is God's rest that the world needs. . . . The church at rest is a sign pointing toward the risen Christ; it is not an end in and of itself. We are light shining the life of Christ in a dark, tired world. Sabbath is countercultural living."[44] By setting aside a weekly day of rest, we model a different way of life that stands in contrast to the often frenetic and hectic pace of our Western world. Sabbath reorients us to shalom and rejects the liberal conceptions of an unencumbered, commodified self. Sabbath observance becomes a form of witness to the world when it enables us to say, *There is enough to go around for all of us*, and *I am enough regardless of what I've*

---

43. Jürgen Moltmann, *Theology of Play*, trans. Reinhard Ulrich (New York: Harper & Row, 1972), 21.
44. Swoboda, *Subversive Sabbath*, 166.

produced.[45] Thus adherence to Sabbath is an act of resistance and an act of hope—it reminds us that God has blessed us abundantly, and, as a result, we can live differently. Taken together, the vision of shalom and the principles of Sabbath form an appropriate framework for understanding ourselves as God's covenant partners.

Jubilee Empowers Us to Restore Shalom

In the introduction to this book, we discussed how the Sabbath principles were most fully articulated in the biblical tradition of Jubilee. This tradition included things like the release of slaves, a return of ancestral lands, and cancellation of debts to demonstrate trust in God's provision. In that chapter, I argued that Jubilee provides the foundations of a biblical social witness that promotes the flourishing of a society in covenant with God. Now, I'd like to demonstrate how Jubilee, a "Sabbath of Sabbaths," parallels Pentecost in God's covenant of abundance, where the universal outpour of the Spirit constitutes a time of rejoicing and the resetting of relationships within the community.

Pentecost is the church's equivalent of Israel's Jubilee—the event that empowers the covenanted person to reestablish shalom. My goal here is to explore two things: (1) how Pentecost can be understood as foundational for the church's public witness and (2) how Pentecost can be understood as a "cosmic Jubilee." While the former insight helps us think about the public ramifications of Pentecost, the latter grounds our entire public theology of renewal. Pentecost as a cosmic Jubilee gives us the framework for engaging the economic and social facets of our constructive arguments, so we will continue to develop this concept throughout the remainder of this book.

Pentecost as the Foundation of the Church's Public Witness

Pentecostal theologian Wolfgang Vondey sees the public witness of Pentecost as a "scandal" that disrupts societal norms and expectations.

45. Walter Brueggemann, "Enough Is Enough," John Mark Ministries, January 3, 2003, https://www.jmm.org.au/articles/1181.htm.

Jesus's life, ministry, and death were subversive in many ways, and Pentecost did not resolve the scandals of Christ's ministry or the cross. Instead, it universalized the scandal as Christ's ministry was transferred to the church at Pentecost.[46] Vondey believes our personhood is fully understood when we, as members of Christ's body, reveal God and God's transformational power that is available through the outpoured Spirit. This is what it means to live an empowered human life that is realized through public witness.

While the Spirit being poured out on *all* flesh indicates that this blessing is available to every person, not all flesh *receives* the Spirit. Only those who willingly enter into covenant with God receive the Spirit. As Vondey writes, "The promise of the Spirit was given to *all* flesh, but the reception of the Spirit only to . . . the community exemplified by the public church."[47] While covenanted life in the Spirit is the goal of human personhood, it must be chosen and not forced. God *could* determine our choices, as an arranged marriage determines what becomes of each partner, but then God would defy the parameters of a freely chosen covenant. God desires and pursues us, but it is our God-given right to choose to enter into God's covenant.

We must remember, however, that our free choice is not *entirely* free; we cannot *not* choose between covenants. If we reject God's covenant, then we, by default, align ourselves with the covenant of the world. We cannot remain neutral or choose a third way—we are either with or against God (Matt. 12:30). Nevertheless, God has given us the right to choose or reject God's covenant of abundance—the covenant that was made possible by the cross and fully instated when the Spirit was poured out on all flesh at Pentecost.

Pentecost as Cosmic Jubilee

While Pentecost should rightly be understood as the impetus of the church's public ministry, can it also be tied exegetically to

---

46. Wolfgang Vondey, *The Scandal of Pentecost: A Theology of the Public Church* (London: T&T Clark, 2024), 78.
47. Vondey, *Scandal of Pentecost*, 190.

the Old Testament concept of Jubilee? If so, we'll have a strong case for making Pentecost the biblical foundation for our public theology of renewal. The Year of Jubilee was celebrated every fifty years after seven Sabbatical cycles. As a time of rest, forgiveness, and release from debt, Jubilee exemplified a way of economic living that truly appreciated God's plan for everyone's flourishing. The Year of Jubilee was, essentially, the Sabbath of Sabbaths—a year that reordered society by restoring families and partnerships. It established social and economic justice by pushing back against every form of exclusion, extraction, and exploitation that arose out of years of economic misfortune.[48] These hardships often led to servitude or slavery as people had no way to pay back their accrued debts. Jubilee ensured that a cycle of poverty would not extend past a single generation.[49]

An appropriate starting point for understanding Pentecost's ties to Jubilee is not Acts but Luke.[50] Luke and Acts should be read together because Acts picks up where the Gospel ends and provides a continuation of the story, describing the activities of the apostles, the spread of Christianity, and the early struggles and growth of the church. Significantly, consistent theological themes run through both Luke and Acts, such as the universality of the gospel, the role of the Holy Spirit, and the emphasis on God's salvation reaching both Jew and Gentile. What is foreshadowed in Luke comes to pass in Acts, and, likewise, what happens in Acts flows from Luke. The Gospel of Luke sets the stage for the mission of Jesus, and Acts narrates how that mission continues through the apostles. Luke and Acts have a unified purpose—they provide a coherent narrative of the unfolding plan of God. By reading Luke and Acts together, we'll see the themes of Pentecost *as* Jubilee emerge.

---

48. Adam Gustine and José Humphreys III, *Ecosystems of Jubilee: Economic Ethics for the Neighborhood* (Grand Rapids: Zondervan Reflective, 2023), 4.

49. Scott Bader-Saye, *Following Jesus in a Culture of Fear: Choosing Trust over Safety in an Anxious Age* (Grand Rapids: Brazos, 2020), 184.

50. The combination of Luke and Acts is sometimes referred to as "Luke-Acts" because they are believed to be two parts of a single work written by Luke.

At the start of his earthly ministry, Jesus went to his hometown of Nazareth and began to teach at the synagogue. There he read from Isaiah (Isa. 61:1–2 in particular) and claimed that the words of Isaiah were fulfilled through him:

> "The Spirit of the Lord is upon me,
>   because he has anointed me
>   to bring good news to the poor.
> He has sent me to proclaim release to the captives
>   and recovery of sight to the blind,
>   to set free those who are oppressed,
> to proclaim the year of the Lord's favor."
>
> And he rolled up the scroll, gave it back to the attendant, and sat down. The eyes of all in the synagogue were fixed on him. Then he began to say to them, "Today this scripture has been fulfilled in your hearing." (Luke 4:18–21)

Here Jesus claims the anointing and empowerment of the Spirit as evidenced by his ministry of bringing good news to the poor, releasing captives, healing blindness, and vindicating the oppressed. Significant to this is verse 19, when Jesus says he is to "proclaim the year of the Lord's favor." Jesus heralds and, as Amos Yong points out, *inaugurates* the year of the Lord's favor, which refers to the "messianic installation of the Day of the Lord announced by the prophets, which in turn relied on the Pentateuchal message regarding the liberative Year of Jubilee."[51] When Jesus announces the inauguration of the kingdom of God, his proclamation is accompanied by healing the sick and delivering the oppressed—he instantiates the kingdom's presence by the power of the Holy Spirit.[52]

Mary Hinkle Shore adds that after Jesus claims to fulfill Isaiah's prophecy of Jubilee, Jesus proclaims and *enacts* Jubilee in the lives

51. Amos Yong, "Jubilee, Pentecost, and Liberation," in *Evangelical Theologies of Liberation and Justice*, ed. Mae Elise Cannon and Andrea Smith (Downers Grove, IL: IVP Academic, 2019), 322.

52. Yong, "Jubilee, Pentecost, and Liberation," 322.

of people he encounters.[53] In Luke 10, for instance, Jesus sends out pairs to heal the sick and announce the coming reign of God. Furthermore, when Jesus heals a woman with a disabling spirit, he says "Woman, you are set free from your ailment" (13:12), indicating the Jubilee principle of freedom from captivity. Jesus's actions also establish shalom. Later in Luke 10 (vv. 38–42), Jesus calls Martha away from her distracted busyness and back to Jesus, the source of her peace. The principles of debt forgiveness and financial justice come up quite a bit as well. In Luke 7, Jesus forgives the sins of a woman who anoints his feet with oil (vv. 36–50), which points to the theme of debt forgiveness. The parable of the rich man and Lazarus tells a story of a reversal of fortune, showing that true fortune is obedience to God's covenant (16:19–31). There are table scenes where Jesus invites strangers to sit in communion with him (14:15–24), helps a guest at midnight (11:5–13), and even invites "enemies" like Zacchaeus to eat (19:1–10).[54] Significantly, Zacchaeus promises to give half of his possessions to the poor and to repay fourfold what he defrauded. This act of restitution reflects the Jubilee principle of financial restoration. Jesus's mission embodies the essence of Jubilee as these and many other instances resonate with the themes of liberation, restoration, and forgiveness associated with Jubilee.

While Acts does not specifically name Pentecost as a type of Jubilee, Luke conveys these themes throughout Luke-Acts, tying them together thematically. Yong puts it well: "Jesus' ministry of empowerment for the poor in Luke is followed by his pouring out of the Spirit in Acts 2:33, so that they (the poor) are given their own voice and, surely through that vocality, enabled to also further herald and inaugurate the redemptive and liberative message of Jubilee in the first-century imperial context."[55] Jubilee is further evidenced in the lives of Christ's followers in Acts. Not only do the disciples learn about economic sharing during Christ's earthly ministry, but, as they

---

53. Mary Hinkle Shore, "Jubilee on the Way: Readings from Luke in the Season after Pentecost," *Journal for Preachers* 45, no. 4 (2022): 3.

54. Shore, "Jubilee on the Way," 6–7.

55. Yong, "Jubilee, Pentecost, and Liberation," 322.

establish the church, they live out "jubilee in a fresh way for a new generation in an urban setting."[56]

As we mentioned earlier, Jubilee was conceptualized under the old covenant, but some scholars question whether Jubilee ever actually occurred. It could be that Jubilee remained more an ideal than a reality in ancient Israel. Nevertheless, in God's covenant of abundance, Jubilee was made manifest by the power of the Holy Spirit. As Kim Tan states, "The jubilee promise that there would be no needy ones among them (Deut. 15:4) was finally fulfilled at Pentecost through the power of the Spirit: 'There was not a needy person among them' (Acts 4:34). Only through the coming of the Spirit was it possible for people to love one another in this radical way."[57] Through God's covenant of abundance, Christ's outpour of the Spirit at Pentecost made Jubilee a reality and enabled radical love and true justice.

This brings us back to Vondey's point that Pentecost did not contradict Jesus's ministry but transferred it to the church. The church is to continue witnessing about the kingdom of God that Jesus initiated. Just as Jesus was anointed and empowered by the Spirit, so too are Christ's followers anointed and empowered when Jesus pours the Spirit out on them at Pentecost (Acts 1:5). Just as we, the church, share in Christ's mission, so too do we share in Christ's anointing and thus the church is filled and empowered to complete his mission.

God's kingdom is evidenced by healings and liberations, just as Jubilee allowed the people and the land to heal and be liberated from socioeconomic hardships. Pentecost is a "cosmic" Jubilee because the Spirit was poured out on *all* flesh, making shalom available to all. The church consists of those who have received the Spirit and are thus specially called to carry on Christ's mission of restoration and renewal. Seeing Pentecost as a cosmic Jubilee helps us focus our public theology of renewal on God's vision to bring all creation into his covenantal community to enjoy shalom, and it helps us recognize the church as the vehicle for accomplishing that vision.

---

56. Kim Tan, "Pentecost, Jubilee, and Nation Building," *Vision* 15, no. 1 (2014): 78.
57. Tan, "Pentecost, Jubilee, and Nation Building," 79.

Conclusion

As is evidenced by the diverse array of citations made throughout this chapter, many scholars from varying theological traditions have come to see the principles of shalom and Sabbath as pivotal for understanding what it means to be a covenant partner with God. What this chapter demonstrates, however, is how a covenantal conception of the self differs drastically from a Western liberal notion of the self. In order to be a powerful public witness in the world, the church must not only recognize this difference but also encourage these biblical principles in the lives of its members. Only then will the church truly exist as an alternative community that expresses God's abundant love.

While nothing really novel has been said about the principles of shalom and Sabbath, if we consider Pentecost as a cosmic Jubilee, it will help us ground our renewal theology in a fresh way. At Pentecost, the empowered and anointed church is commissioned to complete Christ's ministry of bringing good news to the poor, proclaiming release to captives, giving sight to the blind, setting the oppressed free, and proclaiming the year of the Lord's favor. The church's mission, in other words, is to be a minister of Jubilee to a broken world. As we work to restore shalom in our own lives and communities, we'll faithfully bear witness to God's desire for humanity to flourish. As covenanted people, we can all become agents of Jubilee, living out God's promise of a restored world. This chapter sought to establish the foundations for constructing a public theology of renewal; the next two will explore what it means to enact the cosmic Jubilee economically and socially.

5

To Freely Give

*Covenantal Generosity as the Economic Core
of a Renewal Public Theology*

The book of Matthew recounts a story of some Pharisees trying to entrap Jesus (Matt. 22:15–21). They send their disciples to Jesus to ask if they should pay taxes to Caesar. If Jesus says no, he would be commended by the Jews but would be reported to the Romans. If Jesus says yes, he would remain in good favor with the Romans but would be scorned by the Jews. Jesus is caught in a double bind between two allegiances.

Jesus's response to this quandary is at once brilliant and revelatory. It simultaneously silences his critics and demonstrates what motivates the kingdom of God. Jesus responds in this way: "'Show me the coin used for paying the tax.' They brought him a denarius, and he asked them, 'Whose image is this? And whose inscription?' 'Caesar's,' they replied. Then he said to them, 'So give back to Caesar what is Caesar's, and to God what is God's'" (Matt. 22:19–21 NIV).[1]

---

1. I've quoted from the NIV here because it more clearly expresses the meaning of the text.

The reason the coin belongs to Caesar, according to Jesus's logic, is because it is inscribed with Caesar's image and name.[2] In discussion of idols in chapter 1, we saw that they were constructed images of the gods they represented. Thus because the coin bore Caesar's image, it was tied to him as a physical manifestation of his lordship. The coin substantiated Caesar's widespread social and economic power. Furthermore, to bear the name of a god was to declare allegiance to that god. Jesus says to give back to Caesar what clearly belongs to him in his kingdom. Thus Jesus responds to this challenge by appealing, implicitly, to covenant. Caesar is lord of Rome's oppressive, worldly covenant, but God is Lord of the covenant of abundance.

The second half of verse 21 implies what *or who* images God's kingdom. If the coin belongs to Caesar because it bears his image and name, then we must ask, What bears the image and name of Yahweh? In a word, us! People bear God's image (Gen. 1:26), and we, as God's covenant partners, also bear God's name (Exod. 20:7). While Caesar uses gold to demonstrate his power, God uses us. As discussed in chapter 3, we are God's representatives on earth. So while Caesar's economy is focused on worldly values—such as economic growth, wealth accumulation, and the increase of power—God's economy is based on generosity, mutual flourishing, and right relationships with God and others. Both of these economies reflect the character of the covenant's lord. So if God is sovereign over the church, then it is the church's responsibility to ensure that its economic proceedings reflect God's character, which is that of a generous gift giver.

Throughout this chapter, we will look at what economic justice looks like in God's covenant of abundance. This chapter is both a continuation of chapter 4, which began constructing a public theology of renewal, and a response to the critical arguments of chapter 2, which looked at the social shortcomings of free-market reasoning. This chapter is responding, therefore, to the economic face of the golden calf. Fundamentally, this chapter argues that economic thought in a public theology of renewal signifies a shift in mentality

2. Carmen Imes, *Bearing God's Name: Why Sinai Still Matters* (Downers Grove, IL: IVP Academic, 2019), 165–66.

from merchant to giver. We freely give as we covenant with a generous, gift-giving God. By examining the parameters of scarcity and abundance, this chapter recognizes that both indicate the limits of resource allocation. Thus what must be attended to are the mindsets these economic realities can bring about. Whereas God's covenant of abundance encourages an "abundance mindset," market-driven fear instigates a "scarcity mindset." This chapter then considers how Sabbath logic and gleaning principles cultivate an abundance mindset and concludes by considering Jubilee as an overarching principle of covenantal generosity. Because Pentecost can be viewed as a cosmic Jubilee, in which the universal outpouring of the Spirit promotes universal forgiveness and restoration, we can apply this concept to economic justice. Together these principles provide a countercultural response to the free-market reasoning that drives much of our Western economic outlook.

Scarcity and Abundance

The economic core of a public theology of renewal is generosity. In our covenantal framework, generosity is not mere liberality in giving but a way of expressing love and community to others through giving as we make sure everyone has the resources they need to flourish. While covenantal generosity aims to imitate God in giving, we understand that there is a fundamental difference between our ability to give and God's. In the same way that our personal freedom is derived from God's, as we discussed in chapter 4, so is our freedom to give. Miroslav Volf reminds us that God is an infinite giver: "God exists without measure and can give without measure."[3] People, on the other hand, are finite givers and thus must give in measured ways.[4] In other words, God's resources are never exhausted, but people must give in a way that accounts for depletion and replenishment. People cannot be infinite givers in a way identical to God; such a reality is

---

3. Miroslav Volf, *Free of Charge: Giving and Forgiving in a Culture Stripped of Grace* (Grand Rapids: Zondervan, 2005), 62.
4. Volf, *Free of Charge*, 62.

impossible. Rather, we are called to give *like* God—to imitate God's generosity in our material existence. As Volf states, "To give as God gives, but in a way that is humanly possible, is a fine art. But it's an art that can be learned because the art itself is one of the gifts God offers to humanity. We can learn to give wisely and humbly."[5] We have finite resources and energy, so we must learn how to give in a way that both reflects God and does not deplete us.

Covenantal generosity entails, first and foremost, a rootedness in God, the ultimate giver. This is the crucial recognition that all our money and possessions belong to God, and we govern them as stewards. Generosity is an act of faith; it requires that we trust God to supply all that we need even as we share our resources with others. Second, covenantal generosity aims to distribute resources in a way that reflects an *abundance mindset*. This mindset holds that in times of scarcity, if we share, then God provides enough for everyone. Throughout this section, we will flesh out what it means to be guided by an abundance mindset in a culture that values profit and commodification. We'll see that an abundance mindset is guided by a Sabbath logic that stands against the consumeristic values of our Western world.

Economic Scarcity versus the Scarcity Mindset

Perhaps our greatest obstacle in adopting an abundance mindset is our anxiety about scarcity. As Volf writes,

> Limited resources are one of the reasons we don't give. No matter how much we have, our resources are finite, and we ourselves, fragile. Take our amenities away and we feel diminished. Take food and shelter away, and we languish and even die. To care well for ourselves and those entrusted to us, we seek to acquire and keep rather than to give away. To give, we must overcome a hard-wired selfishness born partly of our inescapable finitude. And that's where the God who gives abundantly comes in. Such a God makes giving possible.[6]

5. Volf, *Free of Charge*, 63.
6. Volf, *Free of Charge*, 105.

In fear of not having enough, people respond poorly to scarcity by hoarding what little they do have. It is important to emphasize, however, that scarcity itself is not the problem but, rather, *the fear of scarcity*. Our anxieties are "fueled by a market ideology that keeps pounding on us to take more, to not think about our neighbor, to be fearful, shortsighted, grudging."[7] It is the fear of scarcity that opposes any possibility of abundance.

Nimi Wariboko argues that in economics, scarcity is merely a description of limits regarding resource allocation.[8] Scarcity occurs when unlimited human desire is at odds with finite resources available to fulfill those wants. When resources are limited, decisions must be made about which resources should be allocated and how. Conversely, the "scarcity mindset," a concept popularized in business literature, imagines resources as insufficient for an individual or community. The scarcity mindset believes there is not enough to go around. As Wariboko writes, "This (economic) concept of scarcity differs from scarcity in other contexts or the scarcity mentality. This concept of scarcity says resources are limited but we can through careful allocation and creativity develop new combinations of resources to reduce the gap between perceived needs and available resources or uncover new possibilities for human flourishing."[9] Thus economic scarcity is not the opposite of abundance but a real and significant factor of communal resource allocation in times of need and of plenty. It causes us to thoughtfully approach distribution of goods so everyone can flourish in times of plenty and survive in times of need.[10] Properly understood, economic scarcity *works with* abundance as we approach the "imperative of sustenance with care."[11]

Economic scarcity is morally neutral—it's a mere condition of existence that shifts and changes over time. Evil occurs when a person's

---

7. Walter Brueggemann, "Enough Is Enough," John Mark Ministries, January 3, 2003, https://www.jmm.org.au/articles/1181.htm.

8. Nimi Wariboko, *The Split Economy: Saint Paul Goes to Wall Street* (Albany: SUNY Press, 2020), 161.

9. Wariboko, *Split Economy*, 161.

10. Wariboko, *Split Economy*, 163.

11. Wariboko, *Split Economy*, 163.

greed and anxiety lead to a scarcity mindset that promotes hoarding and unjust resource allocation. These evils occur both individually and socially. They arise in the greedy hearts of people entrapped by a scarcity mindset, and they arise as social evils when societies ignore the economic plight of others in the community and around the world. The former evil affects the character development of an individual, whereas the latter evil subjugates and oppresses entire people groups.

As discussed briefly in chapter 2, a biblical example of an abuse of economic scarcity, and perhaps the first instance of the scarcity mindset in Scripture, is Pharaoh's response to famine in Egypt in Genesis 41. The passage describes Pharaoh's anxiety arising from two troubling, interconnected dreams. In the first dream, he sees seven fat, healthy cows emerging from the Nile River, followed by seven skinny, sickly ones. After that, he dreams of seven plump and healthy ears of corn being consumed by seven thin and withered ears of corn. When none of the advisers can interpret these dreams, Pharaoh turns to the Hebrew prisoner Joseph for help. According to Joseph, the dreams mean Egypt will experience seven years of plenty followed by seven years of famine. To survive the impending famine, Joseph advises Pharaoh to appoint a wise and capable individual to manage the storage of surplus food during the years of plenty.

Through Joseph, God provides Pharaoh insight that would allow him to provide for Egypt and the surrounding nations through famine. As a consequence of abundant economic resources, grains could be stored for when economic scarcity struck to ensure that all would be able to survive. Genesis 41:53–57 demonstrates that the storehouses were intended to provide for Egypt and the rest of the world:

> The seven years of plenty that prevailed in the land of Egypt came to an end, and the seven years of famine began to come, just as Joseph had said. There was famine in every country, but throughout the land of Egypt there was bread. When all the land of Egypt was famished, the people cried to Pharaoh for bread. Pharaoh said to all the Egyptians, "Go to Joseph; what he says to you, do." And since the famine

had spread over all the land, Joseph opened all the storehouses and sold to the Egyptians, for the famine was severe in the land of Egypt. Moreover, all the world came to Joseph in Egypt to buy grain, because the famine became severe throughout the world.

Yet, as the famine continued, scarcity was used more as a tool for oppression and subjugation than as an opportunity for fair resource distribution. Rather than becoming a gracious steward of God's abundance, Pharaoh hoarded Egypt's resources and hired Joseph to manage his monopoly. People who sought food were forced to give up collateral to Pharaoh.[12] First, they gave up their land and their cattle to survive, and by the third year of the famine they gave up *themselves* as slaves. The peasants cried out, "Shall we die before your eyes, both we and our land? Buy us and our land in exchange for food. We with our land will become slaves to Pharaoh; just give us seed, so that we may live and not die and that the land may not become desolate" (Gen. 47:19). By the end of Genesis 47, Pharaoh had hoarded all the surrounding land except for that which belonged to the priests. Accordingly, the "myth of scarcity," the idea that there is not enough to go around, entered the biblical narrative.[13]

Walter Brueggemann believes that Pharaoh's actions are rooted in an anxious desire for self-sufficiency: "Because Pharaoh already has a sufficient food supply, so sufficient that he could feed refugees from other places of famine, we may conclude that his anxiety was not informed by reality. It was rather propelled by an anxious resolve to be self-sufficient."[14] Pharaoh positions Egypt not only to be prosperous through famine but to dominate. Pharaoh covets his neighbor's land and opportunistically uses the famine to acquire it.[15] The scarcity mindset tells Pharaoh there isn't enough to go around, and covetousness and greed cause him to exploit those who are in need. God

12. Walter Brueggemann, "The Liturgy of Abundance, the Myth of Scarcity," *Christian Century* 116, no. 10 (1999): 343.

13. Brueggemann, "Liturgy of Abundance," 343.

14. Walter Brueggemann, *Money and Possessions*, Interpretation (Louisville: Westminster John Knox, 2016), 19.

15. Brueggemann, *Money and Possessions*, 20.

provides a way for all to make it through, but Pharaoh twists economic scarcity to serve his desire for dominance and self-preservation.

Economic scarcity is like a measuring cup or scale used at restaurants for portion control; it serves as an indicator that resources must be thoughtfully distributed. The restaurant has a limited supply of ingredients to serve guests, and so it must portion out appropriate amounts of food so all the expected guests can be evenly served. Many factors can complicate distribution, however. Perhaps many more guests show up to the restaurant than expected, or many guests surprisingly order a particular dish, or a box of ingredients goes missing. Whenever something like this happens, the portions, or the menu, must be reconfigured so everyone can still be served. In the same way, a scarcity of resources necessitates efficient and creative reallocations.

Economic Abundance versus Biblical Abundance

On the flip side, economic abundance indicates that there is a surplus of resources available for allocation or storage. Like scarcity, abundance is related to a defined limit—it can only be understood against a standard of equilibrium. It is wrong, therefore, to view abundance as *limitless* potential. This is the mistake of thinking we have an endless supply of resources like God does. In fact, understanding abundance as limitless potential feeds into the capitalist myth that great wealth is attainable for whoever works hard for it.[16] While free-market capitalism seemingly allows wealth to reproduce itself without restriction, it actually creates great inequalities between levels of income among a nation's citizens. So when capitalism promises limitless abundance, it's actually promising an unequal distribution of wealth for its citizens. For you to get more, someone else must get less.

Biblically, abundance means we have more than enough to distribute; it does not mean we have an endless supply for allocation. As Wariboko states, "Abundance does not mean that material resources

16. Wariboko, *Split Economy*, 40.

in the created order have no limit, no point of exhaustion. Abundance is not absolute, as having no relation to anything, not confined to any bounds. I imagine abundance always as a matter of excess over a certain limit."[17] Therefore, we must avoid pitting abundance against scarcity, as if abundance is a supernatural foil against lack. Both scarcity and abundance require a logical and gracious distribution of resources.

What Wariboko has demonstrated is that abundance necessitates a sharing of resources so *all* can flourish. In times of scarcity we must allocate resources so everyone can make it through *below* a society's usual standard of public provision.[18] Communities must work together creatively to help everyone prosper and come back to a point of flourishing. In times of abundance we must allocate resources to also help others in need reach the society's standard of public provision. There is a social responsibility to having plenty—we're blessed to be a blessing. Scott Bader-Saye points out that in Genesis 12 Abraham and Sarah were chosen to parent a nation that was supposed to be a blessing to the whole world (vv. 2–3). Out of their abundance they were to share their blessings. As Bader-Saye writes, "The gifts of blessing are given in order to be passed on, in order to flow through God's people and beyond them. The logic of blessing is not to pay it back but to pay it forward. Israel is to pay forward to the nations what they have received from God."[19] Israel's public witness would be defined by how it blessed others.

In fact, it seems God's desire for abundance is not for it to be stored but for it to be shared. When God provided manna from heaven, it would rot if the Israelites attempted to store it up (Exod. 16:20). God wanted the Israelites to yearn for God's sustenance; if they stored up provisions, then they would forget that God was the one who provided. That is exactly what happened with Pharaoh during Egypt's famine. Pharaoh forgot that it was God who warned him through

---

17. Wariboko, *Split Economy*, 168.
18. Scott Bader-Saye, *Following Jesus in a Culture of Fear: Choosing Trust over Safety in an Anxious Age* (Grand Rapids: Brazos, 2020), 185.
19. Bader-Saye, *Following Jesus in a Culture of Fear*, 93.

a dream. Pharaoh's mandate to store up food during famine was not typical; it was an exception God made to prepare for a famine that would strike all the land. If Pharaoh had been obedient, God would have supplied everyone food during the famine *through* the Egyptians. Although they were blessed to be a blessing, they hoarded God's provisions and became a curse to all the surrounding areas.

Rebuffing the Scarcity Mindset with Sabbath Generosity

Since economic abundance and economic scarcity are not rivals but mere gauges of the financial times, our primary task in a public theology of renewal is not to learn how to avoid economic scarcity but to learn how to rebuff the scarcity mindset. While it is good practice for any society to work toward the prosperity of all its citizens, as history has shown, unforeseen and unavoidable circumstances will eventually emerge and usher in times of economic scarcity. Even in well-managed economies, there is always the possibility that unexpected events could negatively impact a nation's economy. For instance, the COVID-19 pandemic of the early 2020s had a far-reaching economic impact, with many countries experiencing an unprecedented level of economic scarcity. Without warning, governments around the world were forced to enact lockdown measures in order to contain the spread of the virus. Nations saw large-scale job losses, reduced consumer spending, and a decrease in investment, which led to overall economic decline around the world. The global economic task was to navigate these unprecedented and unscripted times of scarcity.

Those who practice a public theology of renewal can recognize economic scarcity as a pattern of life yet learn to maintain an abundance mindset even in the midst of troubling economic times. This sort of public theology extends the idea that there *is* enough to go around and that we should approach economic scarcity with a generous spirit, looking for ways to share resources to produce common sustenance. This outlook says that scarcity does not have to lead to fear, hoarding, or competition. Instead, scarcity can create an opportunity to build solidarity and community. It allows us to live *toward* and *for* each other, replacing "the dead totem of money that constricts our hearts with a living commitment to each other and to our world."[20]

As mentioned earlier and in chapter 2, the first step to adopting an abundance mindset is to view everything as belonging to God and to view ourselves as stewards of what has been provided. This means we are not the owners of the things we possess but are responsible for caring for and managing them in a way that is covenantally faithful. Since God is a generous provider, we can find confidence in times of plenty *and* in times of want, knowing God will provide for our collective needs. Think about how much more "generous" we become when we use a company card instead of a personal credit card to buy goods or services. If it's on the company card, then we don't fret about getting a good deal, but if it's on our own card, then we suddenly become experts in bargain hunting! It's easier to feel detached from our finances when we know the money belongs to someone else. We no longer feel entitled to anything because we operate from the capital of another. Yet, as stewards of God's resources, we are to be wise and faithful with what we're entrusted. We are given authority as stewards to use our possessions to bring honor to God and to care for and help our communities.

Adopting an abundance mindset requires, once again, utilizing Sabbath logic. As discussed last chapter, Sabbath logic contends that the principles of Sabbath, when followed, produce human flourishing and communal abundance. Sabbath *requires* us to rest, to trust in God's provision, and to prioritize relationship over productivity. In a world that teaches us to strive for more and more possessions, the Sabbath principle of generosity helps us resist the temptations of consumerism as we embrace God's provision. Thus Sabbath generosity animates what should be our posture toward economic justice. Sabbath demonstrates God's providence; by practicing the Sabbath,

20. Bob Massie, "Simplicity, Balance, Wisdom, Generosity: A New Economy," *Reflections* (Spring 2017), https://reflections.yale.edu/article/god-and-money-turning-tables/simplicity-balance-wisdom-generosity-new-economy.

we are enacting the belief that God *will* provide.[21] It harks back to God's provision of manna (Exod. 16), where God's people were given as much as they needed but not as much as they wanted.[22] This provision taught the Israelites to trust God for their "daily bread," not to store up manna for the future (16:20). Likewise, we can be sure that whatever God gives us today will be enough and that God will continue to provide for us day by day.

Sabbath generosity teaches us to live in harmony as a community, enjoying and sharing in God's abundance. Embracing communal mutuality on account of God's providence means denying selfish ambition and control. As Bader-Saye states, "Rightly understood, divine providence frees us of our illusions of control for the sake of God's abundant charity. Generosity is how we participate in the 'flow' of that provision. It happens when we release control and get caught up in something bigger than ourselves. It happens when we come to see ourselves as a portal of divine abundance. It happens when we invite others to participate in the unhindered flow of God's goods."[23] By accepting that we are not in control of our circumstances, we open ourselves up to God's generosity. As we give to others, we become agents of divine abundance. One way to rejoice in God's plenty is to be intentionally generous.

When I was a server in college, I remember hating having to work on Sunday afternoons because not only would I have to miss church but I would have to serve church folks who were notoriously bad tippers. There was always a rush after church when dozens of families sat at our tables in their Sunday best. The guests were usually nice but were often needy and were typically poor tippers. What a weak witness of God's generosity! Reflecting on Sabbath generosity, my wife and I have made it a habit to tip 30–50 percent when we eat out, especially if we eat out on Sundays. We thought it would be a great witness to the servers if we coupled kindness with big tips. In order

21. Bader-Saye, *Following Jesus in a Culture of Fear*, 183.
22. A. J. Swoboda, *Subversive Sabbath: The Surprising Power of Rest in a Nonstop World* (Grand Rapids: Brazos, 2018), 84.
23. Bader-Saye, *Following Jesus in a Culture of Fear*, 180.

to be a good witness of generosity while not breaking the bank, we decided to eat out three times a month instead of four. This is an example of intentional resource allocation—we believe it's better to eat out less often if it means we can tip better when we do.

By practicing Sabbath generosity, we enter a way of living in the world that resists the ways of Western consumerism. We deliberately oppose the life of endless striving, coveting, and workaholism that's devoted to mindless consumption. Sabbath logic emphasizes the importance of slowing down, enjoying what we have, appreciating the small things, and living generously. When the church adheres to Sabbath generosity as a guiding economic principle, it creates a countercultural witness in our materialistic world. But in order to fully comprehend the social effects of Sabbath generosity, we must examine its relationship to work to see how this principle emerges in our everyday lives. We'll see that when work is rightly understood through Sabbath logic, it retains dignity and is viewed as a means to provide for the well-being of others.

Work and Worship in a Sharing Economy

In its insistence on rest, one might assume that Sabbath opposes work. Quite the contrary is true—Sabbath dignifies work. Sabbath supports a strong work ethic that's healthy and life-giving by positioning work in a providential context where both work and rest correspond to God's design. Sabbath does not oppose, negate, or belittle work but opposes *workaholism*. Workaholism is the excessive compulsion to work, often at the expense of one's physical or mental well-being. Although it's sometimes praised in the West, workaholism can only succeed in an environment where productivity is idolatrously valued.

Sabbath Logic Views Work as Worship of God Our Provider

On the seventh day of creation, God stepped back and marveled at the wonders of creation. These wonders were the products of God's own labor. Similarly, the Sabbath serves as a day when we marvel at

God's handiwork, both in the world and in our lives. When we rest in Sabbath abundance, we are not forgetting work but recognizing and enjoying the fruits of our work in providential context. In other words, we don't honor the work in itself but honor the work as it relates to God's provision for us. As Swoboda writes, "Sabbath is God's eternal way of helping us worship our good God and not worship the good work he has given us to do."[24] Sabbath helps us resist the worship of work and rightly situates work as a good gift from God.

Kaemingk and Willson contend that a healthy, integrated concept of work and worship was fully present in the garden of Eden. They write, "The garden functioned as both a workplace and a temple. . . . Their work and worship were one and the same. Their diverse acts of material cultivation and spiritual adoration were a seamless collection of movements that all processed toward the glory and worship of God."[25] Every aspect of life, even work, was seen as a worshipful response to God. The moment we fail to see work in this way, we adopt a dualism that either devalues work's dignity or succumbs to individualistic conceit at the idea of what we can accomplish in a given day.

Often, Western churches promote a dualism that sees no connection between Sunday worship and what takes place at the marketplace.[26] A dualist understands the Sabbath commandment to "remember the Sabbath day and keep it holy" (Exod. 20:8) to mean that *only* the Sabbath is sacred, which implies that God is Lord *only* over the Sabbath. The Sabbath *is* meant to be set apart as a special day,[27] but God is still sovereign every day of the week. The commandment does not restrict worship to *only* the Sabbath, nor does it prohibit us from worshiping *through* our work. In fact, we honor the Sabbath by

---

24. Swoboda, *Subversive Sabbath*, 33.
25. Matthew Kaemingk and Cory Willson, *Work and Worship: Reconnecting Our Labor and Liturgy* (Grand Rapids: Baker Academic, 2020), 53.
26. Kaemingk and Willson, *Work and Worship*, 87.
27. "Holy" (*qadosh* in Hebrew) means "consecrated" or "set apart." *Holman Illustrated Bible Dictionary*, revised and expanded, ed. Chad Brand, Eric Alan Mitchell, Steve Bonds, E. Ray Clendenen, Trent C. Butler, and Bill Latta (Nashville: B&H, 2015), 1401.

embracing the work we do on the other days of the week. Throughout the week, we can choose to work with integrity, diligence, and care, and we can look at each workday as an offering of worship to God. In this way we honor the spirit of Sabbath by allowing our work to be an outward expression of our commitment to God. Work is an important source of dignity, purpose, and community for individuals. When we devote a day to rest, reflection, and worship, our work throughout the week is imbued with a properly aligned purpose.

When we lose sight of God's lordship over our work, we might think of professional accomplishments as personal feats. When we fail to connect our achievements to God's provision, "we imagine that our bonuses and promotions are the result of our own diligence, hard work, brilliance, or good fortune. We make our own harvest. We decide where it goes. And we do this all alone. Or, of course, we begin to attribute our newfound fortunes to some other invisible hand."[28] Alternatively, viewing our achievements as God-given gifts allows us to recognize that we are not self-made individuals but stewards of divinely bestowed talents and resources. When we achieve success, remembering God's lordship keeps us from focusing on material gain or worldly triumphs. When we fail, we can find comfort in knowing our worth is not determined by our worldly achievements.

Sabbath Logic Views Work as an Opportunity for Generosity

Sabbath not only gives us a chance to rest in abundance but also encourages us to consider how we can share our blessings with those in need. In their book *Ecosystems of Jubilee*, authors Adam Gustine and José Humphreys contend that the kingdom of God promotes a "sharing economy" where those in the kingdom work together toward shalom. A sharing economy subverts the "culturally accepted notion of an economy of privatized, competitive ownership"[29] and promotes an economy that views God as owner and us as stewards.

---

28. Kaemingk and Willson, *Work and Worship*, 87.
29. Adam Gustine and José Humphreys III, *Ecosystems of Jubilee: Economic Ethics for the Neighborhood* (Grand Rapids: Zondervan Reflective, 2023), 149.

We share in God's provision so as to promote solidarity in a flourishing community.

According to Gustine and Humphreys, the gleaning laws of Leviticus 19 provide a basis for a sharing economy. Verses 9–10 state, "When you reap the harvest of your land, you shall not reap to the very edges of your field or gather the gleanings of your harvest. You shall not strip your vineyard bare or gather the fallen grapes of your vineyard; you shall leave them for the poor and the alien: I am the LORD your God." Furthermore, Deuteronomy 24:19–21 instructs farmers to leave their gleanings for the poor, widows, orphans, and foreigners. These laws forced the wealthy to consider the marginalized, reinforcing the idea that they are all connected through community. Rather than storing leftovers to secure their own futures, landowners were called by God to "free the edges of their fields as a means for creating opportunity for the poor to flourish in community."[30] While the scarcity mindset would say to store up leftovers to protect against an unknown future, an abundance mindset looks at the leftovers as an opportunity to bless those in present need. Gleaning is thus the biblical mandate to share from one's abundance. Doing so helps create economic justice in a greedy world.

The book of Ruth contains a classic story that illustrates the course of justice through gleaning. Ruth, a young Moabite widow, gathers crops in fields belonging to Boaz, a wealthy Israelite landowner. Boaz not only allows Ruth to glean but also protects her and provides her with extra assistance. The story ends with Boaz and Ruth marrying and living faithfully together. Not only did the practice of gleaning provide for the poor, but it also promoted communal inclusivity, which led to social justice. As it turns out, Ruth, a poor, widowed foreigner, became the great-grandmother of King David. More significantly, Jesus also descends from Ruth via David's lineage. Thus the practice of gleaning was not just an act of charity but also a great demonstration of communal inclusion and social justice, which eventually led to the birth of Israel's Messiah.

30. Gustine and Humphreys, *Ecosystems of Jubilee*, 72.

If we take the gleaning laws as a foundation for a sharing economy, two questions may arise: What does a sharing economy look like for the individual? And what does a sharing economy look like for a church community? An obvious way individuals can participate in a sharing economy is through tithing. A tithe is a percentage of one's income, usually 10 percent, that is given to a church or a ministry. Through tithing, people are encouraged to live on 90 percent of their earnings and use 10 percent to bless others. Tithing is part of the Mosaic law (Lev. 27:30; Num. 18:21–24; Mal. 3:10) and is inspired by earlier biblical precedents in which the faithful set aside the firstfruits of the ground as an offering to God (Gen. 4:3; 14:20; Prov. 3:9). As an act of worship, tithing recognizes that all money and resources belong to God. It says, in effect, that God has provided more than what's needed, so one can use the firstfruits of this provision to bless others in need. Consequently, tithers participate in a cycle of generosity and abundance when the church or ministry uses the money to provide assistance to disadvantaged church members and members of the community.[31]

Similarly, churches and ministry organizations participate in a sharing economy when they look for ways to "pay blessings forward," becoming channels of God's abundance.[32] A powerful example of this is the Salvation Army, a holiness denomination with its own churches and worship services that is also an international ministry organization known for its charitable and humanitarian work. It was founded in England in 1865 by William Booth with the goal to meet the material needs of people in Christ's name, without discrimination.[33] The Salvation Army collects donations all over the world and uses the money to support emergency disaster relief, homeless shelters, addict rehabilitation, youth and children's programs, family

31. In order to provide full transparency, many churches and ministries offer financial reports of their yearly income and expenses. This allows constituents to see how their tithes and offerings are being used. Accountability is important for churches, as this helps protect against embezzling, fraud, financial misconduct, and other unjust allocations of resources.

32. Bader-Saye, *Following Jesus in a Culture of Fear*, 93.

33. "About," The Salvation Army, https://www.salvationarmyusa.org/usn/about/.

and community centers, and food banks. These efforts are carried out through the organization's global network of volunteers and staff, who are committed to meeting the needs of the most vulnerable members of society. When churches and ministry organizations share what they have with others, they enact the same acts of generosity Christ demonstrated throughout his earthly ministry. By imitating Christ through humanitarian efforts, we honor God's abundance and demonstrate God's love in a way that is lasting and tangible.

Participating in a sharing economy means that the realization of God's plan for another's provision may come through us. God desires for us to be generous and to give of ourselves just as God has done for us. By helping others, we are not only helping those in need but, in turn, being conformed to the ways of Christ. Yet most Christians in the West *do not* practice generosity through tithes or donations. Mike Holmes from *Relevant Magazine* published an article in 2013, which was updated in 2023, titled "What Would Happen If Christians Actually Tithed?" Holmes looked at tithe statistics and saw that American Christians currently give only 2.5 percent in tithe per capita.[34] If all Christians in the US actually tithed 10 percent, churches and ministries would have an additional $165 billion to distribute. To put that number in context, with $165 billion, in a five-year span, Christians would be able to relieve hunger globally, solve issues with water and sanitation globally, completely fund mission work overseas, and still have over $100 billion to help people around the world.[35] So why doesn't the American church tithe? Perhaps churchgoers have given in to a scarcity mindset that says there isn't enough to go around.

It's important to note, however, that participating in God's sharing economy is less about rigid allocations of money than it is about the posture of an individual's heart in giving. In Mark 12:41–44, Jesus and the disciples watched a crowd put money into the treasury.

---

34. Mike Holmes, "What Would Happen If Christians Actually Tithed?," *Relevant Magazine*, December 6, 2023, https://relevantmagazine.com/faith/church/what-would-happen-if-church-tithed/.

35. Holmes, "What Would Happen If Christians Actually Tithed?"

While many rich people offered large sums of money, a poor widow put in two small copper coins. Jesus responded to this, saying, "Truly I tell you, this poor widow has put more into the treasury than all the others. They all gave out of their wealth; but she, out of her poverty, put in everything—all she had to live on" (Mark 12:43–44 NIV).[36] The widow had an abundance mindset even though she was poor, and her small gift was more generous than the gifts of anyone else in the crowd. According to the gleaning principle, the others who gave to the treasury should have helped the poor widow—this would have created justice in their community. Instead, the story presents us with a juxtaposition: on one side are the wealthy people, who rigidly followed customs but walked right past a woman in need, and on the other side is the woman in need, who had a posture of generosity in her heart and gave the little she had. As mentioned at the start of this chapter, economic justice in a public theology of renewal entails a radical shift from the mentality of merchant to the mentality of giver. If Christians would adopt this mentality, then perhaps tithing wouldn't feel like a burden. As we reject the consumeristic ways of the world, we'll become cheerful givers in God's sharing economy.

Economic Justice through Cosmic Jubilee

Along with fostering a sharing economy, the church could apply Jubilee principles to its covenantal outlook on economic justice. Here we might find insight from one of Jesus's more difficult parables. In Luke 16:1–13 Jesus tells a parable of a dishonest manager who is accused of wasting his master's possessions. The master confronts the manager, telling him he will be dismissed. In response, the manager comes up with a shrewd plan—he decides to reduce the debts of his master's debtors, thus making them indebted to him personally. This way, he hopes to gain favor with them by granting them

---

36. I've quoted from the NIV here because this translation more clearly expresses the meaning of the text.

assistance or hospitality. Astonishingly, when the master discovers what the manager did, he compliments the manager for his shrewdness. The parable concludes with a moral lesson about being shrewd with worldly wealth. By emphasizing the importance of being faithful and trustworthy in handling resources, Jesus encourages his followers to use worldly wealth wisely and prudently. This passage is confounding. Why is a corrupt manager celebrated? And what does this have to do with Jubilee?

Mary Hinkle Shore offers some insight: "The dishonest manager recognizes that material goods are for drawing people together. Thus he is commendable in a way that most middle class Americans are not. To those who live in a culture where self-sufficiency is the highest value, the parable offers reorientation to the values of Jubilee. Communion, rather than self-sufficiency, is God's aim for all that God has made."[37] The manager was generous only when he was using someone else's money. But therein lies the point—if we consider our wealth not our own but God's, then we can have a right understanding on how to generously use our wealth for the good of our community. As mentioned in chapter 2, the first (economic) step of God's covenant of abundance is to understand everything as belonging to God and to understand ourselves as stewards who are entrusted to manage God's possessions. Only when the manager was about to be fired did he manage the master's wealth with prudence and generosity. Jubilee was established so that debts wouldn't last beyond a generation and so that wealth was rightly understood as something we are entrusted with, rather than something we possess. As debts were canceled every fifty years, family hopes and aspirations were reset as well. By easing the debts of the master's debtors, the manager provided economic alleviation for families trapped in debt, allowing new households to escape misfortune caused by previous generations. Thus this confounding parable reinforces many of the principles of Jubilee.

---

37. Mary Hinkle Shore, "Jubilee on the Way: Readings from Luke in the Season after Pentecost," *Journal for Preachers* 45, no. 4 (2022): 6.

Jubilee Provides Freedom from Both Death and Wealth

As Brueggemann points out, an economy based on debt is one that has chosen wealth over God.[38] Such an economy creates and maintains power through wealth. The wealthy subjugate the poor by hoarding wealth and stifling social mobility. The poor take on a reality of servitude and can often see no way out of the debt that has amassed. Jubilee is a way out of these financial struggles. As Brueggemann writes, "In a society of debt, what is required is cancellation of debt, exactly the intent of the Jubilee year and the 'year of release.'"[39] Scripture portrays a "God of covenantal emancipation" who aims at establishing a flourishing economic life for all, not one of immobilizing servitude.[40] The task of the church today is to "give primary attention to servitude and debt, and the way in which these destructive practices continue to skew the real life of the world."[41] As part of its public witness, the church ought to work to create solutions to alleviate the suffering of those in need.

Jubilee also helps to free the rich who are held captive by their own wealth.[42] While the rich are not recipients of injustice, a market morality drives their actions and desires, thereby leaving them bound to a worldly covenant. In Mark 10:17–31, Jesus offers the rich young ruler a way out of his bondage to wealth, but the young man refuses to forsake his allegiance to money. The economic justice brought about by Jubilee smooths out economic inequalities and reorients the people of God as a society of equals—a society that assures dignity for all.[43]

Jubilee Creates a Community of Economic Equality

In a public theology of renewal, we can view Pentecost—the cosmic Jubilee—as the basis of the church's economic structures.

---

38. Walter Brueggemann, "Emancipating Debt: Biblical Jubilee and Contemporary Economics," Church Anew, accessed October 7, 2023, https://churchanew.org/brueggemann/emancipating-debt-biblical-jubilee-and-contemporary-economics.

39. Brueggemann, "Emancipating Debt."

40. Brueggemann, "Emancipating Debt."

41. Brueggemann, "Emancipating Debt."

42. Gustine and Humphreys, *Ecosystems of Jubilee*, 22.

43. Daniela Augustine, *The Spirit and the Common Good: Shared Flourishing in the Image of God* (Grand Rapids: Eerdmans, 2019), 112.

Pentecostal ethicist Daniela Augustine sees Pentecost as the birth-place of the kingdom of God's leveling, life-giving economy. She writes,

> On the day of Pentecost, the sociopolitical and economic reality of the kingdom of God is birthed in the womb of the church by the Spirit. What the Spirit creates is holy for it is the social form of the trinitarian communal life embodied within humanity—it is the life of the Holy God translated within the human *socium*. The economics of the Spirit transform the community of faith into God's household so that, in return, it may make the world into a home for all. The Spirit exposes the unsanctified nature of the market and reveals the sacred-ness of the world, created and given to humanity as a gift toward a holy communion with God and neighbor.[44]

The Spirit moves us away from a transactional view of life, where the focus is on what we can gain, to a transformational view, where the focus is on what we can give. The Spirit creates an economy of shar-ing and love, where the needs of others are as important as our own.

We are impelled to share and to live for the good of the other because the Spirit was poured out on *all* flesh. The universal outpour of the Spirit renders all of creation sacred and shows that we are all interconnected. As Wolfgang Vondey writes, "The recogniz-able social reality of the public church is based on a recognizable spiritual reality. Because flesh and spirit are interdependent in the embodiment of that community, the renewed prophetic community formed by the Holy Spirit required a fellowship of the flesh in which the boundaries of wealth, health and power are abolished in all its dimensions."[45] In this way, the Spirit creates a potent fellowship of body and spirit, where all members of Christ's body are equal and bound together.

The church—the communal body of Christ—is saturated by the Spirit beginning at Pentecost, causing it to become the means by

44. Augustine, *Spirit and the Common Good*, 127.
45. Wolfgang Vondey, *The Scandal of Pentecost: A Theology of the Public Church* (London: T&T Clark, 2024), 234.

which humanity is restored to its original vocation. To this point Augustine writes, "The Spirit manifests the church as the new, anointed, cosmic *homo adorans*, ordained to circumscribe all creation in union with the Creator."[46] Thus the economic responsibility of the church is to establish economic justice by sharing family resources to help others.[47] This is evidenced by the way the early church created an ethos of household sharing in the first century. Consider how Peter instructs the church: "Be hospitable to one another without complaining. Like good stewards of the manifold grace of God, serve one another with whatever gift each of you has received" (1 Pet. 4:9–10). Peter wants the church to demonstrate a culture of hospitality and generosity, where each member is encouraged to use his or her gifts for the common good. For the remainder of this chapter, I'd like to highlight three inspiring ministries and organizations that emulate the cosmic Jubilee in today's socioeconomic reality.

Enacting Cosmic Jubilee for Economic Justice

Trinity Moravian Church

A wonderful trend that took off during the height of the COVID pandemic was churches buying up local medical debts.[48] Medical debts are often sold to secondary-market debt collectors for pennies on the dollar. The national nonprofit organization RIP Medical Debt was founded in 2014 by two former debt-collection executives. Since their task as executives was to buy up debt at lower prices, they realized they could form an organization that would use donations to buy large amounts of debt. Thus RIP Medical Debt was born.[49] This organization partners with anyone who seeks to relieve the medical debts of a region. As of this

---

46. Augustine, *Spirit and the Common Good*, 140.
47. Augustine, *Spirit and the Common Good*, 140.
48. Gustine and Humphreys, *Ecosystems of Jubilee*, 157.
49. This organization recently changed its name to Undue Medical Debt. See "Our Mission & History," Undue Medical Debt, accessed June 25, 2024, https:// unduemedicaldebt.org/mission-and-history/.

writing, over $10 billion in medical debt has been relieved for nearly seven million people in the US.[50] Although anyone can start a campaign to erase medical debts, many of the campaigns are administered by churches. One church, Trinity Moravian Church of Winston-Salem, North Carolina, recently made national headlines for their ongoing campaigns, which they've named the "Debt Jubilee Project."[51] In an attempt to fundraise, the church made an advertisement that said:

> The United States is the only industrialized nation where an accident or illness can drive you into bankruptcy or poverty. We can't change the system, but we can make a difference. The Debt Jubilee Project of Trinity Moravian Church is seeking to raise the money to purchase and forgive a half-million dollars in medical debt owed by people here in Forsyth County. Imagine the impact on a family that's been struggling under that kind of debt to receive a letter unexpectedly that announces, "Your debt is forgiven." It's sort of a real-world parable of what God does for us.[52]

Through this ad Trinity Moravian Church is critiquing the failures of a market economy's handling of health care and offering a biblically based solution that will help thousands of people. Not only are they demonstrating a strong public witness for the church, but they are demonstrating how the kingdom of the world has failed.

50. "Our Impact: Our Outcomes & Impact," Undue Medical Debt, https://un duemedicaldebt.org/our-outcomes/.

51. See A. J. Willingham, "A Church Is Canceling People's Medical Debt for Pennies on the Dollar," CNN, April 26, 2023, https://www.cnn.com/2023/04/26/us /debt-jubilee-medical-trinity-moravian-cec/index.html; La Croix International Staff, "United States: 'Small' Trinity Moravian Church Cancels $3 Million of Medical Debt among Poor People," LaCroix International, June 25, 2024, https://international.la -croix.com/news/religion/united-states-small-trinity-moravian-church-cancels-3-mil lion-of-medical-debt-among-poor-people/17649#:~:text=The%20campaign%20 raised%20%2415%2C048%20in,had%20been%20bought%20and%20forgiven; Sheelah Kolhatkar, with David Remnick, "How to Buy Forgiveness from Medical Debt," *New Yorker*, July 31, 2023, https://www.newyorker.com/podcast/political -scene/how-to-buy-forgiveness-from-medical-debt.

52. "Debt Jubilee Project," Trinity Moravian, July 31, 2022, https://www.youtube .com/watch?v=psMDv0lJfuo&t=44s.

Alfred Street Baptist Church

Another church that has made headlines for its Jubilee-inspired generosity is Alfred Street Baptist Church in Alexandria, Virginia.[53] In January of 2019, Alfred Street participated in a churchwide fast in which they abstained from certain things that were distracting them from their spiritual lives, such as drinking alcohol, eating sweets, or scrolling on social media. They also undertook a "financial fast" that eliminated nonessential spending. For this fast, the pastors asked the congregants to donate the money they saved during their financial fast to give back to the community. They ended up raising $150,000, and as a historically black church, they thought it best to invest in the futures of young black men and women in their community. They donated $50,000 to help Bennet College, an HBCU (historically black college or university) based in Greensboro, North Carolina, restore their accreditation, and they donated $100,000 to Howard University, an HBCU based in Washington, DC, to pay off the outstanding tuition balances of thirty-four students.[54] The lack of resources available to many minority students made this donation particularly important. By investing in these institutions, Alfred Street helped create a foundation for future generations of African Americans to earn a college degree and become community leaders.

Greenline Housing Foundation

Finally, a nonprofit organization that was inspired by the "Gospel imperative to pursue justice" is Greenline Housing Foundation.[55]

53. See Katie Kindelan, "After a Month-Long Fast, Church Pays Off $100,000 in Debt for 34 College Students," ABC News, February 15, 2019, https://abcnews.go.com/GMA /Living/month-long-fast-church-pays-off-100000-debt/story?id=61046793; Morgan Smith, "'A Huge Weight off of My Shoulders': Virginia Church Pays Howard Students' Debt," *Washington Post*, February 10, 2019, https://www.washingtonpost.com/local/ed ucation/a-huge-weight-off-of-my-shoulders-virginia-church-pays-howard-students-debt /2019/02/10/71424f42-2ae6-11e9-b011-d8500644dc98_story.html; Elizabeth Bruenig, "Churches Step in Where Politicians Will Not," *New York Times*, November 27, 2020, https://www.nytimes.com/2020/11/27/opinion/covid-medical-debt-church-charity.html.

54. Laurel Wamsley, "Historic Black Church Donates $100,000 to Pay Off Debts of Howard U. Students," NPR, February 12, 2019, https://www.npr.org/2019/02/12/693953771 /historic-black-church-donates-100-000-to-pay-off-debts-of-howard-u-students.

55. "About Us," Greenline Housing Foundation, https://greenlinehousing.org/about/.

Greenline was founded by Jasmin Shupper, a former insurance underwriter and former director of business at Fellowship Church in Monrovia, California. Shupper recognized that in the US, real estate is commonly passed down from generation to generation to build wealth. Many minorities, however, are disadvantaged because their parents or grandparents did not have houses or land to pass down. This reality came about not because of a lack of effort or desire but largely because of discriminatory practices such as redlining. Redlining, which took place in the US during the mid-twentieth century, involved loans or insurance being denied to people based on their race, ethnicity, or background. A bank or other financial institution would literally draw red lines on maps around a neighborhood they deemed to be at high risk for loans, often because it was occupied by predominantly African American or other minority communities. Mortgage loans and other financial services were systematically denied to residents of these neighborhoods, making it extremely difficult for them to buy homes or improve their existing ones.[56] Only in 1968 did it become illegal nationwide to discriminate on the basis of race in real estate sales, rentals, and financing.[57]

Shupper founded Greenline to create economic justice for people of color by bridging the financial gap for those who are trying to buy houses to start a legacy for their families. Greenline receives financial support through crowdfunding and then offers down-payment grants, home-maintenance assistance grants, and financial education to future and current homeowners who are in a racial minority. Resources like these can help people of color realize dreams of homeownership that they might otherwise have been unable to achieve due to financial limitations. This is how Greenline describes its mission: "Greenline exists because of this history [the history of redlining] and how that history informs our current reality. We are restoring the lost opportunity to access homeownership and its economic and

56. Terry Gross, "A 'Forgotten History' of How the U.S. Government Segregated America," NPR, May 3, 2017, https://www.npr.org/2017/05/03/526655831/a-forgotten-history-of-how-the-u-s-government-segregated-america.

57. "About Us," https://greenlinehousing.org/about/.

generational benefits. What we do is about more than just a down payment. It's about justice. It's about equity. It's about repair."[58] By providing access to homeownership, Greenline is doing its part to repair the wrongs of the past.

The Impact of Enacting Jubilee Principles Today

Each of these ministries or organizations demonstrates Jubilee principles. RIP Medical Debt and Trinity Moravian Church demonstrate Jubilee principles by canceling debts of strangers in their community. They are emulating God by being pure givers—givers who give without any expectation of reciprocation. Alfred Street Baptist Church also canceled debts but for students in the community. Not only does this help the students, but it helps strengthen the community in general when the students graduate and enter the workforce. Both ministries draw on Jubilee principles as they pay blessings forward. Greenline Housing Foundation follows Jubilee principles by creating an equitable housing system that provides everyone with the opportunity to build wealth and a better future for themselves and their families. This organization helps to flatten out financial inequalities just as the Year of Jubilee did for the Israelites. God's cosmic Jubilee is enacted when churches and Christian organizations strive to bring about economic justice in the world.

Conclusion

Bader-Saye points out that "providence does not guarantee protection; rather, it assures us of God's provision (making a way for us to go on) and redemption (restoring what is lost along the way)."[59] In other words, God's providence is not an escape from hardship and times of scarcity but a promise that God will take care of us even in times of need. We must remember, however, that God's covenant of

---

58. "Why Greenline?," Greenline Housing Foundation, https://greenlinehousing.org/why-greenline/.
59. Bader-Saye, *Following Jesus in a Culture of Fear*, 125.

abundance is not individualistic but communally focused as it calls us to bear economic responsibilities for each other. When God's *whole community* lives in covenant, then no matter the circumstance, we will be provided for, and what's lost will be redeemed. God's covenant of abundance calls us to share in God's provision and to establish economic justice for those who are in need. Since a good and generous God is the Lord of our covenant, we must emulate God's generosity. This will generate economic justice in our communities and establish a powerful, countercultural witness of generosity in the world.

In this chapter I sought to establish a covenantal response to the free-market ideology that drives much of our Western economic thought. First, we saw that scarcity and abundance can form in us various mindsets that govern our financial behavior. In contrast, God's covenant of abundance fosters an abundance mindset, while market-driven fear promotes a scarcity mindset. I then further explicated Sabbath logic, considering biblical practices that cultivate an abundance mindset. In particular, we looked at gleaning principles for a sharing economy and saw that Jubilee is an overarching principle of covenant generosity. If Pentecost is a cosmic Jubilee, then we can apply Jubilee's restorative ideas to our current economic situations. In God's covenant of abundance, we are led by the Spirit of Pentecost to be a witness of generosity to the world.

6

To Freely Depend

*Mutuality and Hospitality as the Social Core
of a Renewal Public Theology*

Paul begins Galatians 5—the famous chapter that profiles the fruit of the Spirit—talking about the nature of covenantal freedom. He writes, "It was for freedom that Christ set us free; therefore keep standing firm and do not be subject again to a yoke of slavery" (v. 1 NASB).[1] As mentioned in chapter 1 of this book, although Christians are set free from the yoke of slavery, that does not mean they can stay perpetually unbound. First, the slavery Christians are freed from is the slavery of flesh. Second, later in the same passage Paul urges Christians to use their freedom to live for one another, which once again binds them, but this time to each other rather than to their flesh. He writes, "For you were called to freedom, brothers and sisters; only do not turn your freedom into an opportunity for

1. This passage is quoted from the NASB, which, in my view, better depicts what is meant by serving one another.

the flesh, but serve one another through love. For the whole Law is fulfilled in one word, in the statement, 'You shall love your neighbor as yourself.' But if you bite and devour one another, take care that you are not consumed by one another" (vv. 13–15 NASB). Here Paul is referring to the social dynamics of covenantal freedom—God's covenant partners are to serve one another in love. In doing so, Christians are newly bound to God and to each other in covenant.

Walking by the Spirit overcomes the pull of our fleshly desires (Gal. 5:16–24) and also shows us how to live with and for one another: "If we live by the Spirit, let us also walk by the Spirit. Let us not become boastful, challenging one another, envying one another" (vv. 25–26 NASB). In walking by the Spirit, we learn how to love others as God loves us and how to live together in peace. As a community, we restore shalom. The goal of this chapter is to explore what social justice looks like in God's covenant of abundance. This chapter is a continuation of chapters 4 and 5, in which I began constructing a public theology of renewal by profiling civic life in the Spirit and detailing economic justice in a sharing economy. Here we will once again see how Pentecost, as cosmic Jubilee, helps restore shalom in our world through the church. Thus this chapter considers the social aspects of our public theology, looking particularly at how Pentecost rectifies various forms of injustice and inequality that exist within our society.

We'll first look at the limits of autonomous freedom and the social responsibilities that accompany humanity's existence as "beings-in-community." Because humans are, by nature, communally oriented, we'll argue that liberalism promotes something unnatural in its call to voluntarist individualism. We'll see how a covenantal social ethic is neither individualist nor socialist but posits a freely chosen, communally oriented way of being. Next we'll look at what a thick, prophetic witness looks like in God's covenant of abundance. This is important because it explicates the purpose and extent of our social engagement as a communally oriented church that strives for justice on its way to shalom. Finally, we'll end this chapter in the same way we ended chapter 5—by considering real-life examples of ministries that embody a social witness of Jubilee today. These profiles will help us envision how to demonstrate a radical and sacrificial commitment to the needs of others, becoming a Spirit-led prophetic voice in the public square.

Freedom and Responsibility

When the church displays covenantal fidelity to God, it creates a community of mutuality between its members that is guided and formed by God. The book of Acts demonstrates that the early church was just such a community:

> Now the whole group of those who believed were of one heart and soul, and no one claimed private ownership of any possessions, but everything they owned was held in common. With great power the apostles gave their testimony to the resurrection of the Lord Jesus, and great grace was upon them all. There was not a needy person among them, for as many as owned lands or houses sold them and brought the proceeds of what was sold. They laid it at the apostles' feet, and it was distributed to each as any had need. (Acts 4:32–35)

This example of sharing and mutuality demonstrates the church's desire to minister to the needs of everyone in the community. The church was guided by generosity and unity, recognizing that in Christ they were all inextricably bound. While this passage outlines what a covenantal social ethic looks like in practice, I'll argue next that it does not call us to adopt a form of socialism, nor does it endorse individualism. As we'll see, the example in Acts promotes economic justice through voluntary sharing and promotes social justice through mutuality. This social ethic is free because it is voluntary, but it is also socially responsible because it addresses the needs of others. Importantly, I will argue, this sort of social ethic is directed at the church and not the state.

Voluntary Sharing versus Socialism

Because Acts 4 sees the church denying private ownership and holding all things in common (v. 33), some have argued that the early church established a form of socialism. For instance, Karl Kautsky, an early Marxist theorist and historian and a contemporary of Vladimir Lenin and Leon Trotsky, argued that the first-century Christian communities operated on socialist principles as they shared resources and emphasized communal ownership. He argued that the early church practiced "primitive Christian communism"—a form of proto-socialism, where lower-class and marginalized Christians came together to support one another in opposition to the dominant social order. Primitive Christian communism differs from modern communism in that the church existed as a small community that merely sought to distribute wealth and standardize consumption, whereas modern communism was a totalizing ideology that needed state power to sustain the concentration of wealth and production.[2] Nevertheless, Kautsky argues, even if the early church wasn't sanctioned and empowered by the state, it was still guided by socialist principles.

Moving beyond the early church's example in Acts 4, Hak Joon Lee argues that democratic socialism is the closest economic system to the vision of a covenantal economy today. He states,

> Sabbath economics is need based, and subsistence and sustenance oriented, and seeks not affluence but adequacy. It provides social support for the fulfillment of personal potential and the enhancement of the common good. It balances and respects both freedom and the public good, both creativity and solidarity. It emphasizes socially responsible citizens and publicly minded economic policies. And it offers social support and cultivates personal motivation for fulfilling personal potential and enhancing the common good.[3]

2. Karl Kautsky, *Foundations of Christianity: A Study in Christian Origins* (New York: International Publishers, 1925), 467–68.

3. Hak Joon Lee, *Christian Ethics: A New Covenant Model* (Grand Rapids: Eerdmans, 2021), 322.

Lee sees democratic socialism as a third way between capitalism and communism, one that "upholds both civil-political and economic social rights."[4] Lee is right to describe a covenantal social ethic as fostering social responsibility, but I hesitate to align it with any worldly economic system. A covenantal social ethic posits a freely chosen, communally oriented way of being. It is not organized by a national government, nor does it mechanize its redistribution of wealth.[5] Rather, when the church adopts and faithfully participates in a covenantal social ethic, it stands as a witness to the rest of the world. In this way, the church's witness will be a living and active form of faith, not simply a Christianized rearticulation of a worldly economic system.

Linking a covenantal social ethic to any secular government is problematic in at least three ways: (1) it's an imperfect comparison because the local church is a voluntary community that lives within a state; (2) it implicitly promotes the polity of a Babylonian state; and (3) it needlessly politicizes the vital social principles of Acts 4. We must remember that the early church flourished under imperial authority. Christians established a polity of sharing and mutuality *while* submitting to centralized power under autocratic rule. What Acts 4 demonstrates is how to live for each other in mutuality—a lesson available to all believers irrespective of location or political context. Entering God's covenant of abundance is a holistic matter of the heart, not a matter of national identity. We are commissioned to make disciples of all nations, not to see what sort of government looks the most like Acts 4.

---

4. Lee, *Christian Ethics*, 322.
5. Art Lindsley argues that Jubilee doesn't require a redistribution of wealth or forgiveness of debts outright; rather, it celebrates the completed payment of a debt. He believes that the concept of Jubilee served as a mechanism to prevent perpetual poverty and ensure the stability of society. Rather than simply canceling debts, the Jubilee involved a process of debt restructuring or repayment (Art Lindsley, "Does God Require the State to Redistribute Wealth? An Examination of Jubilee and Acts 2–5," in *For the Least of These: A Biblical Answer to Poverty*, ed. Anne Bradley and Art Lindsley [Grand Rapids: Zondervan, 2014], 92–115). Yet Lev. 25 describes Jubilee as calling for both the return of ancestral lands and the release of slaves. This suggests there is a broader economic and social reset at play, rather than a simple restructuring of debts.

Mutuality versus Individualism

While the biblical covenantal social ethic we have discussed cannot be considered socialist, it also cannot be considered individualist. The liberal overemphasis on individualist voluntarism disregards the social and communal aspects of our human constitution, which often relieves the liberal from a sense of communal responsibility. Humans are socially formed, and we have inescapable communal ties. David Koyzis makes the excellent point that liberal societies have difficulties realizing that human beings are created for life in community. Adherents of liberalism find it hard to "admit that people may be under legitimate obligations and other constraints irreducible to their voluntary agreement."[6] Liberalism envisions the community as autonomous people living nearby who voluntarily subscribe to governing laws. As such, liberals believe their responsibility toward others is limited to not harming anyone. Conversely, a covenantal concept of community sees individuals as inescapably bound together in covenant. Through community, people negotiate who they are, what they value, and how they should live. A covenantal mindset encourages individuals to think beyond self-interests and to bear responsibility for others.

As discussed in chapter 4, a covenantal view of personhood views people as having *both* individual *and* communal responsibilities. Because we are born into communities, we are by nature communal and have been socialized by a community. The project of communal socialization is inevitable. An individual who abandons his or her community will simply grasp onto the linguistic parameters of another. An individual who lives like a hermit away from people will still have been socialized by a community early on in their development. No matter the circumstance, communal socialization is an innate part of the human condition. Social and moral agency requires being situated by a communal context that comprises family, religion, locality, and more.

6. David Koyzis, *Political Visions and Illusions: A Survey and Christian Critique of Contemporary Ideologies*, 2nd ed. (Downers Grove, IL: IVP Academic, 2019), 61.

Furthermore, to be an authentic member of any community, we also claim that community's history. The struggles of the community belong to everyone in the community, and as such, *we have a responsibility to reckon with both the good and the bad aspects of the community, which includes its history.* Communities do not come out of nowhere. They are intergenerational and carry long, traceable lineages that make communities the way they are. Jana Thompson argues that "liberal ahistoricism" is wrong in its ideas that a political society's institutions can be justified without any reference to history and that the people of the society have no historical obligations or entitlements to the past.[7] Because communities are intergenerational and have shared heritages of memories, they also have shared responsibilities of past transgressions.[8] If a great evil has been committed by the community, the community and its members must reckon with this history. If, for instance, someone enters into the US community as an immigrant, he or she is claiming both the benefits and the problems of the US. The US has racial issues that stem from slavery and persist to this day. If someone wants to authentically become part of the US community, he or she will take on this struggle as well.[9]

Here we must ask ourselves, Does the Western church view itself as a community bound together in covenant or as a group of autonomous people who live in close proximity and voluntarily subscribe to biblical laws and customs? Although the church may claim to be united by covenant, its actions suggest otherwise; the Western church's individualism, which separates the moral agent from its communal reality, reveals liberalism's pervasive influence. But if people are authentic members of God's covenantal community, then they

---

7. Jana Thompson, "Apology, Historical Obligations and the Ethics of Memory," *Memory Studies* 2, no. 2 (2009): 197.

8. They are intergenerational because (1) there is generational overlap between generations that share and pass along heritages; (2) the interests of members are intergenerational; and (3) the making, fixing, and maintaining of institutions is an intergenerational task. Thompson, "Apology, Historical Obligations and the Ethics of Memory," 205.

9. Thompson's argument is often used as a moral grounds for calling a society to atone for historical injustices like slavery, but a thorough assessment of this issue is outside the bounds of this book.

must live in mutuality, *for* each other. Individuals must *be* the church to each other in community. It is in this way that the church can become a powerful witness in the world. As church members live in gracious mutuality with each other, the church's light will shine brightly and expose how unhuman liberal autonomy in society can be. Humans flourish as beings-in-community, but they languish as solitary beings. Just as a branch dies when it is cut off from a tree, so people lose vitality when they are cut off from community. The power of the covenantal community is that people are not merely connected to one another but all connected to God, the giver and sustainer of life. Together, God and God's people form a covenantal community that provides the necessary sustenance for flourishing.

Communal Belonging and Hospitality

Since people are communal, it can generally be said that people bear communal responsibilities. This is even more true for people who are members of a covenant community. Freedom in a covenant community is not merely about individual autonomy but also about fostering a sense of belonging within the community. Essentially, communal freedom is a balance between individual interests and a sense of responsibility toward other community members. Mutual accountability is vital for communal freedom as members support, guide, and correct each other. Those who belong to the community recognize that their individual freedoms are exercised within the framework of a shared vision and shared values. This sort of freedom entails a person's willingness to contribute time, resources, and aid for the benefit of the community's common values.

In chapter 5 we talked about generosity as an important Sabbath principle that helps establish shalom in our lives and the world. We can view *hospitality* as a form of generosity but in the social sphere. As we are generous with our time, resources, and care, we show hospitality to those in need, which helps restore shalom in their lives and in our shared reality. Sociologist Matthew Vos writes passionately about why helping those in need is part and parcel of our Christian witness:

When Christians publicly express a "keep away from us" sentiment, will those in great need who stand at our borders with their hungry children see Jesus in us? Are we treating them as we would wish to be treated were our circumstances reversed? Will we be known as the hands and feet of Jesus? Will the needy and marginalized say, "Oh good, it's the Christians . . . things will be okay"? Or will our embodiment of the good news of Jesus Christ be seen as a sham—just another disappointment for people struggling for basic human dignity?[10]

Vos's questions are challenging but pertinent. If we claim to be covenant partners in God's covenant of abundance, then we *must* be hospitable and generous with our resources.

Local churches, as communities in their own right, form their own communal contexts within broader national contexts. Concurrently, however, the local church is also part of a broader global church community. This community is global and transnational, and it stretches beyond denominational and organizational structures. It is the "invisible" church—the universal body of believers united by God in covenant. While we may be born into local communities, we are *re*born into the invisible church community. God extends an invitation of membership to all; hence, all are welcome. As a loving, gracious, and generous community, the church, both visible and invisible, must follow God's lead and invite "outsiders" into community. The social ramifications of this statement are twofold: (1) the church must be a safe place for the disenfranchised within the community, and (2) the church must be a safe place for the "stranger" who comes from outside the community.

Hospitality for the Disenfranchised

As representatives of God's kingdom on earth, the church should be a place of refuge, acceptance, and support for those who are marginalized or disenfranchised. James tells us that "religion that is pure and undefiled before God the Father is this: to care for orphans

10. Matthew S. Vos, *Strangers and Scapegoats: Extending God's Welcome to Those on the Margins* (Grand Rapids: Baker Academic, 2022), 113.

and widows in their distress" (James 1:27), meaning that the church has a responsibility to care for the most vulnerable members of society. When we welcome those who are considered socially disadvantaged, we flatten out the unjust power dynamics instilled by society. We reject the notion that orphans and widows lack social value or that anyone needing communal support is a burden to society. The orphans and widows within our society, analogically speaking, are those facing social barriers: children in foster care; vulnerable elderly people; low-income families; minority and immigrant communities; the unhoused (due to poverty, unemployment, or mental illness); people with physical, intellectual, or developmental disabilities; and victims of domestic violence and abuse. Many LGBTQ+ people also experience discrimination, bullying, and even violence.

The church is called to care for the disenfranchised of our society without condition. It should not concern us if it was sin, carelessness, bad financial decisions, or external forces that put them at risk. We must respect and dignify them and meet their needs simply because they are made in God's image too. Jesus dined with sinners (Luke 15:1–2), dignified prostitutes (Luke 7:36–50), helped lepers (Matt. 8:1–4; Mark 1:40–45; Luke 17:11–19), and befriended corrupt tax collectors (Matt. 9:9–13; Mark 2:13–17; Luke 5:27–32). Jesus showed love to the disenfranchised of society, so if we call ourselves followers of Christ, we must do the same.

Hospitality for the Stranger

Being part of both the invisible (universal) and the visible (local) church should affect the way we think about refugees and immigrants. While the invisible church is universal and unrestricted by national boundaries, the visible church is located within the borders of a nation, so it invariably confronts matters of migration. When a refugee or immigrant, legal or not, is seeking welcome at our home, which of our allegiances takes precedence? Should we double down on our national identities and shun the outsider to protect our home? Or should we evoke our kingdom identities and see all people as kin? This issue is even more compounded when the immigrants are Christians and members of our same covenant. Do we give precedence to our covenantal kin or our national communities?

On many occasions in the old and new covenants, God's people are called to extend kinship to people on the margins, specifically to those who are disposed and without community.[11] For instance, one of the old covenant laws says not to oppress the "stranger" and reminds the Israelites that they were once strangers in Egypt (Exod. 22:21; see also Lev. 19:34). The word "stranger" in these passages is sometimes translated as "resident alien" or "foreigner" and always refers to outsiders who are in need of a community. The Israelites are instructed to treat them as natives—as insiders or kin. As Jesus establishes the new covenant, he uses the same language to talk about the dispossessed when he talks about who will enter the kingdom of God:

> Come, you who are blessed by my Father, inherit the kingdom prepared for you from the foundation of the world, for I was hungry and you gave me food, I was thirsty and you gave me something to drink, I was a stranger and you welcomed me, I was naked and you gave me clothing, I was sick and you took care of me, I was in prison and you visited me. . . . Truly I tell you, just as you did it to one of the least of these brothers and sisters of mine, you did it to me. (Matt. 25:34–36, 40)

Here Jesus aligns with the old covenant commandments to care for strangers. Even more remarkably, Jesus calls the strangers his family, which shows how personally Jesus takes our care for strangers. Just as in the old covenant rejecting a stranger was rejecting God,[12] so in the new covenant turning away a stranger is rejecting Christ.

Jesus does not mince words in Matthew 25 when he says that caring for the stranger is caring for him. In fact, he goes on to say that those who ignore the displaced in their plight are accursed and will go into the eternal fire prepared for the devil and his angels (v. 41).

---

11. Mark R. Glanville and Luke Glanville, *Refuge Reimagined: Biblical Kinship in Global Politics* (Downers Grove, IL: IVP Academic, 2021), 13.

12. Vos, *Strangers and Scapegoats*, 133.

The answer to the question about which of our allegiances should take precedence is clear—Jesus calls his followers to be *for* the least of these. Scott Bader-Saye points out that it is an "ethic of safety" based in fear that gives us uncharitable hearts. He writes, "We do not open our lives to strangers, fearing they will take advantage of our hospitality. Fear makes Jesus's ethic of risky discipleship look crazy, unrealistic, and irresponsible."[13] Yet it is precisely this—the embrace of strangers and love of enemies—that will prove our allegiance to God and lead to real change in the world. God's vision of shalom is to draw us back into right relationship with God and each other. By caring for the displaced, we not only show our obedience to God but contribute to God's vision of shalom.

A Thick, Prophetic Witness

Now that we've understood humans as beings-in-community and have addressed the significance of communal mutuality and social hospitality, we can explore what it means to become a good witness in society. While chapter 5 addressed the economic side of public witness, this section fleshes out the social side of witness, which entails forming and extending an authentic community, enacting God's mission in the world, and promoting justice in society. Jesus's teaching and ministry clearly demonstrate outward-looking social engagement as integral to establishing shalom in the world.

Love as Foundational to Public Witness

Many of Jesus's parables illustrate themes of compassion, justice, mercy, and the importance of caring for others, which inherently involve social engagement. For instance, in the parable of the good Samaritan (Luke 10:25–37), Jesus tells his audience about a Samaritan helping a wounded Jewish man. Because Samaritans were regarded by Jews as religious and social others, Jesus demonstrates that the

13. Scott Bader-Saye, *Following Jesus in a Culture of Fear: Choosing Trust over Safety in an Anxious Age* (Grand Rapids: Brazos, 2020), 40.

true definition of "neighbor" is anyone who extends mercy indiscriminately to others (v. 37). The parable of the prodigal son (Luke 15:11–32) highlights themes of forgiveness, reconciliation, and restoration as a father welcomes home a wayward son without condition. Rather than judging and stigmatizing those who have strayed, Jesus teaches us to show everyone compassion and mercy. Finally, justice is demonstrated in the parable of the rich man and Lazarus (Luke 16:19–31). Here Jesus contrasts the lives of a wealthy man and a poor beggar named Lazarus. In the afterlife, the two men carry on a conversation, and we see that the rich man is suffering as a consequence of ignoring Lazarus's plight while they were both alive. Here Jesus warns us against neglecting the needs of the poor and marginalized, showing that God's justice will be served either in this life or in the next. Taking these parables together, we see the formation of a social ethic guided by loving kindness, compassion, merciful forgiveness, and justice for all.

For Jesus, social action is always an outflow of love. Consider, for instance, when Jesus gives his disciples a "new commandment" during his final days on earth. Before Jesus is arrested and crucified, he shares an intimate moment with his disciples. He stoops low and washes all their feet—even the feet of Judas, who will later betray him. Afterward he says, "I give you a new commandment, that you love one another. Just as I have loved you, you also should love one another. By this everyone will know that you are my disciples, if you have love for one another" (John 13:34–35). Jesus says our greatest witness *to him* is our love for one another. In other words, we look and act like Jesus when we love the way Jesus loved. Jesus tells us to love our neighbors (Matt. 22:37–39; Mark 12:30–31; Luke 10:27) and our enemies (Matt. 5:44; Luke 6:27–28). If we are to be Christ's witnesses on earth, then we must love indiscriminately, the way he did.

Cultivating a Thick Public Witness

Our public witness must be multifaceted, extending beyond the mere effort of individual conversion that is *solely* rooted in the expression of propositional truth. While we should always speak and share the truth, our witness must be rooted in a *lived reality* that is shaped by our identity as God's covenant partners. This reality should govern our daily lives and our interactions with others. Such a witness recognizes how inescapably interconnected the myriad facets of our lives really are and how God is Lord over it all. In his book *A Public Missiology*, missiologist Gregg Okesson argues that the church has developed a "thin" approach to public witness that focuses only on conversion. He writes, "Salvation is more than individual conversion. Public missiology requires a robust understanding of salvation . . . , along with a complex analysis of public life."[14] As such, Okesson argues for a "thick" witness that exists within a "thick society."[15] Since congregants already participate in many different facets of life, they can bear witness of Christ in the thick public realm from within.[16]

"Public," according to Okesson, should be pluralized as "publics," since there are many different spaces in which people interact. He defines a "public" as a "common space of togetherness where people participate with one another in life and form opinions through the circulation of different texts."[17] There are many different types of publics—political, economic, social, and cultural—that coexist and interact. For instance, a single person might be part of a professional network, a church, an educational institution, a particular sports fandom, a particular ethnic group, a political group, an arts group, and a social group all at once. Each of these publics uniquely shapes the person, and some of those publics often interpenetrate. A woman's school friend might also be a huge Lakers fan, or a man's church buddy might also be a coworker (and a huge Lakers fan!). This overlap of publics creates a complex sense of the world that requires a thick, multifaceted witness. As Okesson states, "To the extent that publics interpenetrate with each other, there is the possibility that

14. Gregg Okesson, *A Public Missiology: How Local Churches Witness to a Complex World* (Grand Rapids: Baker Academic, 2020), 23.
    15. Okesson, *Public Missiology*, 23.
    16. Okesson, *Public Missiology*, 5.
    17. Okesson, *Public Missiology*, 63.

they themselves can be interpenetrated with the lordship of Jesus Christ as embodied by a community of believers located in a specific place."[18] If Jesus truly is Lord of our lives, then our Christian witness should extend into every public, affecting our entire lives.

A thick public witness of God's covenant of abundance means that the shalom principles of generosity, love, grace, and reconciliation must permeate through every sector of our lives. I've argued that Christians must first practice these principles in the church, forming a generous, loving, and gracious community that faithfully demonstrates God's covenant and welcomes everyone to join. In other words, our witness must practice what it preaches. Our witness must also reflect Christ's ministry in word *and* deed. Jesus preached to the masses but also fed and healed them. When Christians participate in humanitarian efforts, they enact Christ's love in the community. This is embodied well by former US president Jimmy Carter. A hallmark of Carter's postpresidential humanitarian work was his commitment to promoting peace, democracy, human rights, and public health worldwide through the Carter Center. Carter was also involved with Habitat for Humanity for several decades, helping low-income families build affordable housing. On many occasions, Carter attributed his humanitarian work to his faith, positing that God had instilled in him a feeling of responsibility toward others.[19] Likewise, Christians can minister like Christ in word and deed, and the church can emulate what a truly generous and giving community looks like.

Our witness must also be present and persuasive in public discourse. As discussed in chapter 4, we have dual citizenship as God's covenant partners: we're citizens of the state through a social contract, and we're citizens of the kingdom of God as God's children. Because we are both contracted (state citizenship) and covenanted (kingdom citizenship), we can authentically engage both realms. First, the Western church must discard the idols of liberal freedom

---

18. Okesson, *Public Missiology*, 59.

19. Betsy Shirley, "The Faith of Jimmy Carter," *America: The Jesuit Review*, April 11, 2018, https://www.americamagazine.org/arts-culture/2018/04/11/faith-jimmy-carter.

and exist as a holy, unique, alternative community in the worldly borders of Babylon. Guided by a covenantal social ethic, the church's first witness to the world is a lived witness. Second, as discussed above, the church must reflect Christ's ministry on earth. When it does these two things, the church will be an authentic community whose proclamation of Christ carries weight. These two things *must* precede the church's presence in public discourse, or the church will quickly be called out for hypocrisy and for presenting a conflicted, politicized witness. That being said, because Christians are dual citizens, they have the opportunity and right to voice their perspectives on matters of policy and civic engagement. The key here, as discussed in chapter 4, is to persuade people through word and deed and not to coerce anyone into any position through force. A thick witness means we'll bring a loving and persuasive witness to every sector of life—to churches and outreaches and also to our job and the grocery store.

Since Christians can be persuasive in public discourse, a thick witness should also stand against social injustices perpetuated by the society. Unfortunately, some Christian communities seem to have an either/or mentality that erroneously portrays evangelism and political engagement as competing against each other.[20] Because matters of social justice are often categorized as part of a partisan political agenda,[21] some Christians may feel uneasy about publicly supporting a cause that has been politicized. However, as we've seen in Christ's ministry, evangelism and social justice are not mutually exclusive but complementary. Christ walks in truth *and* compassion. Time and time again throughout Scripture we see Christ standing up for and befriending social outcasts and angering the religious establishment in doing so. Christ was not worried about political labels, nor did he give in to social pressures to conform to any political establishment. We must not worry about how Babylon has politicized particular

20. Elizabeth D. Rios, "Pentecostals, the Church and Justice," Pentecostals & Charismatics for Peace & Justice, January 27, 2019, https://pcpj.org/2019/01/27/pen tecostals-the-church-and-justice/.

21. Andy Smarick and Bruno V. Manno, "Reclaiming Social Justice," *Public Discourse: The Journal of the Witherspoon Institute*, May 19, 2020, https://www .thepublicdiscourse.com/2020/05/63239/.

social matters but, instead, do what's right in God's eyes. But as we follow Christ's lead, we must ask ourselves, What does it mean to extend love to others as we prophetically stand up for the oppressed?

Exemplifying Thick Public Witness: The Azusa Street Revival

Recently, several scholars have claimed that the Azusa Street Revival of 1906 offers tremendous resources for developing a prophetic public witness that addresses the powers and principalities of the state.[22] William J. Seymour, a Louisiana native and son of former slaves, led the revival. Seymour was called to ministry and then trained under Charles Parham in Topeka, Kansas. Seymour then moved to the West and ended up hosting prayer meetings at a small house in Los Angeles. These meetings grew so rapidly that Seymour and company had to move the meetings into an abandoned African Methodist Episcopal church at 312 Azusa Street. A revival broke out and Seymour and his team began hosting multiple services a day for three years.[23] People from all over the world attended the revival and even ended up starting the first Pentecostal denominations.[24]

Though a multiyear religious revival in America is remarkable enough, what's even more incredible is that it was led by a black man during the Jim Crow era. Beyond that, the leaders of the revival saw it

22. See Estrelda Alexander, *Black Fire: One Hundred Years of African American Pentecostalism* (Downers Grove, IL: InterVarsity, 2011); Keri Day, *A Radical Vision of Religious and Democratic Belonging* (Stanford: Stanford University Press, 2022); and Michael McClymond, "'I Will Pour Out of My Spirit upon All Flesh': An Historical and Theological Meditation on Pentecostal Origins," *Pneuma: The Journal of the Society for Pentecostal Studies* 37, no. 3 (2015): 356–74.

23. Cecil Robeck Jr., *The Azusa Street Mission and Revival: The Birth of the Global Pentecostal Movement* (Nashville: Thomas Nelson, 2006), 4–6.

24. Although some scholars hold to a polygenesis of Pentecostalism, it would be fair to see the Azusa Street Revival as the *symbolic* birthplace of the Pentecostal movement. See Allan Anderson, *To the Ends of the Earth: Pentecostalism and the Transformation of World Christianity* (Oxford: Oxford University Press, 2013); Adam Stewart, "From Monogenesis to Polygenesis in Pentecostal Origins: A Survey of the Evidence from the Azusa Street, Hebden, and Mukti Missions," *PentecoStudies* 13, no. 2 (2014): 151–72; Everett Wilson, "They Crossed the Red Sea, Didn't They? Critical History and Pentecostal Beginnings," in *The Globalization of Pentecostalism: A Religion Made to Travel*, ed. Murray Dempster and Byron Klaus (Eugene, OR: Wipf & Stock, 1999), 85–115.

as a *type* of Pentecost that washed away the color line and any other socially constructed divisions. Just a few years prior to the revival, W. E. B. Du Bois famously wrote that "the problem of the twentieth century is the problem of the color line."[25] In response, Seymour and his team proclaimed that in the revival "the 'color line' was washed away in the blood of Christ."[26] When it comes to justice-seeking prophetic witness, Pentecostal public theologian Estrelda Alexander points out that the Azusa Street Revival could be interpreted as "radical activism" in that it blatantly subverted the racial norms of Jim Crow America.[27]

The revival audaciously challenged the American power dynamics concerning race, status, and gender. Not only did the revival decenter America's social mores, but it did so in the spirit of Pentecost, where the Spirit was poured out indiscriminately upon male and female, young and old, slave and free (Acts 2:18). This connection was so clear to early Pentecostals that "any effort to marginalize, deny, or devalue anyone's participation in the supernatural praxis of the beloved community on the basis of gender or economic status stands as a witness against the Holy Spirit."[28] The revival extended an implicit ethical mandate that all participants shared equal status.[29] Alexander sees the prophetic witness of the Azusa Street Revival as evidenced by the breaking down of all sorts of manmade[30] social barriers.[31] The Pentecostal Spirit being poured out again at Azusa Street was viewed by Seymour and the revival leaders as a "vehicle for

25. W. E. B. Du Bois, *The Soul of Black Folk: Essays and Sketches* (Chicago: A. C. McClurg & Co., 1903), 13.

26. Frank Bartleman, *Azusa Street* (New Kensington, PA: Whitaker House, 1982), 51. Bartleman, a historian, was an attendee of the revival and recalled this general interpreted narrative.

27. Estrelda Alexander, *The Spirit of the Lord: Renewal Spirituality, Biblical Justice, and the Prophetic Witness of the Church* (Lanham, MD: Seymour, 2022), 162.

28. Cheryl J. Sanders, "Social Justice: Theology as Social Transformation," in *The Routledge Handbook of Pentecostal Theology*, ed. Wolfgang Vondey (London: Routledge, 2020), 439.

29. Sanders, "Social Justice," 439.

30. I intentionally write "manmade" to imply the patriarchal powers at play in the construction of these social barriers.

31. Alexander, *Spirit of the Lord*, 85.

unifying a divided church and world."[32] Many of the revival leaders were direct descendants of slaves and saw special significance in Acts 2:18, which states,

> Even upon my slaves, both men and women,
> in those days I will pour out my Spirit,
> and they shall prophesy.

The revival displayed not just acceptance of the marginalized but their empowerment. For Alexander, the revival demonstrated three "God-given resources" available to any Spirit-empowered Christian who seeks to engage and promote justice in society today: *pneumatological unction, pneumatological urgency,* and *prophetic audacity.*[33] *Pneumatological unction* means that as the Spirit indwells, gifts, sets apart, and empowers believers, they are given an anointing to carry on Christ's prophetic ministry of sharing the gospel with the poor, proclaiming the release of captives, healing the blind, and freeing the oppressed (Luke 4:18).[34] These anointed Christians are driven by a *pneumatological urgency* that says justice for the oppressed is a pressing matter that cannot wait.[35] They'll feel a resolve to stand up for the oppressed the way Christ stood up for the woman caught in adultery (John 8:1–11), they'll defend the disenfranchised the way Christ defended the Samaritan woman at the well (John 4:1–42), and they'll help mend the broken the way Jesus healed the blind beggar Bartimaeus (Mark 10:46–52; see Matt. 20:29–34; Luke 18:35–43). Finally, the anointed Christian will move in *prophetic audacity*—with the boldness to confront injustice in a way that reflects God's desire for reconciliation.[36]

Alexander warns, however, that our prophetic witness must carry out *God's* cause of justice, not our own.[37] True justice is an endeavor

32. Alexander, *Spirit of the Lord*, 107.
33. Alexander, *Spirit of the Lord*, 165–66.
34. Alexander, *Spirit of the Lord*, 167.
35. Alexander, *Spirit of the Lord*, 171.
36. Alexander, *Spirit of the Lord*, 171.
37. Alexander, *Spirit of the Lord*, 178.

that is carried out according to God's will, not ours. God's will is to establish shalom through love. God desires shalom—peace and flourishing—and redemption for all, even our enemies who persecute us (Matt. 5:44–45) and especially our oppressors. Theologian Clifton Clarke sees injustice as "the measure of the absence of *shalom* within a society,"[38] and the only way to overcome injustice is through love. William Seymour understood this and knew that God's justice would be demonstrated subversively through divine love. Frank Bartleman, an eyewitness at the revival, recounts, "Divine love was wonderfully manifest in the meetings. The people would not even allow an unkind word said against their opposers or the churches. The message was the love of God."[39] The crucial message of the Azusa Street Revival was the primacy of God's love. By practicing an uncompromising loving kindness even toward those who opposed what was happening, the revival functioned as a countercultural force. For Seymour, Alexander, and Clarke, perfect love is the key to social justice and unity.[40] Likewise, we must let God's perfect love animate our thick, prophetic witness in the world.

The universal outpouring of the Spirit at Pentecost was seen not as a one-time event but as a *continual outpouring* of the Spirit onto recipients who were willing and ready to walk in power and grace. To early Pentecostals, justice-seeking was not just an incidental side effect of the Spirit's outpour, nor was it an optional mandate; instead, it was "an undeniable, inescapable unction imparted with the gift of the Holy Spirit."[41] Thus we can view Pentecost as the starting point of an ongoing journey of faith (of which Azusa Street is an expression) where justice-seeking is an integral step toward restoring shalom.

---

38. Clifton Clarke, *The Love Remedy: The Cure for a Racially Divided World* (Porter Rach, CA: Alliance, 2020), 120.

39. Bartleman, *Azusa Street*, 51.

40. Steven Land, "William Seymour: The Father of the Holiness-Pentecostal Movement," in *From Aldersgate to Azusa Street: Wesleyan, Holiness, and Pentecostal Visions of the New Creation*, ed. Henry Knight III (Eugene, OR: Pickwick, 2010), 225.

41. Alexander, *Spirit of the Lord*, 128.

Jubilee Creates a Community of Social Equality

As the cosmic Jubilee, Pentecost universalizes the effects of the cross. Understood socially, all inequities and oppressions that were caused by sin are overcome by Christ's sacrifice on the cross. Paul, after making reference to water baptism as the sign of the new covenant, states, "God made you alive together with him, when he forgave us all our trespasses, erasing the record that stood against us with its legal demands. He set this aside, nailing it to the cross. He disarmed the rulers and authorities and made a public example of them, triumphing over them in it" (Col. 2:13–15). Not only did Jesus forgive us our sins on the cross, but he triumphed over "rulers and authorities"—the corrupt powers of the social sphere. Sin and sinful powers were once and for all defeated on the cross. Then *death itself* was defeated by the resurrection (Rom. 6:9–10). This is what it means to be free in covenant: Through Jesus's death and resurrection, death has lost its power. We can now have everlasting life in Christ and be saved from the bondage of sin.

Although some may see the ascension as the culminating point of Christ's ministry on earth, theologian Frank Macchia argues persuasively that because "God gave God" to all believers at Pentecost, we should see the cross, ascension, *and* Pentecost as one event.[42] Jesus reveals his own lordship once and for all when he pours out his Spirit at Pentecost. James Dunn agrees, writing, "The climax and purposed end of Jesus' ministry is not the cross and the resurrection, but the ascension and Pentecost."[43] It is through the universal outpour of the Spirit at Pentecost that the ascended Christ is made available to every believer and to every community of believers.[44] This event is cosmic, as the Spirit of the risen Christ was poured out on *all flesh*.

Furthermore, we see the cosmic Jubilee of Pentecost breaking down manmade social divisions. First, a flattening out of social privileges

---

42. Frank Macchia, *Jesus the Spirit Baptizer: Christology in Light of Pentecost* (Grand Rapids: Eerdmans, 2018), 64.

43. James D. G. Dunn, *Baptism in the Holy Spirit* (London: SCM, 1970), 44.

44. Gordon Smith, *Evangelical, Sacramental, & Pentecostal: Why the Church Should Be All Three* (Downers Grove, IL: IVP Academic, 2017), 26.

occurred when "all of them" in the upper room—men, women, young, old, slave, and free—were filled with the Holy Spirit and given tongues of fire to speak in other languages (Acts 2:3–4). This gifting allowed them to preach to crowds of mixed ethnicities and cultures in their native tongues (vv. 5–13). As the crowds gathered, Peter stood up and declared that sons, daughters, and even slaves will prophesy, and young and old will see visions and dreams (vv. 17–18). This means egalitarian justice was displayed through the indiscriminate distribution of spiritual gifts. From this empowerment, not only were the social inequities flattened out for those in the upper room, but three thousand people from various tongues and tribes were saved (v. 41). Thus the birth of the church is marked by the Jubilee principles of freedom, justice, restoration, solidarity, and hospitality. We see in Pentecost the most powerful move toward shalom on this side of the eschaton.

Enacting Cosmic Jubilee for Social Justice

I would like to conclude this section by demonstrating how particular parachurch ministries embody Jubilee principles to foster social justice today. These ministries advocate for the disenfranchised through Jubilee action.

Practice Mercy

A great example of a ministry working with displaced immigrants is the Texas-based organization Practice Mercy. This ministry works mainly along the Texas-Mexico border to serve vulnerable migrant women and children.[45] Their mission is to empower immigrants and Indigenous families by restoring their hope and dignity through friendship and by supplying practical provisions. Using a holistic approach, their ministry offers prayer and spiritual support, and provides critical supplies to struggling immigrant communities. Along the border many migrants live in makeshift refugee camps, so the

---

45. "Who We Are," Practice Mercy Foundation, https://practicemercy.org/about-2/.

Practice Mercy staff goes from tent to tent to form deep, humanizing friendships. They pray with the families and offer basic counseling services to the young girls and women, many of whom have become rape victims at these camps. They also refer many of these individuals to professional organizations and shelters. As they visit the tents, the staff ask the people about their personal needs. The team then distributes clothing, footwear, vitamins, and toiletries, and helps cover medical expenses. The team also helps find the women and children temporary accommodations and aids them with travel.[46]

Practice Mercy's founder, Alma Ruth, often advocates for the migrant population and raises awareness in both the church and the broader society of migrants' lived experiences. Ruth, a Mexican immigrant herself, founded Practice Mercy in 2019 after noticing a lack of humanitarian support from the church at the border. She said, "You can count with your fingers the faith-based organizations that were involved in helping the refugee camp. . . . A lot of photo ops, but people of faith serving on a weekly basis, . . . you can count them with your fingers."[47] Practice Mercy was founded because of Ruth's desire to have a constant Christian presence in the lives of migrants who are experiencing some of the most difficult times in their lives. By being a present, loving witness, Practice Mercy extends shalom to the vulnerable by helping them feel valued and seen.

Hope the Mission

Another great ministry, Hope the Mission, is a Los Angeles–based Christian organization that seeks to eradicate poverty, hunger, and homelessness through immediate and long-term assistance. The ministry, founded by Ken Craft, defines hope as "a message of love, support and freedom for a better tomorrow."[48] They have a

---

46. "What We Do," Practice Mercy Foundation, https://practicemercy.org/work/.
47. Alma Ruth, quoted in Bekah McNeel, "Thanking God for Miracles, Asylum Seekers Enter US," *Christianity Today*, June 10, 2021, https://www.christianitytoday.com/news/2021/june/remain-in-mexico-ends-biden-trump-asylum-christian-help.html.
48. "About Us," Hope the Mission, https://hopethemission.org/about-us/.

covenantal understanding of freedom that entails helping people get free from the grips of poverty. Of their many services, they provide hot meals, housing, health services, and "healing" through programs that lead to wholeness and self-sufficiency. Their statement of philosophy describes the vision behind their multifaceted approach: "Hope the Mission is committed to offering second chances to everyone we serve. We understand that homelessness and the challenges people face are complex. That's why we provide a range of services, from shelter and housing to emotional support, mental health services, and financial assistance. Our approach involves preventing homelessness, helping in times of crisis, and finding long-term solutions. We aim to empower individuals to rebuild their lives and thrive."[49]

One of their more innovative projects was establishing the first tiny home village at Chandler Boulevard, in Los Angeles. Working with Councilman Paul Krekorian and Mayor Eric Garcetti, they secured a half-acre plot to build forty tiny homes manufactured by Pallet Shelter. The sixty-four square foot tiny homes all have two beds, heating, air-conditioning, windows, and a desk. These homes were designed to be "transitional" housing to bridge the gap between homelessness and permanent housing solutions.[50] Each tiny home guest is given "three meals a day, case management, housing navigation, and access to mental health and substance use treatment."[51] Since the housing at Chandler Boulevard opened, the city of Los Angeles has funded and built five more tiny home villages across the city.[52] By dignifying and meeting the needs of unhoused and impoverished groups across Los Angeles, Hope the Mission enacts Jubilee for people who might otherwise be hopeless.

49. "About Us," https://hopethemission.org/about-us/.

50. "Chandler," Hope the Mission, https://hopethemission.org/our-programs/tiny-homes/chandler/.

51. "Hope the Mission: Tiny Homes," *Overflow: Christian Assembly Magazine*, Christian Assembly Church, Los Angeles, November 2023, https://cachurch.com/wp-content/uploads/2023/11/2023-Kingdom-Magazine.pdf, 19.

52. "Tiny Homes," Hope the Mission, https://hopethemission.org/our-programs/tiny-homes/.

Harambee Ministries

Finally, a wonderful ministry that is breaking generational racial inequalities through education and the arts is the faith-based organization Harambee Ministries. Harambee was founded in 1982 by Dr. John Perkins, who had a vision to defeat the "school-to-prison pipeline" in Pasadena, California. The American Civil Liberties Union defines the "school-to-prison-pipeline" as "the policies and practices that push our nation's schoolchildren, especially our most at-risk children, out of classrooms and into the juvenile and criminal justice systems."[53] This pipeline perpetuates cycles of poverty, incarceration, and disenfranchisement, disproportionately affecting lower-income black and brown communities. Perkins believed that cycles of violence and poverty could be broken if people would reconcile with God and each other, and if the larger society would resource underserved communities.[54] To break these cycles, Harambee offers performing arts programs, after school programs, tutoring, and a program for high school students named Build University.[55] Their intentional programming also points students to follow Jesus as a form of discipleship. When students learn how to lead and be creative, they perform better at school and have a brighter future. The word "Harambee," which means "let's get together and push" in the Kiswahili language,[56] has become the rallying cry to bring the community together and change the lives of countless marginalized young people.

The Impact of Enacting Jubilee Principles Today

Each of these organizations demonstrates Jubilee principles enacted on pertinent social issues. Practice Mercy Foundation demonstrates Jubilee principles by showing hospitality to the "stranger" at the border. Because of Practice Mercy's presence at the border,

---

53. "What Is the School-to-Prison Pipeline?," ACLU, June 6, 2008, https://www.aclu.org/documents/what-school-prison-pipeline.

54. "About," Harambee Ministries, https://www.harambeeministries.org/about.

55. "Programs," Harambee Ministries, https://www.harambeeministries.org/programs.

56. "About," https://www.harambeeministries.org/about.

the migrant women and children who are suffering might begin to say, "Oh good, it's the Christians . . . things will be okay."[57] Hope the Mission demonstrates radical hospitality to the poor and hopeless by providing them food, drink, and a place to lay their head. Harambee Ministries breaks generational cycles of discrimination by offering creative, educational programs to underserved youth. Each of these ministries demonstrates a thick, prophetic witness as they engage in multifaceted programs of care. For them, ministering is not mere lip service but entails meeting the social needs of society's most vulnerable people. Paul tells us that we will fulfill the law of Christ when we "bear one another's burdens" (Gal. 6:2). In so doing we enact shalom in a world that desperately needs it.

Conclusion

God's covenant of abundance is life-giving. Not only do we gain new life in Christ, but we become God's agents on earth to instill new life in others. We become Christ's hope peddlers—bards who sing songs of redemption and reconciliation in a broken world. And as our words match our actions, the good news once again becomes *good*. This chapter sought to understand what social responsibility entails in a renewal public theology. We found that it entails (1) rejecting liberalism's penchant for individualism, (2) serving others in a posture of love, and (3) advocating for the disenfranchised through Jubilee action. These three steps construct a communally oriented way of being that reflects God's enactment of shalom in the world.

This chapter also closes out the constructive arguments of the book. It is my hope that this public theology demonstrates what a faithful Christian public witness can look like today. May the words of Christ spoken to the believers before the ascension ring true for us on this day: "But you will receive power when the Holy Spirit has come upon you, and you will be my witnesses in Jerusalem, in all Judea and Samaria, and to the ends of the earth" (Acts 1:8).

57. Vos, *Strangers and Scapegoats*, 113.

CONCLUSION

The Promise of Freedom

Imagine the world at shalom. Such a world is not merely a place devoid of conflict but a vibrant world plaited with threads of harmony, justice, and love. The wolf lies down with the lamb, and every creature lives in harmony with its fellow inhabitants (Isa. 11:6–9). The cities are filled with people from all social backgrounds and walks of life walking hand in hand, their faces glowing with the acceptance of a loving community. Here the unhoused find shelter, the hungry are fed, and the downtrodden are lifted high. Every person is a valued member of a society that respects all people as family. In such a world, leaders govern with wisdom and compassion, guided not by selfish ambition but by a deep sense of responsibility to God and their fellow kin. And as they are so led, citizens of this kingdom feel a deep sense of belonging, knowing that they are loved beyond measure by God and each other. Such a world is not merely a pipe dream or a distant hope but a promised reality. It reflects God's vision for humanity described in Revelation 21, where the world is remade by Christ the returned king, and peace and justice reign as an overflow of God's abundant love.

As God's covenant partner you were likely able to imagine this world for two reasons: (1) you have a theological imagination that has been shaped by Scripture, your Christian community, and your personal experiences with God; and (2) you've experienced moments of shalom throughout your life. Whenever the Spirit breaks through into your present circumstances, you experience a glimpse of shalom—in this intermediate stage between Pentecost and Christ's return, you experience a foretaste of the world set to rights.[1] When we imagine a world at shalom, we imagine the world God intends to bring about.[2] In fact, in Christ's earthly ministry God already started the process of bringing this world about, and God has commissioned the church to continue working toward this aim until Christ's return. Because we have our *telos*—a clear visualization of our end goal—we can continue to enact God's vision for the world today.

But what if we *don't* have a rich theological imagination or a Christian narrative framework from which to interpret our experiences? What if a person views shalom as a fantasy or a fool's paradise? In these cases, we must demonstrate that such a community can indeed exist. This is what it means for the church to be a public witness in the world—to show the world that God's promise of a world at shalom is not only possible but presently made visible by the church.

The *problem of freedom* is that much of the Western church defiles God's vision of shalom when it adopts liberal concepts of freedom into its ecclesial structures. The church shows the world a tainted witness in a syncretized form of Christianity. The idolatrous church has one foot in Scripture and one in its national identity, an identity that is guided by self-interest and self-indulgence. Instead of showing the world a community at peace where justice and love reign supreme, the church heralds and reinforces the ideals of the state. To close out this

---

1. N. T. Wright, *Surprised by Hope: Rethinking Heaven, the Resurrection, and the Mission of the Church* (New York: HarperCollins, 2008), 249. Wright talks about the intermediate state as between the resurrection and the second coming, but I purposefully moved the starting point to Pentecost, as this was the final act of God's work of redemption through Christ on earth.

2. N. T. Wright, *Surprised by Hope*, 107.

book, let's explore what the promise of covenantal freedom entails and what the church's responsibility is in the world today.

Our Prophetic Task

The *promise of freedom* is that the church can once again proclaim God's vision of shalom by rejecting our Western idols and by living out the biblical principles of shalom—namely, Sabbath generosity, mutuality, and hospitality. This covenantal freedom is one that sets us free from the desires of the flesh and the oppressions of the world. Not only are we ultimately freed from death and the consequences of sin, but we are freed in our present circumstances from the fears and anxieties of bondage, both spiritual and physical, caused by sin and by corrupt earthly powers. In Christ, the one who conquered sin and death, we have victory over the powers of darkness, and by the Spirit that dwells in us we are empowered to make disciples of all nations, sharing the transformative power of God's grace and the liberating work of Christ and the Spirit. Thus the promise of freedom extends from our personal and ecclesial union with Christ to the world, as everyone is invited to experience life in abundance by the Spirit.

Our prophetic task throughout this book was to rebuke the Western church's tendency to syncretize with liberalism and then to energize a new vision of an undefiled church that faithfully bears witness to the kingdom of God. Ironically, this new reality is not new at all but ancient.[3] It is the biblical vision of God's covenant of abundance imagined for our world today. To carry out this prophetic task, we first grounded the book's arguments in two sets of Scripture passages. For our critical arguments, we referred to Exodus 19–20 (the construction of the law and the Mosaic covenant, particularly through the Ten Commandments) and Exodus 32 (the golden-calf episode) to demonstrate what sort of communal, public orientation God desired for the Israelites. Like that of the idolatrous Israelites, the Western

---

3. Walter Brueggemann, *The Prophetic Imagination*, 2nd ed. (Minneapolis: Fortress, 2001), 59–60.

church's main problem is syncretic idolatry, which comes about as a consequence of conflating a covenantal conception of freedom with a liberal conception of autonomous freedom. The book's constructive arguments are grounded in Leviticus 25's description of Jubilee and Acts 2's account of Pentecost, which empowers God's covenant of abundance. One of this book's more novel ideas is that Pentecost can be read as a "cosmic Jubilee." As God's Spirit is poured out on all flesh, social and economic inequalities are flattened out and shalom is reestablished.

Part 1 fleshed out the book's critical arguments first by demonstrating how liberal conceptions of freedom derive from extrabiblical notions of justice, such as "justice as fairness" (Kant and Rawls) and "justice as entitlement" (Locke and Nozick). Both of these conceptions rely on an individualist sense of autonomous freedom that sees agents as capable of determining their own courses of action, rather than being subjected to external forces. When the church adopts this notion of social freedom, it syncretizes either to an assimilated church that tries to preserve autonomous freedom for individuals, even while in covenant, or to the nationalistic church that fossilizes the concept of autonomous freedom as a God-given right. Alternatively, a biblical conception of freedom considers the relational dynamics between God and God's people, characterized by both freedom and responsibility within a covenantal relationship.

Another notion of freedom that can be idolized by the church is the free-market reasoning that is associated with liberal economics. An unchecked market perpetuates cycles of yearning and consumption that eventually shape a person's values and desires. When this happens, markets become idolized and a market morality replaces any sense of trust in God's provision. When the church adopts this notion of economic freedom, it syncretizes and either becomes a dualistic church that allows God to govern spiritual matters and the free market to govern fiscal matters or becomes a materialistic church that merges biblical concepts of prosperity with market reasoning. Both cases are idolatrous because God is forced to share the throne with money. A biblical concept of money and possessions views all things as belonging to God and views people as stewards. This covenantal view on economics rightly understands money and possessions as gifts from a generous God. So while we are free to enjoy God's abundance in our lives, we are also called to extend our abundance by blessing and helping others.

As we uncover various ways the Western church has slipped into syncretism, we must ask how Christians should view themselves as citizens of both the kingdom of God and the state. The liberal state claims to be neutral, but we've seen that it indeed comes with an encumbered sense of what it means to be a citizen, and some of what this entails conflicts with what it means to be a member of God's kingdom. As such, Christians must be careful to pledge their totalized allegiance only to the kingdom of God, even while they live peaceably as good, contracted citizens of a state. Every worldly regime is Babylon, so Christians must align with the laws of the land only if they do not conflict with God's laws. Whenever they do conflict with God's laws, Christians can still respect the laws of the land by conscientiously objecting and bearing whatever consequences follow. This general approach allows Christians to always uphold their true allegiance to God's kingdom, regardless of the Babylonian state in power.

Part 1's critical arguments are necessary for our public theology because they trace where we've gone wrong. To work as prophets we must first call out the corrupt powers and lament the ways in which injustice has prevailed. Yet prophetic utterances are meant not to keep us in a state of lament but to energize us to create a new vision of a better reality. This is the main point of part 2—to offer the church a new vision of public engagement for a public theology based on God's covenant of abundance. Thus the arguments of part 2 are not critical but constructive. First, we discussed what a covenanted sense of personhood entails. It rejects the liberal ideas that people can be unencumbered and commodified and instead posits the notion that humans are holistic "beings-in-community." We are communally formed and bound together, and we thus bear responsibility toward each other. Because God's goal for humanity is to exist in a state of shalom, God established Sabbath laws to help us preserve a robust, holistic sense of self. Various Sabbath principles such as rest, play, and generosity help us rightly reorient ourselves to God and creation.

We can view Pentecost as a cosmic Jubilee that flattens out inequalities and unifies believers on a global scale. This has both economic and social implications. Economically, the church can practice Jubilee principles when it contributes to a "sharing economy" that pictures God as provider and us as stewards of the resources God has entrusted us with. Gleaning principles teach us to be generous with what God has provided so we can be a blessing to others who are negatively affected by scarcity. A sharing economy pictures people working together and pooling resources so everyone in a community can make it through tough times. When Christians participate in a sharing economy and shift their mindsets to view prosperity as how much they are able to bless others, they practice economic justice in God's covenant of abundance.

Christians can also practice social justice in covenant when they view themselves as beings-in-community who bear social responsibility for one another. Freedom in covenant is communal; it's not about individual autonomy but about fostering a sense of belonging in community. Christ calls us to live in mutuality and hospitality with each other because it is only then that we reflect God's heart for those who suffer in displacement and marginalization. God is for the least of these—the widows and orphans, the social outcasts and the refugees. Living in God's covenant of abundance entails showing social hospitality toward those in need by sharing our time and resources and serving others in a posture of love. We must also participate in outward-looking social engagement to establish shalom in the world. The church cannot stand idly by when injustices occur in our world. We are not called to take up the political causes of Babylon, but we are called to present a thick public witness that demonstrates loving kindness, compassion, mercy, and forgiveness to everyone in society, especially to those who suffer injustice. Pentecost breaks down manmade social divisions and establishes a social ethics rooted in divine love. We'll see the Jubilee principles of freedom, justice, restoration, solidarity, and hospitality enacted when we are entrenched in and empowered by the Spirit of God. This is our prophetic task—to be the church, empowered by the Holy Spirit, that cultivates shalom in the world.

The Church's Public Responsibility

One of the most famous prayers in modern times is Reinhold Niebuhr's "Serenity Prayer," which states, "God grant me the serenity to accept the things I cannot change, the courage to change the things I can, and the wisdom to know the difference."[4] This prayer demonstrates a wise approach to public action. We should not worry or develop anxieties over things we can't change, yet we're called to action when we *can* change things. While Christians can advocate for policies at a national level to bring about change, they can never establish a total expression of the kingdom of God on this side of the eschaton. Hence the church's goal should never be to establish a theocracy in Babylon. Political influence is the right of any citizen, but political coercion for a religious cause defies the heart of our faith. Nor should we attempt to bring about change through force. This is what the conquistadors and the crusaders did. Coercion works against the kingdom of God and spreads a syncretic version of our faith that's biblically unrecognizable. What we can and must do first is change our own polity as a church so it reflects Scripture through and through. Our witness will be attractive because of our love and care toward each other and toward strangers. Hence, we will *inspire* change rather than force it.

Because the church's communal context exists within broader national contexts, the church will be a witness to the nations when it demonstrates what a loving community of generosity, mutuality, and hospitality looks like. When the church is holy and unique, it reveals

---

4. According to Elisabeth Sifton, Niebuhr's daughter, Niebuhr composed and first recited the Serenity Prayer in 1943 at a Sunday morning service at Heath Union Church in Heath, Massachusetts. See Elisabeth Sifton, *Serenity Prayer: Faith and Politics in Times of Peace and War* (New York: Norton, 2005), 18.

Christ to the world. As James K. A. Smith states, "The church is a body politic that invites us to imagine how politics could be otherwise."[5] Then, as the church fulfills its obligations under God's covenant of abundance—as it serves and embraces the least of these—it truly becomes a vision of the kingdom of God, and it becomes a blessing to the world. In fact, God's covenant of abundance reiterates and reinterprets God's universal mandate to *be* a blessing to the world.

Although a message of universality is present all the way back in the Abrahamic covenant, it is realized through Christ's redemption in God's covenant of abundance.[6] God's intent was always to bring redemption to the whole world through covenant, but the old covenant was *centripetal*, as nations were to be drawn to covenant through Israel's witness, whereas the new covenant is *centrifugal*, as God's priestly people are to go out to the world and demonstrate God's witness of love.[7]

God's people in the old covenant make up the particular nation of Israel, whereas in the new covenant God's people are the church, which is composed of members from all nations. The new covenant marks a shift from being a *covenant nation* to being a *covenant community* that draws from all nations.[8] In fact, Peter makes the move to include Gentiles in the new covenant because they too are filled with the Spirit.[9] Instances like the Spirit being poured out on Cornelius (a Gentile) convinced Peter that the new covenant, a covenant of abundance, also includes Gentiles (Acts 10:44–48). The centrifugal responsibility of the church is, therefore, to go out into all nations and bring anyone who receives the message into the kingdom of God. Thus our reimagined priestly role of the church is to go out, reflect the kingdom of God, and bear witness to King Jesus. The church's

5. James K. A. Smith, *Awaiting the Kingdom: Reforming Public Theology* (Grand Rapids: Baker Academic, 2017), 16.

6. Christopher J. H. Wright, *The Mission of God: Unlocking the Bible's Grand Narrative* (Downers Grove, IL: IVP Academic, 2006), 223.

7. C. Wright, *Mission of God*, 223.

8. Carmen Imes, *Bearing God's Name: Why Sinai Still Matters* (Downers Grove, IL: IVP Academic, 2019), 175.

9. Imes, *Bearing God's Name*, 173.

public and political witness in a pluralist society is nothing less than being Christ's covenantal ambassadors.

Conclusion

If we are to image Christ in the public square and to walk in both holiness and compassion, we'll see that some of our actions will be deemed conservative and others progressive. We cannot allow social pressure and the fear of being labeled determine our actions in society. All we need to worry about is faithfulness to Christ, who calls us to love God with all our heart, soul, and mind (Matt. 22:37) *and* to love our neighbor as ourselves (22:39). Loving God fully will create in us a countercultural witness of holiness in our communities, and loving others will create a witness of compassion in the world. Just as Jesus tied these commandments together, so must they complement each other in the public realm.

This book has traversed a lot of ground and covered many topics. Although we relied on Scripture to make every argument, some points will inevitably bear my perspective, interpretive frame. Nevertheless, as a church we must let Christ's words define our public witness. Without mincing words, Christ has not only called us to love God (Matt. 22:37–38) and honor God's law (5:17–18) but challenged us to love all people indiscriminately—our neighbors (22:39) and our enemies (5:44). He has called us to do unto others what we would have them do to us (7:12). He has called us to seek reconciliation (5:24–25). He has called us to forgive our offenders (18:21–22). He has called us to serve others (20:26–28). He has called us to show hospitality to the poor (Luke 14:12–14). He has called us to give generously (6:38). He has called us to go the second mile (Matt. 5:38–42). He has called us to deny ourselves (Luke 9:23). And in the Great Commission, God has called us to make disciples, indiscriminately, of *all* nations (Matt. 28:19–20). He has called us to choose the kingdom of this world or the kingdom of God (6:33). Are you a Christian first or a national citizen first? Christian, pick your allegiance.

INDEX